THE INFINITE LOOP

NOTHING BUT THE TRUTH

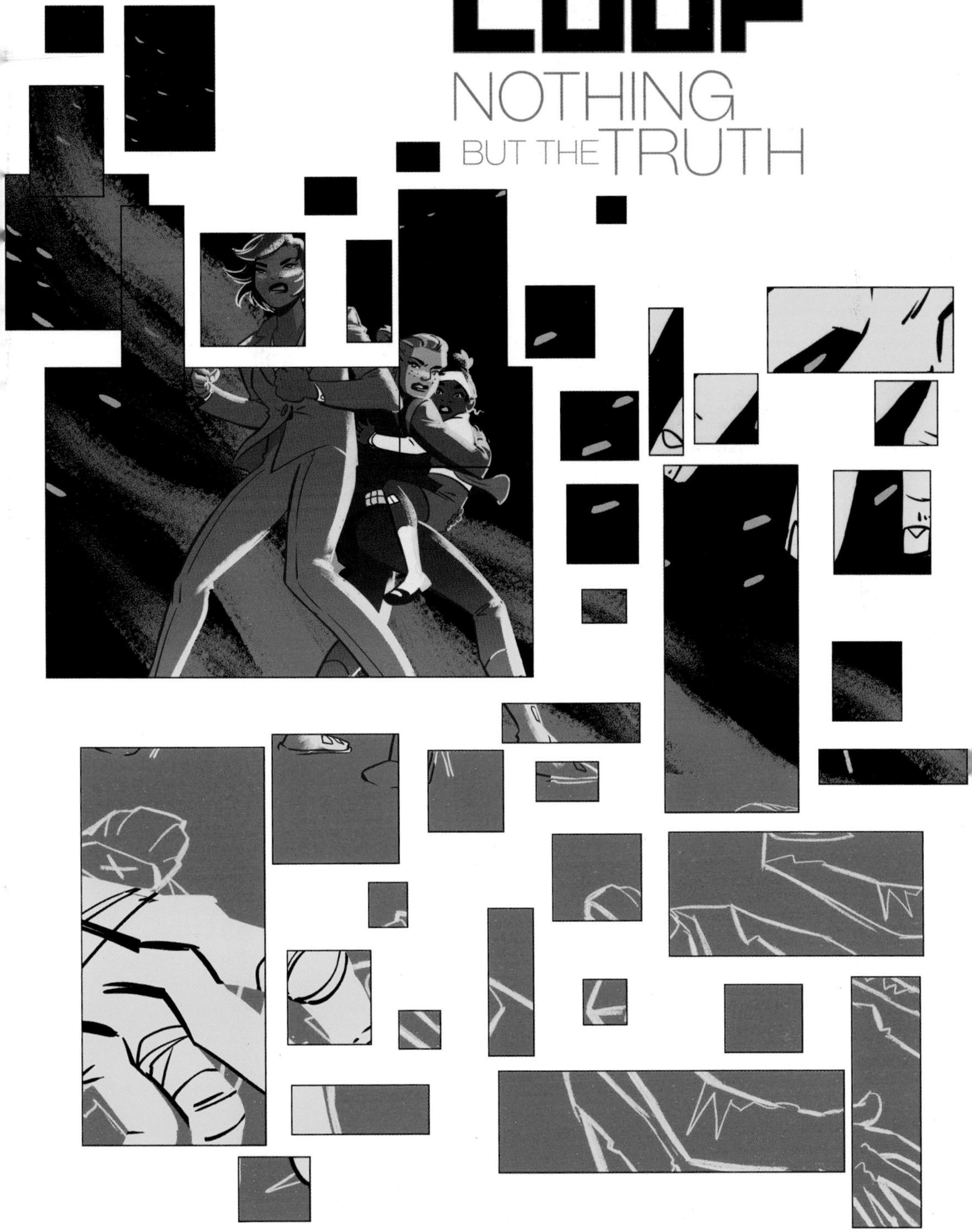

Written by
PIERRICK COLINET
& ELSA CHARRETIER

Art by
DANIELE DI NICUOLO

Additional Art by
ELSA CHARRETIER (Issue #4)

ISBN: 978-1-68405-241-7

21 20 19 18   1 2 3 4

WWW.IDWPUBLISHING.COM

Greg Goldstein, President & Publisher
Robbie Robbins, EVP & Sr. Art Director
Chris Ryall, Chief Creative Officer & Editor-in-Chief
Matthew Ruzicka, CPA, Chief Financial Officer
David Hedgecock, Associate Publisher
Laurie Windrow, Senior Vice President of Sales & Marketing
Lorelei Bunjes, VP of Digital Services
Eric Moss, Sr. Director, Licensing & Business Development
Ted Adams, Founder & CEO of IDW Media Holdings

Become our fan on Facebook facebook.com/idwpublishing
Follow us on Twitter @idwpublishing
Subscribe to us on YouTube youtube.com/idwpublishing
See what's new on Tumblr tumblr.idwpublishing.com
Check us out on Instagram instagram.com/idwpublishing

THE INFINITE LOOP
NOTHING BUT THE TRUTH

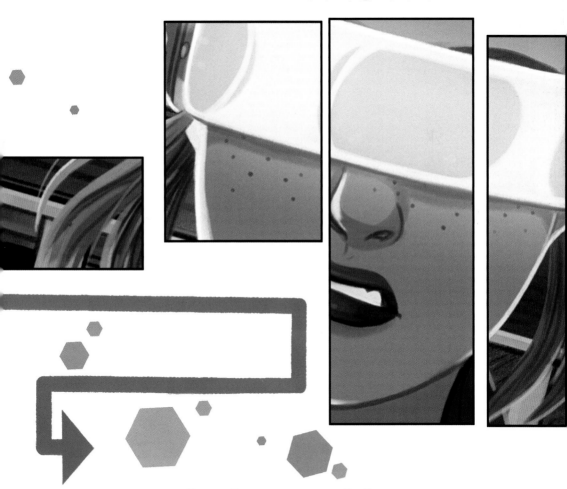

Colors by **SARAH STERN**   Letters by **ED DUKESHIRE**

Series Co-Editor: **CHASE MAROTZ**   Series Editor: **SARAH GAYDOS**

Cover Art by **ELSA CHARRETIER**

Collection Edits by **JUSTIN EISINGER** and **ALONZO SIMON**

Collection Design by **CLAUDIA CHONG**

Publisher: **GREG GOLDSTEIN**

Art by
ELSA CHARRETIER

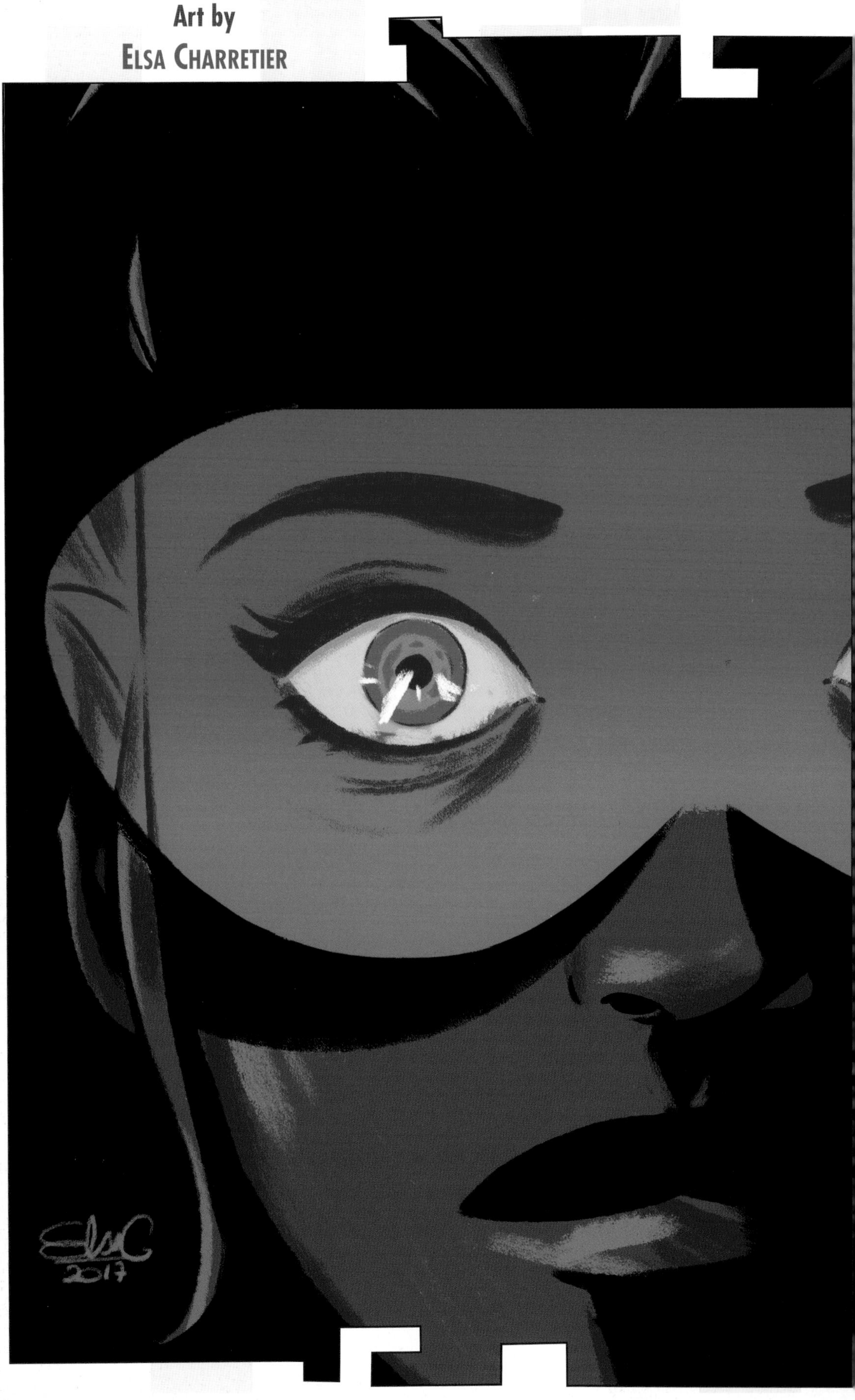
ElsaC
2017

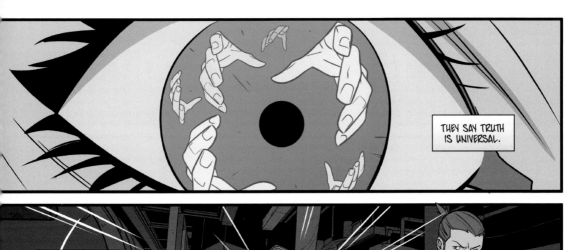

THEY SAY TRUTH IS UNIVERSAL.

I SAY OUR PERCEPTION OF TRUTH IS NOT.

TAKE RIGHT NOW. YOU SEE A MOB OF BLOODTHIRSTY ZOMBIES, AND FRANKLY, I DON'T BLAME YOU.

WHAT I SEE ARE DESPERATE PEOPLE. DESPERATE TIMES. DESPERATE MEASURES.

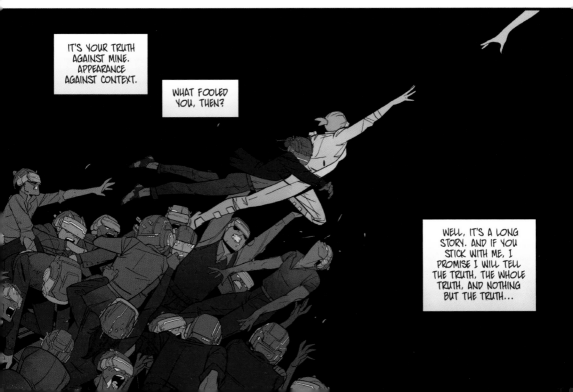

IT'S YOUR TRUTH AGAINST MINE. APPEARANCE AGAINST CONTEXT.

WHAT FOOLED YOU, THEN?

WELL, IT'S A LONG STORY. AND IF YOU STICK WITH ME, I PROMISE I WILL TELL THE TRUTH, THE WHOLE TRUTH, AND NOTHING BUT THE TRUTH...

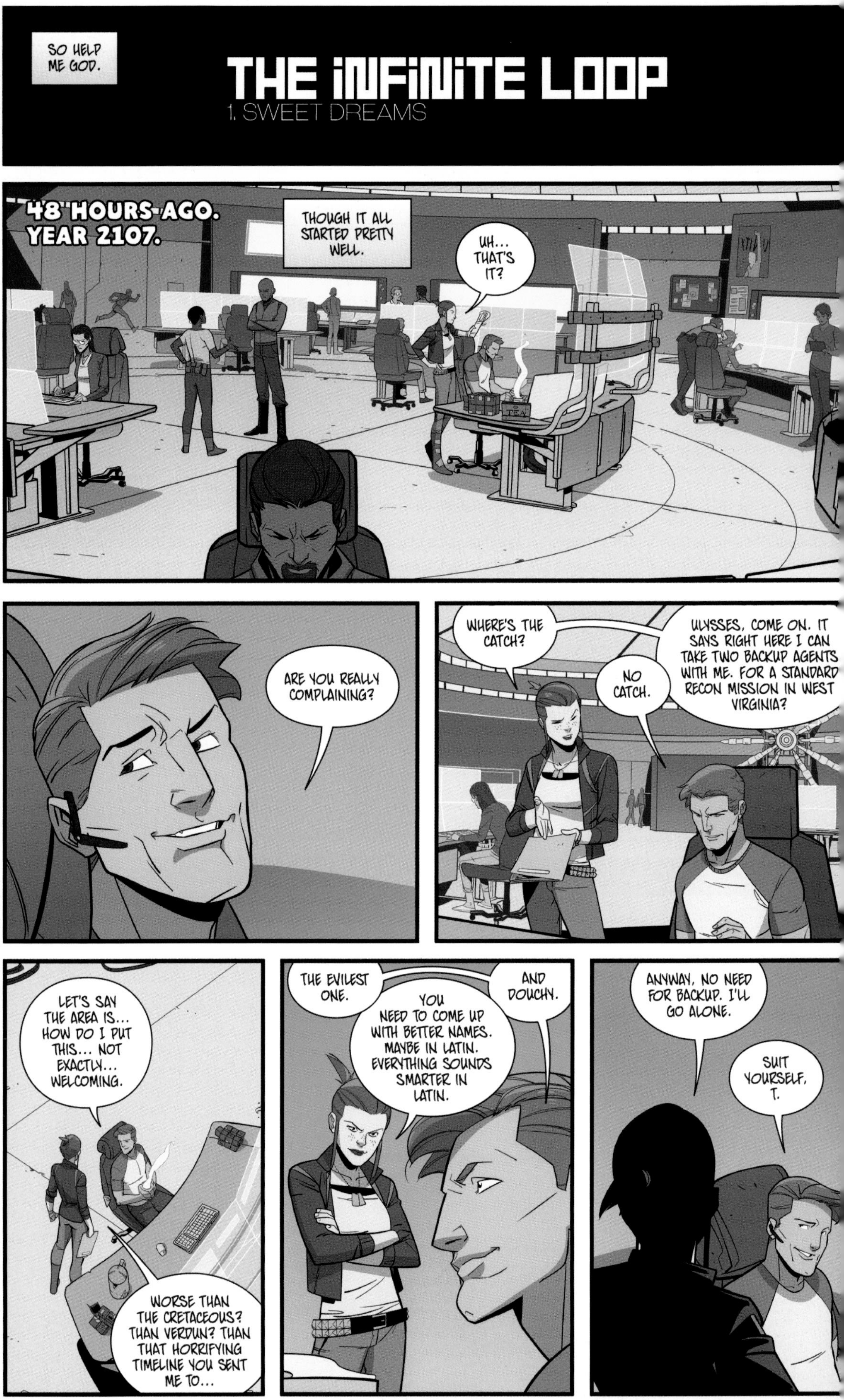

SO HELP ME GOD.
THE INFINITE LOOP
1. SWEET DREAMS
48 HOURS AGO. YEAR 2107.
THOUGH IT ALL STARTED PRETTY WELL.
UH... THAT'S IT?
ARE YOU REALLY COMPLAINING?
WHERE'S THE CATCH?
ULYSSES, COME ON. IT SAYS RIGHT HERE I CAN TAKE TWO BACKUP AGENTS WITH ME. FOR A STANDARD RECON MISSION IN WEST VIRGINIA?
NO CATCH.
LET'S SAY THE AREA IS... HOW DO I PUT THIS... NOT EXACTLY... WELCOMING.
WORSE THAN THE CRETACEOUS? THAN VERDUN? THAN THAT HORRIFYING TIMELINE YOU SENT ME TO...
THE EVILEST ONE.
AND DOUCHY.
YOU NEED TO COME UP WITH BETTER NAMES. MAYBE IN LATIN. EVERYTHING SOUNDS SMARTER IN LATIN.
ANYWAY, NO NEED FOR BACKUP. I'LL GO ALONE.
SUIT YOURSELF, T.

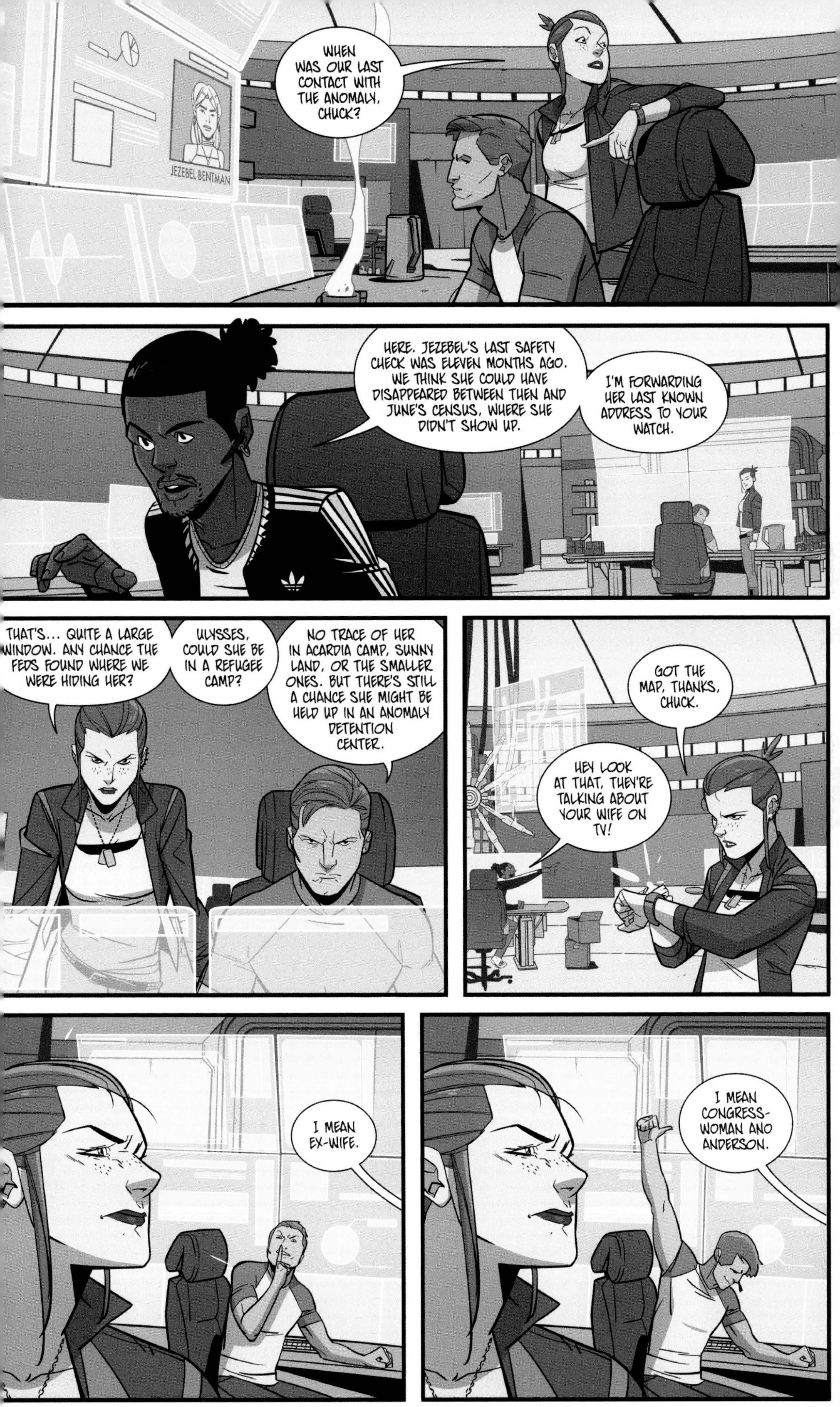
WHEN WAS OUR LAST CONTACT WITH THE ANOMALY, CHUCK?
JEZEBEL BENTMAN
HERE. JEZEBEL'S LAST SAFETY CHECK WAS ELEVEN MONTHS AGO. WE THINK SHE COULD HAVE DISAPPEARED BETWEEN THEN AND JUNE'S CENSUS, WHERE SHE DIDN'T SHOW UP.
I'M FORWARDING HER LAST KNOWN ADDRESS TO YOUR WATCH.
THAT'S... QUITE A LARGE WINDOW. ANY CHANCE THE FEDS FOUND WHERE WE WERE HIDING HER?
ULYSSES, COULD SHE BE IN A REFUGEE CAMP?
NO TRACE OF HER IN ACARDIA CAMP, SUNNY LAND, OR THE SMALLER ONES. BUT THERE'S STILL A CHANCE SHE MIGHT BE HELD UP IN AN ANOMALY DETENTION CENTER.
GOT THE MAP, THANKS, CHUCK.
HEY LOOK AT THAT, THEY'RE TALKING ABOUT YOUR WIFE ON TV!
I MEAN EX-WIFE.
I MEAN CONGRESS-WOMAN ANO ANDERSON.

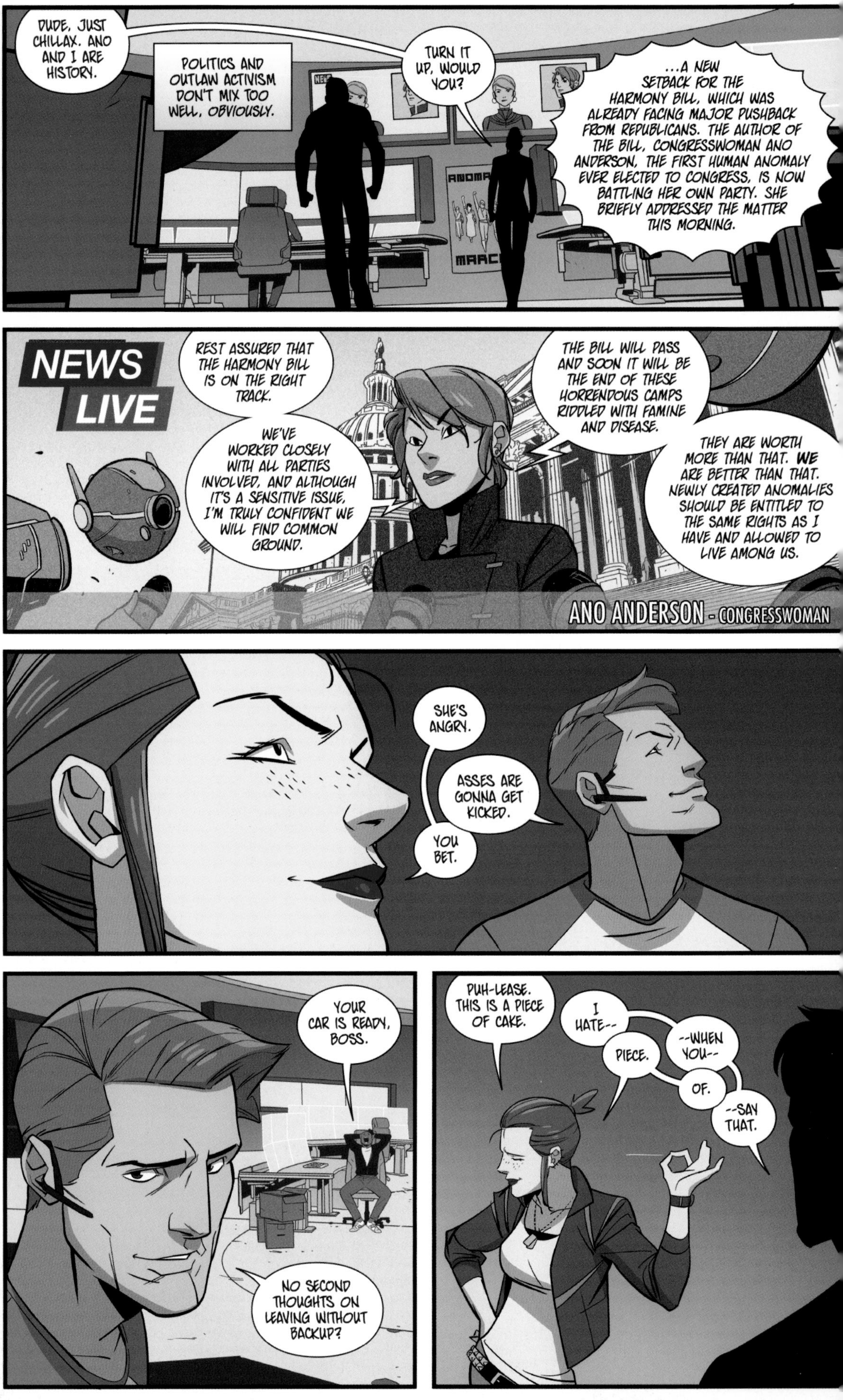

DUDE, JUST CHILLAX. ANO AND I ARE HISTORY.
POLITICS AND OUTLAW ACTIVISM DON'T MIX TOO WELL, OBVIOUSLY.
TURN IT UP, WOULD YOU?
...A NEW SETBACK FOR THE HARMONY BILL, WHICH WAS ALREADY FACING MAJOR PUSHBACK FROM REPUBLICANS. THE AUTHOR OF THE BILL, CONGRESSWOMAN ANO ANDERSON, THE FIRST HUMAN ANOMALY EVER ELECTED TO CONGRESS, IS NOW BATTLING HER OWN PARTY. SHE BRIEFLY ADDRESSED THE MATTER THIS MORNING.
NEWS LIVE
REST ASSURED THAT THE HARMONY BILL IS ON THE RIGHT TRACK.
WE'VE WORKED CLOSELY WITH ALL PARTIES INVOLVED, AND ALTHOUGH IT'S A SENSITIVE ISSUE, I'M TRULY CONFIDENT WE WILL FIND COMMON GROUND.
THE BILL WILL PASS AND SOON IT WILL BE THE END OF THESE HORRENDOUS CAMPS RIDDLED WITH FAMINE AND DISEASE.
THEY ARE WORTH MORE THAN THAT. WE ARE BETTER THAN THAT. NEWLY CREATED ANOMALIES SHOULD BE ENTITLED TO THE SAME RIGHTS AS I HAVE AND ALLOWED TO LIVE AMONG US.
ANO ANDERSON - CONGRESSWOMAN
SHE'S ANGRY.
ASSES ARE GONNA GET KICKED.
YOU BET.
YOUR CAR IS READY, BOSS.
NO SECOND THOUGHTS ON LEAVING WITHOUT BACKUP?
PUH-LEASE. THIS IS A PIECE OF CAKE.
I HATE--
PIECE.
--WHEN YOU--
OF.
--SAY THAT.

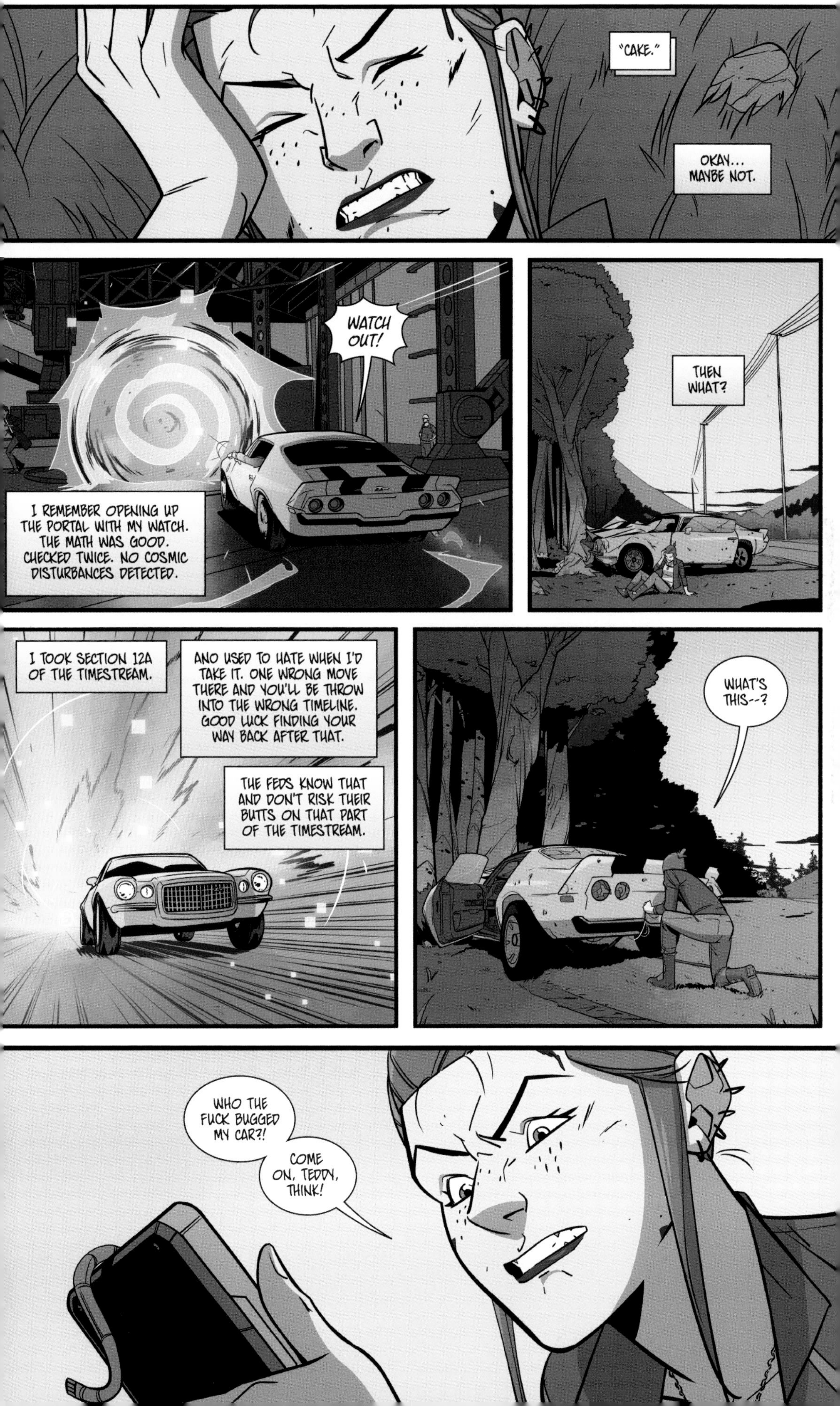
"CAKE."
OKAY... MAYBE NOT.
I REMEMBER OPENING UP THE PORTAL WITH MY WATCH. THE MATH WAS GOOD. CHECKED TWICE. NO COSMIC DISTURBANCES DETECTED.
WATCH OUT!
THEN WHAT?
I TOOK SECTION 12A OF THE TIMESTREAM.
ANO USED TO HATE WHEN I'D TAKE IT. ONE WRONG MOVE THERE AND YOU'LL BE THROW INTO THE WRONG TIMELINE. GOOD LUCK FINDING YOUR WAY BACK AFTER THAT.
THE FEDS KNOW THAT AND DON'T RISK THEIR BUTTS ON THAT PART OF THE TIMESTREAM.
WHAT'S THIS--?
WHO THE FUCK BUGGED MY CAR?!
COME ON, TEDDY, THINK!

WHAT HAPPENED NEXT?

BLACK CAR. NO LICENSE PLATE.

MILITARY CAR BODY ENGINEERED TO RESIST STRONG TIMESTREAM DISTURBANCES.

RANDOM DUDES IN BLACK WITH HUMORLESS FACES AND POWER ISSUES.

OH GOD, THIS IS PRIVATE MILITIA.

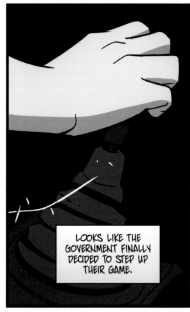

LOOKS LIKE THE GOVERNMENT FINALLY DECIDED TO STEP UP THEIR GAME.

DON'T GET ME WRONG, I'M ALL ABOUT THE CAT-AND-MOUSE GAME, BUT MAN...

...THESE GUYS ARE THE WORST KIND OF SORE LOSERS.

IT'S LIKE THEY'RE JUST HERE FOR THE K--

BLAM

MY POINT EXACTLY!

CHANGE OF PLANS, FUCKERS!

PHOMP

ANO WOULD WANT ME TO PLAY IT COOL AND NOT TRY ANYTHING STUPID.

PHOMP

BUT YOU GUYS ARE FORCING MY HAND HERE.

PHOMP

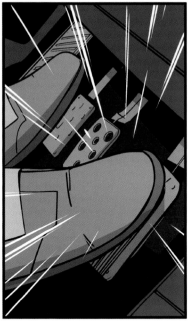

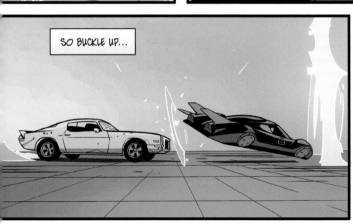

SO BUCKLE UP...

...BECAUSE I'M SENDING YOU NEANDERTHALS...

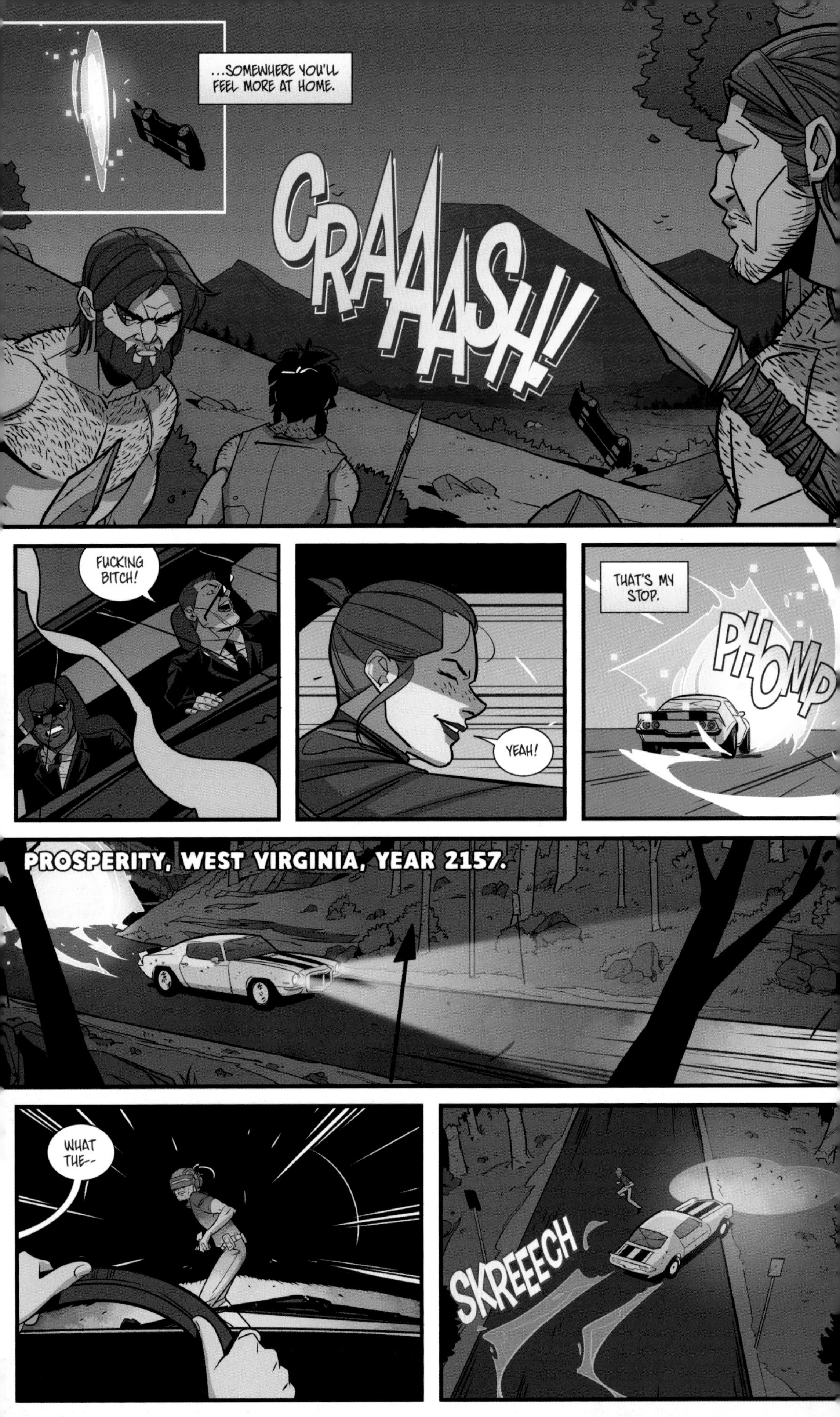
...SOMEWHERE YOU'LL FEEL MORE AT HOME.
CRAAASH!
FUCKING BITCH!
YEAH!
THAT'S MY STOP.
PHOMP
PROSPERITY, WEST VIRGINIA, YEAR 2157.
WHAT THE--
SKREEECH

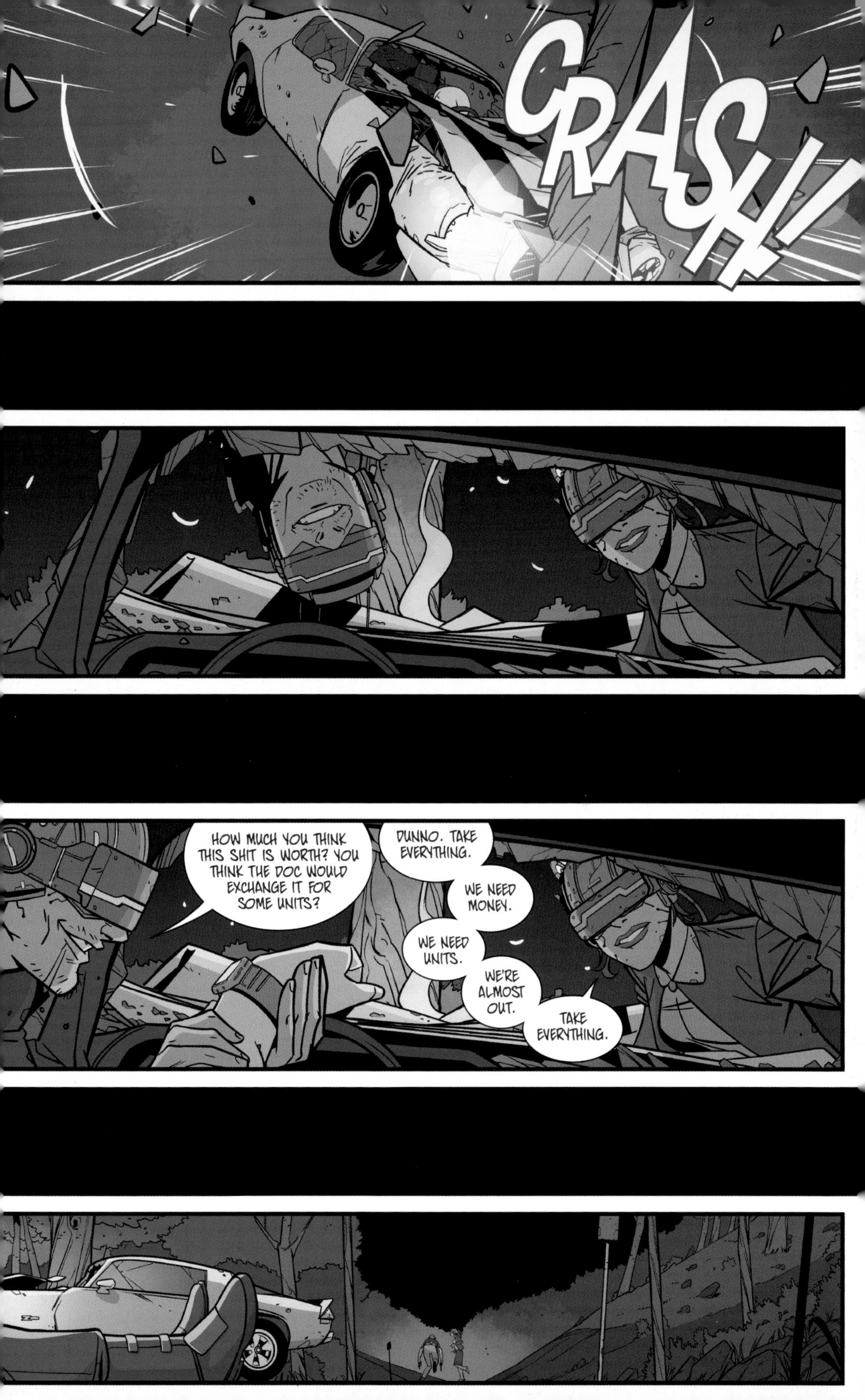
CRASH!!
HOW MUCH YOU THINK THIS SHIT IS WORTH? YOU THINK THE DOC WOULD EXCHANGE IT FOR SOME UNITS?
DUNNO. TAKE EVERYTHING.
WE NEED MONEY.
WE NEED UNITS.
WE'RE ALMOST OUT.
TAKE EVERYTHING.

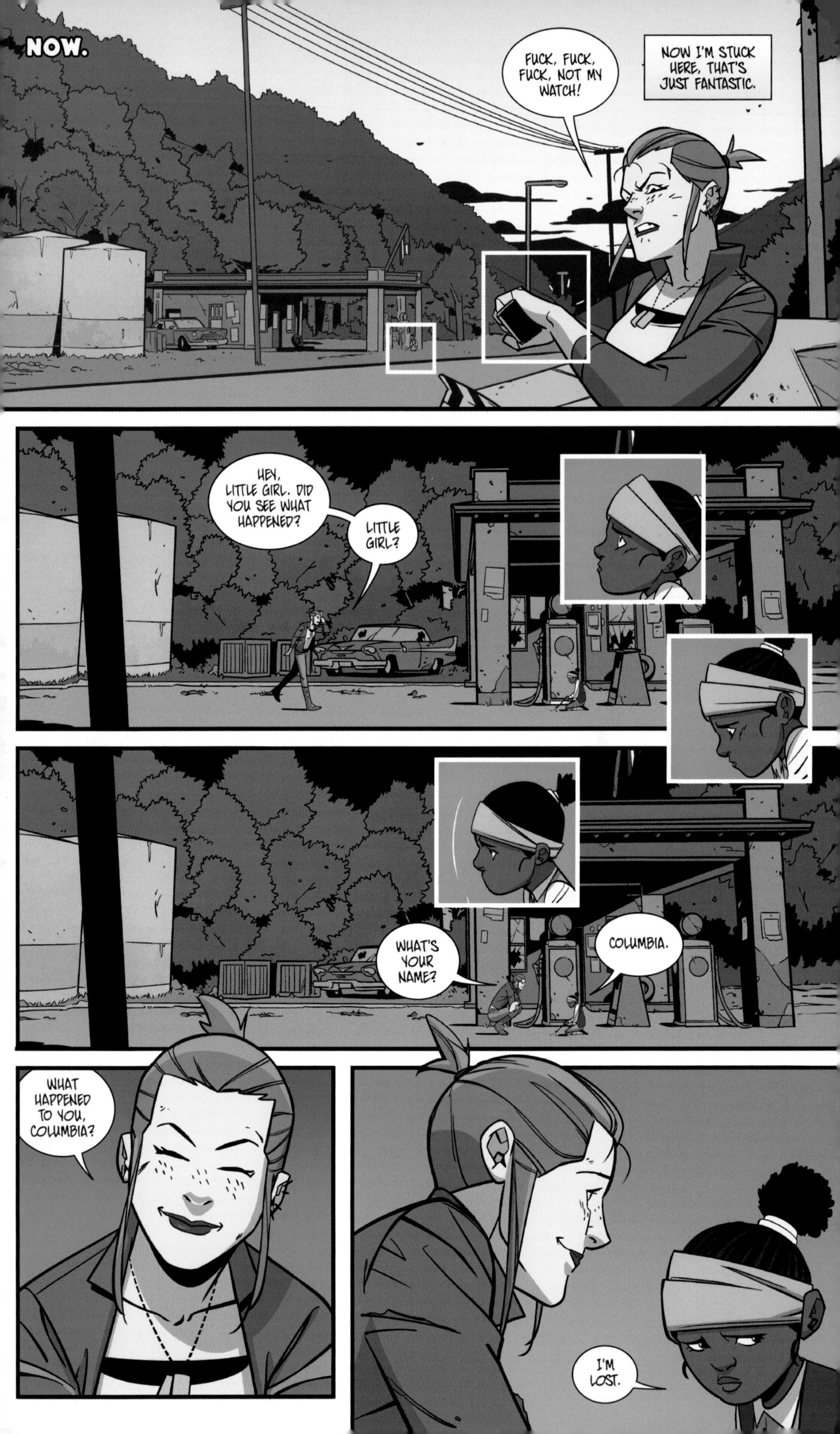
NOW.
FUCK, FUCK, FUCK, NOT MY WATCH!
NOW I'M STUCK HERE, THAT'S JUST FANTASTIC.
HEY, LITTLE GIRL. DID YOU SEE WHAT HAPPENED?
LITTLE GIRL?
WHAT'S YOUR NAME?
COLUMBIA.
WHAT HAPPENED TO YOU, COLUMBIA?
I'M LOST.

THAT MAKES TWO OF US. HOW ABOUT WE STICK TOGETHER? WHAT DO YOU SAY?

I'M SURE WE CAN HELP EACH OTHER OUT.

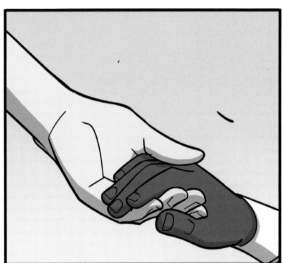

WHY CAN'T I EVER STAY OUT OF TROUBLE?

welcome to *Prosperity* an Appalachian Gem

IT'S LIKE I NEVER LEARN.

DOC'S REHABILITATION CENTER

WANT WANTED

-ILLEGAL TIME T -ILLEGAL TIME TRAVELER- M

$ 500,0 $ 500,000

REWA REWARD

OPENING SOON

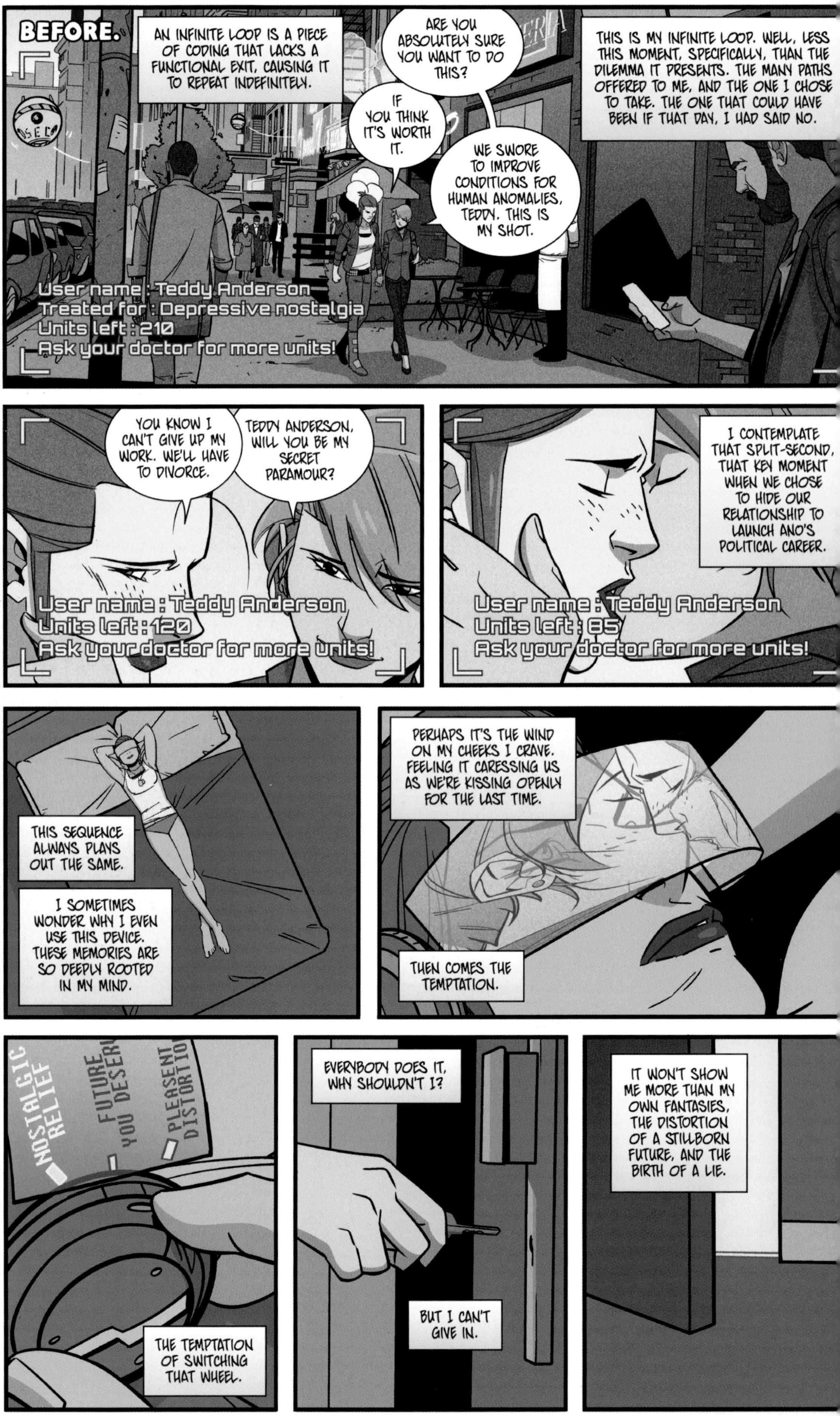

BEFORE.
AN INFINITE LOOP IS A PIECE OF CODING THAT LACKS A FUNCTIONAL EXIT, CAUSING IT TO REPEAT INDEFINITELY.
ARE YOU ABSOLUTELY SURE YOU WANT TO DO THIS?
IF YOU THINK IT'S WORTH IT.
WE SWORE TO IMPROVE CONDITIONS FOR HUMAN ANOMALIES, TEDDY. THIS IS MY SHOT.
THIS IS MY INFINITE LOOP. WELL, LESS THIS MOMENT, SPECIFICALLY, THAN THE DILEMMA IT PRESENTS. THE MANY PATHS OFFERED TO ME, AND THE ONE I CHOSE TO TAKE. THE ONE THAT COULD HAVE BEEN IF THAT DAY, I HAD SAID NO.
User name : Teddy Anderson
Treated for : Depressive nostalgia
Units left : 210
Ask your doctor for more units!
YOU KNOW I CAN'T GIVE UP MY WORK. WE'LL HAVE TO DIVORCE.
TEDDY ANDERSON, WILL YOU BE MY SECRET PARAMOUR?
User name : Teddy Anderson
Units left : 120
Ask your doctor for more units!
I CONTEMPLATE THAT SPLIT-SECOND, THAT KEY MOMENT WHEN WE CHOSE TO HIDE OUR RELATIONSHIP TO LAUNCH ANO'S POLITICAL CAREER.
User name : Teddy Anderson
Units left : 85
Ask your doctor for more units!
THIS SEQUENCE ALWAYS PLAYS OUT THE SAME.
I SOMETIMES WONDER WHY I EVEN USE THIS DEVICE. THESE MEMORIES ARE SO DEEPLY ROOTED IN MY MIND.
PERHAPS IT'S THE WIND ON MY CHEEKS I CRAVE. FEELING IT CARESSING US AS WE'RE KISSING OPENLY FOR THE LAST TIME.
THEN COMES THE TEMPTATION.
NOSTALGIC RELIEF
FUTURE
THE TEMPTATION OF SWITCHING THAT WHEEL.
EVERYBODY DOES IT, WHY SHOULDN'T I?
BUT I CAN'T GIVE IN.
IT WON'T SHOW ME MORE THAN MY OWN FANTASIES, THE DISTORTION OF A STILLBORN FUTURE, AND THE BIRTH OF A LIE.

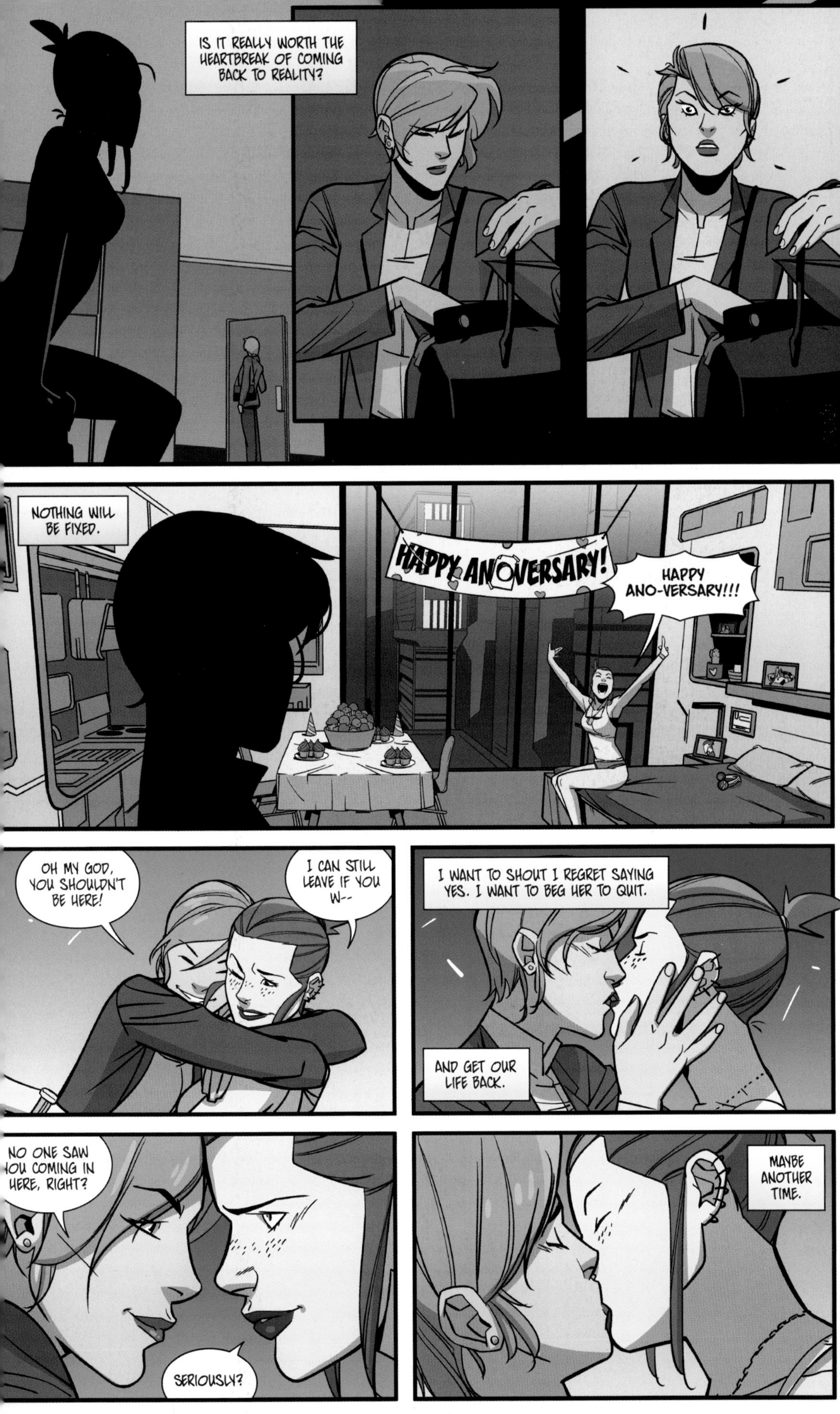

IS IT REALLY WORTH THE HEARTBREAK OF COMING BACK TO REALITY?
NOTHING WILL BE FIXED.
HAPPY ANOVERSARY!
HAPPY ANO-VERSARY!!!
OH MY GOD, YOU SHOULDN'T BE HERE!
I CAN STILL LEAVE IF YOU W--
I WANT TO SHOUT I REGRET SAYING YES. I WANT TO BEG HER TO QUIT.
AND GET OUR LIFE BACK.
NO ONE SAW YOU COMING IN HERE, RIGHT?
SERIOUSLY?
MAYBE ANOTHER TIME.

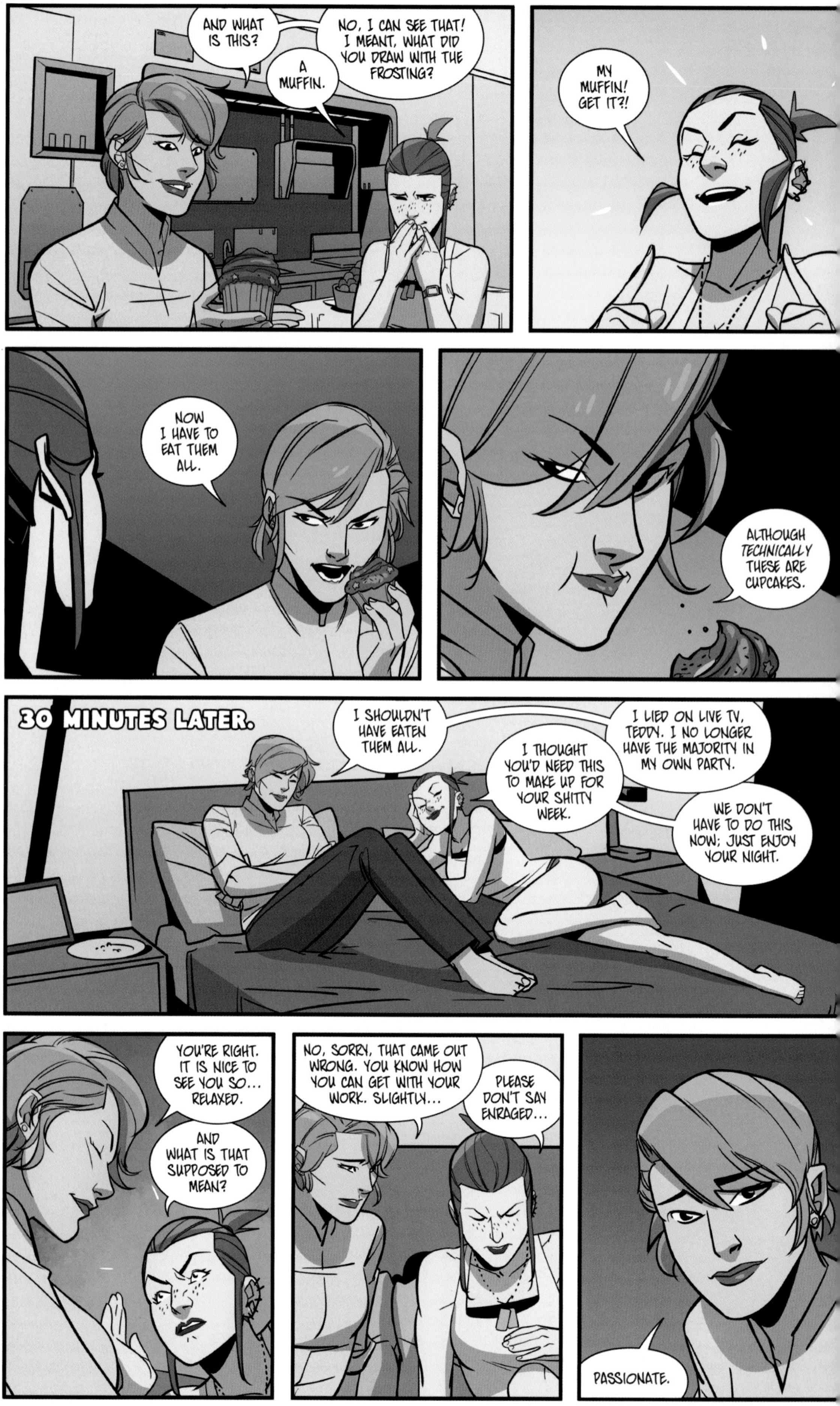
AND WHAT IS THIS?
A MUFFIN.
NO, I CAN SEE THAT! I MEANT, WHAT DID YOU DRAW WITH THE FROSTING?
MY MUFFIN! GET IT?!
NOW I HAVE TO EAT THEM ALL.
ALTHOUGH TECHNICALLY THESE ARE CUPCAKES.
30 MINUTES LATER.
I SHOULDN'T HAVE EATEN THEM ALL.
I THOUGHT YOU'D NEED THIS TO MAKE UP FOR YOUR SHITTY WEEK.
I LIED ON LIVE TV, TEDDY. I NO LONGER HAVE THE MAJORITY IN MY OWN PARTY.
WE DON'T HAVE TO DO THIS NOW; JUST ENJOY YOUR NIGHT.
YOU'RE RIGHT. IT IS NICE TO SEE YOU SO... RELAXED.
AND WHAT IS THAT SUPPOSED TO MEAN?
NO, SORRY, THAT CAME OUT WRONG. YOU KNOW HOW YOU CAN GET WITH YOUR WORK. SLIGHTLY...
PLEASE DON'T SAY ENRAGED...
PASSIONATE.

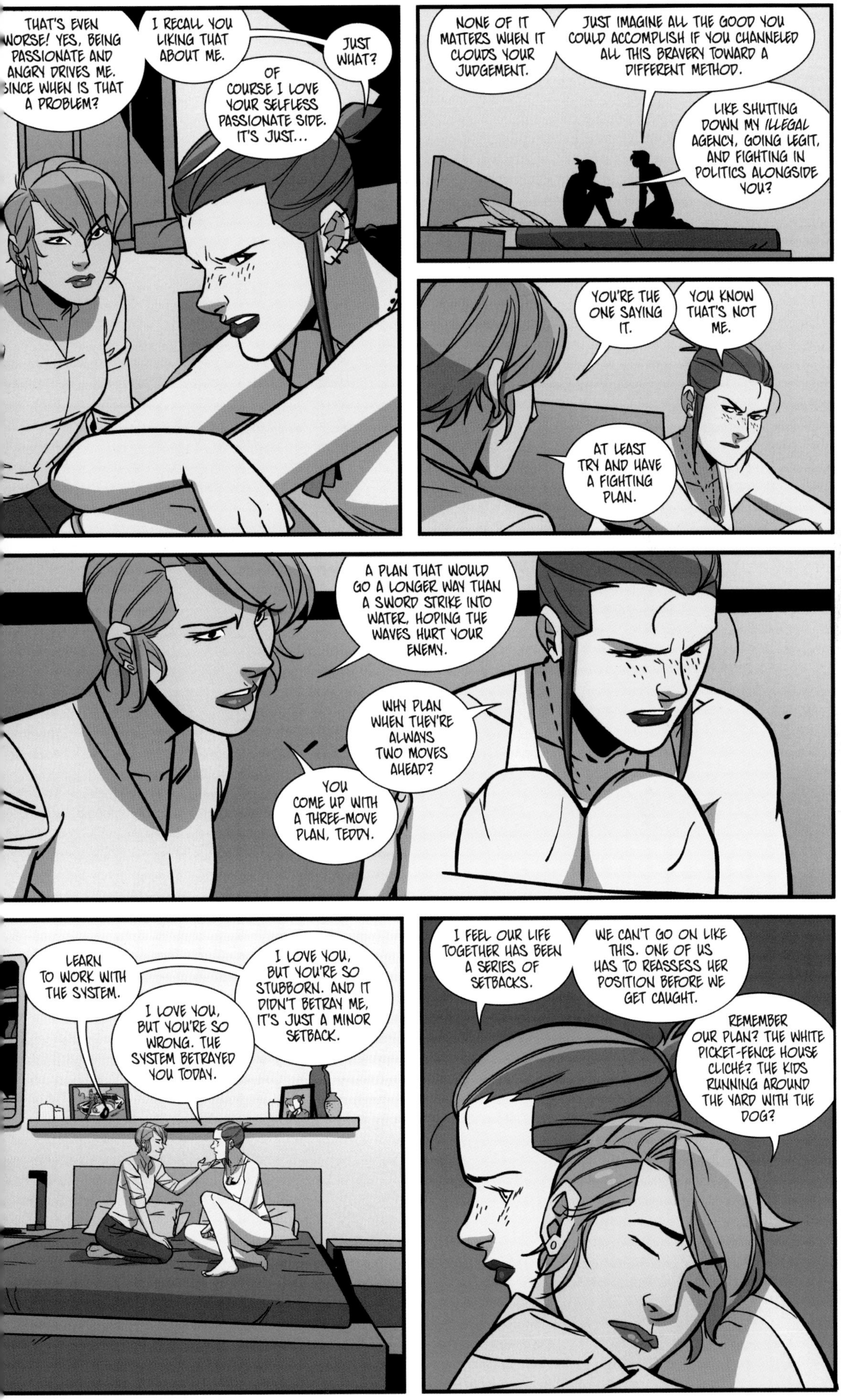
THAT'S EVEN WORSE! YES, BEING PASSIONATE AND ANGRY DRIVES ME. SINCE WHEN IS THAT A PROBLEM?
I RECALL YOU LIKING THAT ABOUT ME.
OF COURSE I LOVE YOUR SELFLESS PASSIONATE SIDE. IT'S JUST...
JUST WHAT?
NONE OF IT MATTERS WHEN IT CLOUDS YOUR JUDGEMENT.
JUST IMAGINE ALL THE GOOD YOU COULD ACCOMPLISH IF YOU CHANNELED ALL THIS BRAVERY TOWARD A DIFFERENT METHOD.
LIKE SHUTTING DOWN MY *ILLEGAL* AGENCY, GOING LEGIT, AND FIGHTING IN POLITICS ALONGSIDE YOU?
YOU KNOW THAT'S NOT ME.
YOU'RE THE ONE SAYING IT.
AT LEAST TRY AND HAVE A FIGHTING PLAN.
A PLAN THAT WOULD GO A LONGER WAY THAN A SWORD STRIKE INTO WATER, HOPING THE WAVES HURT YOUR ENEMY.
WHY PLAN WHEN THEY'RE ALWAYS TWO MOVES AHEAD?
YOU COME UP WITH A THREE-MOVE PLAN, TEDDY.
LEARN TO WORK WITH THE SYSTEM.
I LOVE YOU, BUT YOU'RE SO WRONG. THE SYSTEM BETRAYED YOU TODAY.
I LOVE YOU, BUT YOU'RE SO STUBBORN. AND IT DIDN'T BETRAY ME, IT'S JUST A MINOR SETBACK.
I FEEL OUR LIFE TOGETHER HAS BEEN A SERIES OF SETBACKS.
WE CAN'T GO ON LIKE THIS. ONE OF US HAS TO REASSESS HER POSITION BEFORE WE GET CAUGHT.
REMEMBER OUR PLAN? THE WHITE PICKET-FENCE HOUSE CLICHÉ? THE KIDS RUNNING AROUND THE YARD WITH THE DOG?

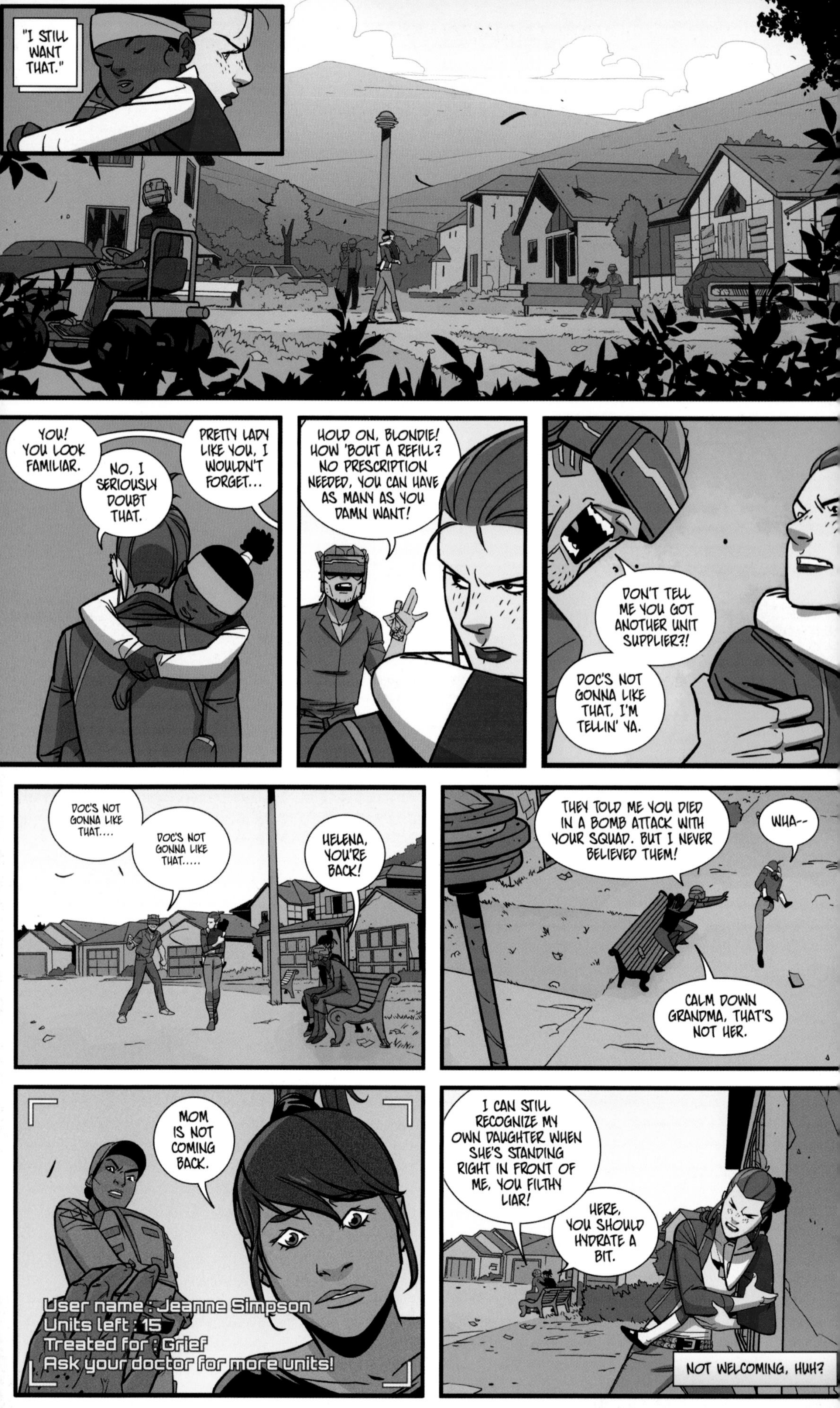
"I STILL WANT THAT."
YOU! YOU LOOK FAMILIAR.
NO, I SERIOUSLY DOUBT THAT.
PRETTY LADY LIKE YOU, I WOULDN'T FORGET...
HOLD ON, BLONDIE! HOW 'BOUT A REFILL? NO PRESCRIPTION NEEDED, YOU CAN HAVE AS MANY AS YOU DAMN WANT!
DON'T TELL ME YOU GOT ANOTHER UNIT SUPPLIER?!
DOC'S NOT GONNA LIKE THAT, I'M TELLIN' YA.
DOC'S NOT GONNA LIKE THAT....
DOC'S NOT GONNA LIKE THAT.....
HELENA, YOU'RE BACK!
THEY TOLD ME YOU DIED IN A BOMB ATTACK WITH YOUR SQUAD. BUT I NEVER BELIEVED THEM!
WHA--
CALM DOWN GRANDMA, THAT'S NOT HER.
MOM IS NOT COMING BACK.
User name : Jeanne Simpson
Units left : 15
Treated for : Grief
Ask your doctor for more units!
I CAN STILL RECOGNIZE MY OWN DAUGHTER WHEN SHE'S STANDING RIGHT IN FRONT OF ME, YOU FILTHY LIAR!
HERE, YOU SHOULD HYDRATE A BIT.
NOT WELCOMING, HUH?

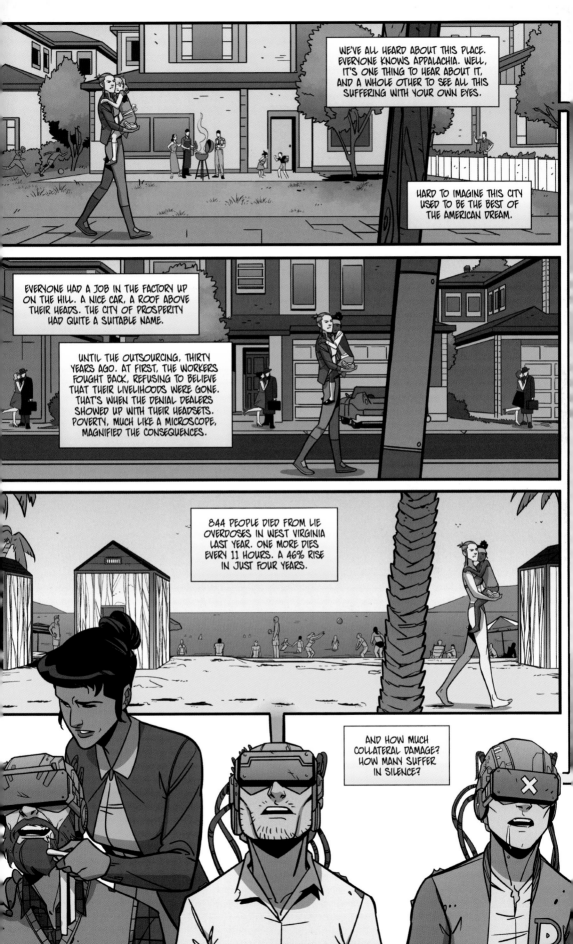

WE'VE ALL HEARD ABOUT THIS PLACE. EVERYONE KNOWS APPALACHIA. WELL, IT'S ONE THING TO HEAR ABOUT IT, AND A WHOLE OTHER TO SEE ALL THIS SUFFERING WITH YOUR OWN EYES.

HARD TO IMAGINE THIS CITY USED TO BE THE BEST OF THE AMERICAN DREAM.

EVERYONE HAD A JOB IN THE FACTORY UP ON THE HILL. A NICE CAR, A ROOF ABOVE THEIR HEADS. THE CITY OF PROSPERITY HAD QUITE A SUITABLE NAME.

UNTIL THE OUTSOURCING, THIRTY YEARS AGO. AT FIRST, THE WORKERS FOUGHT BACK, REFUSING TO BELIEVE THAT THEIR LIVELIHOODS WERE GONE. THAT'S WHEN THE DENIAL DEALERS SHOWED UP WITH THEIR HEADSETS. POVERTY, MUCH LIKE A MICROSCOPE, MAGNIFIED THE CONSEQUENCES.

844 PEOPLE DIED FROM LIE OVERDOSES IN WEST VIRGINIA LAST YEAR. ONE MORE DIES EVERY 11 HOURS. A 46% RISE IN JUST FOUR YEARS.

AND HOW MUCH COLLATERAL DAMAGE? HOW MANY SUFFER IN SILENCE?

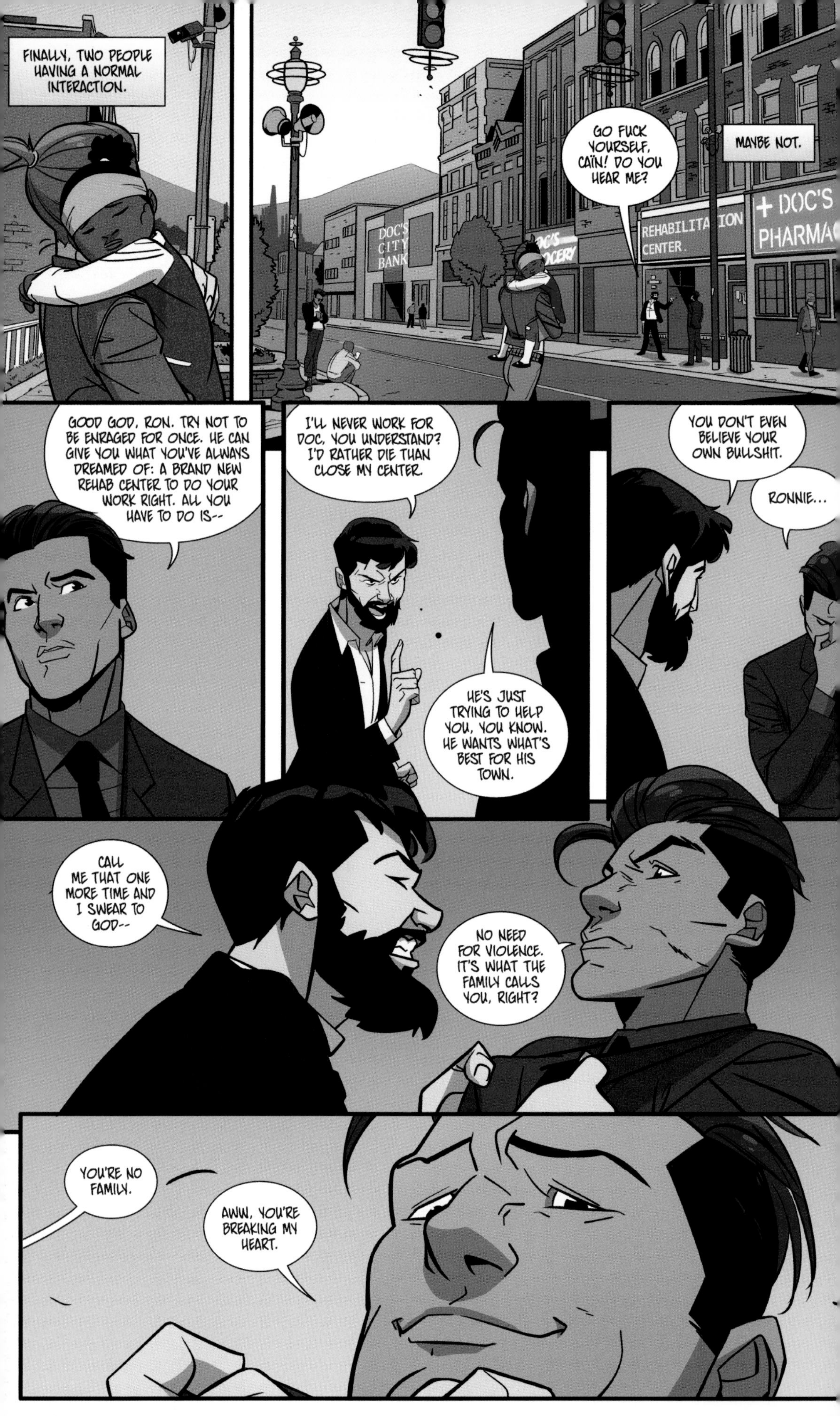
FINALLY, TWO PEOPLE HAVING A NORMAL INTERACTION.
DOC'S CITY BANK
GO FUCK YOURSELF, CAÏN! DO YOU HEAR ME?
REHABILITATION CENTER.
+ DOC'S PHARMAC
MAYBE NOT.
GOOD GOD, RON. TRY NOT TO BE ENRAGED FOR ONCE. HE CAN GIVE YOU WHAT YOU'VE ALWAYS DREAMED OF: A BRAND NEW REHAB CENTER TO DO YOUR WORK RIGHT. ALL YOU HAVE TO DO IS--
I'LL NEVER WORK FOR DOC, YOU UNDERSTAND? I'D RATHER DIE THAN CLOSE MY CENTER.
HE'S JUST TRYING TO HELP YOU, YOU KNOW. HE WANTS WHAT'S BEST FOR HIS TOWN.
YOU DON'T EVEN BELIEVE YOUR OWN BULLSHIT.
RONNIE...
CALL ME THAT ONE MORE TIME AND I SWEAR TO GOD--
NO NEED FOR VIOLENCE. IT'S WHAT THE FAMILY CALLS YOU, RIGHT?
YOU'RE NO FAMILY.
AWW, YOU'RE BREAKING MY HEART.

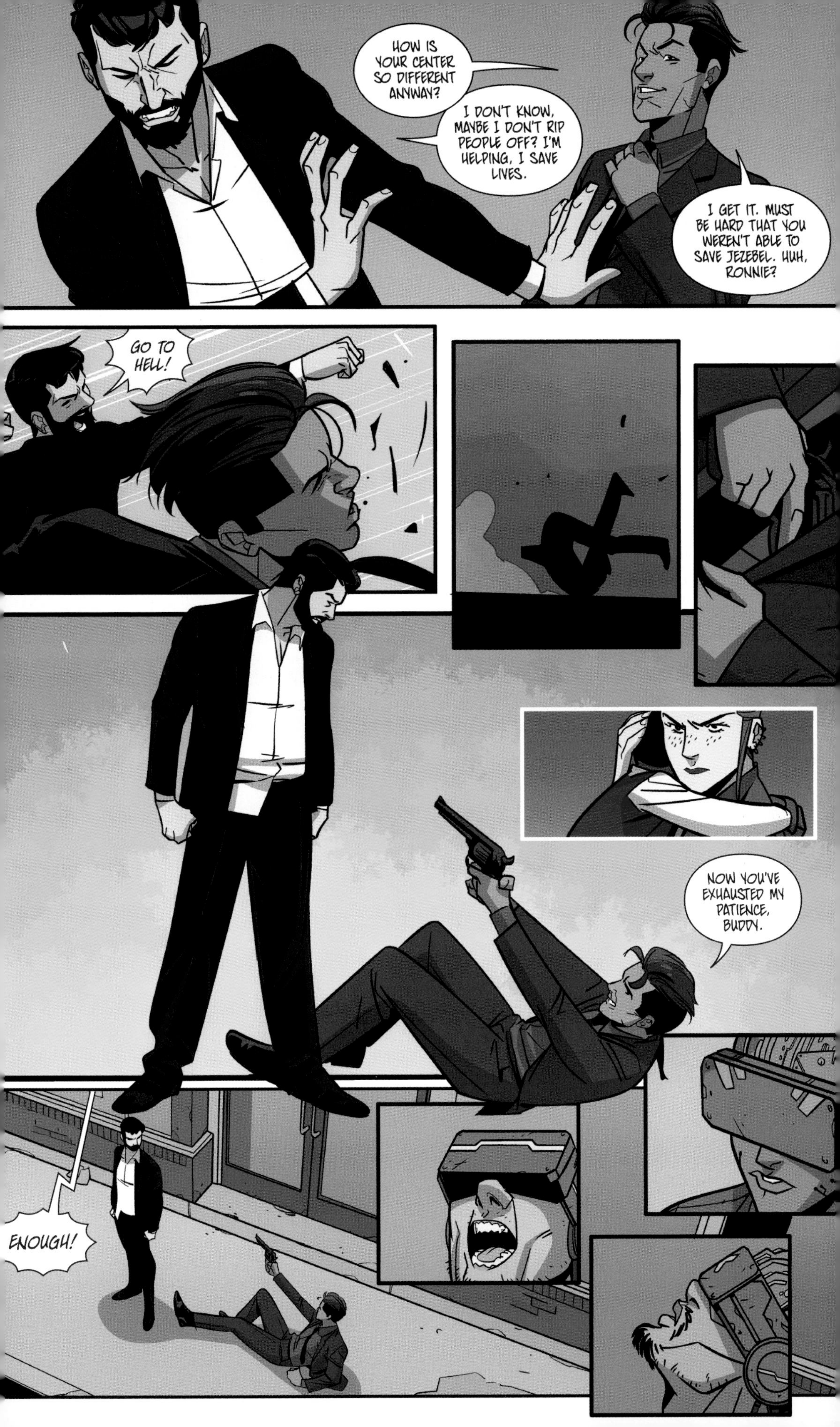
HOW IS YOUR CENTER SO DIFFERENT ANYWAY?
I DON'T KNOW, MAYBE I DON'T RIP PEOPLE OFF? I'M HELPING, I SAVE LIVES.
I GET IT. MUST BE HARD THAT YOU WEREN'T ABLE TO SAVE JEZEBEL. HUH, RONNIE?
GO TO HELL!
NOW YOU'VE EXHAUSTED MY PATIENCE, BUDDY.
ENOUGH!

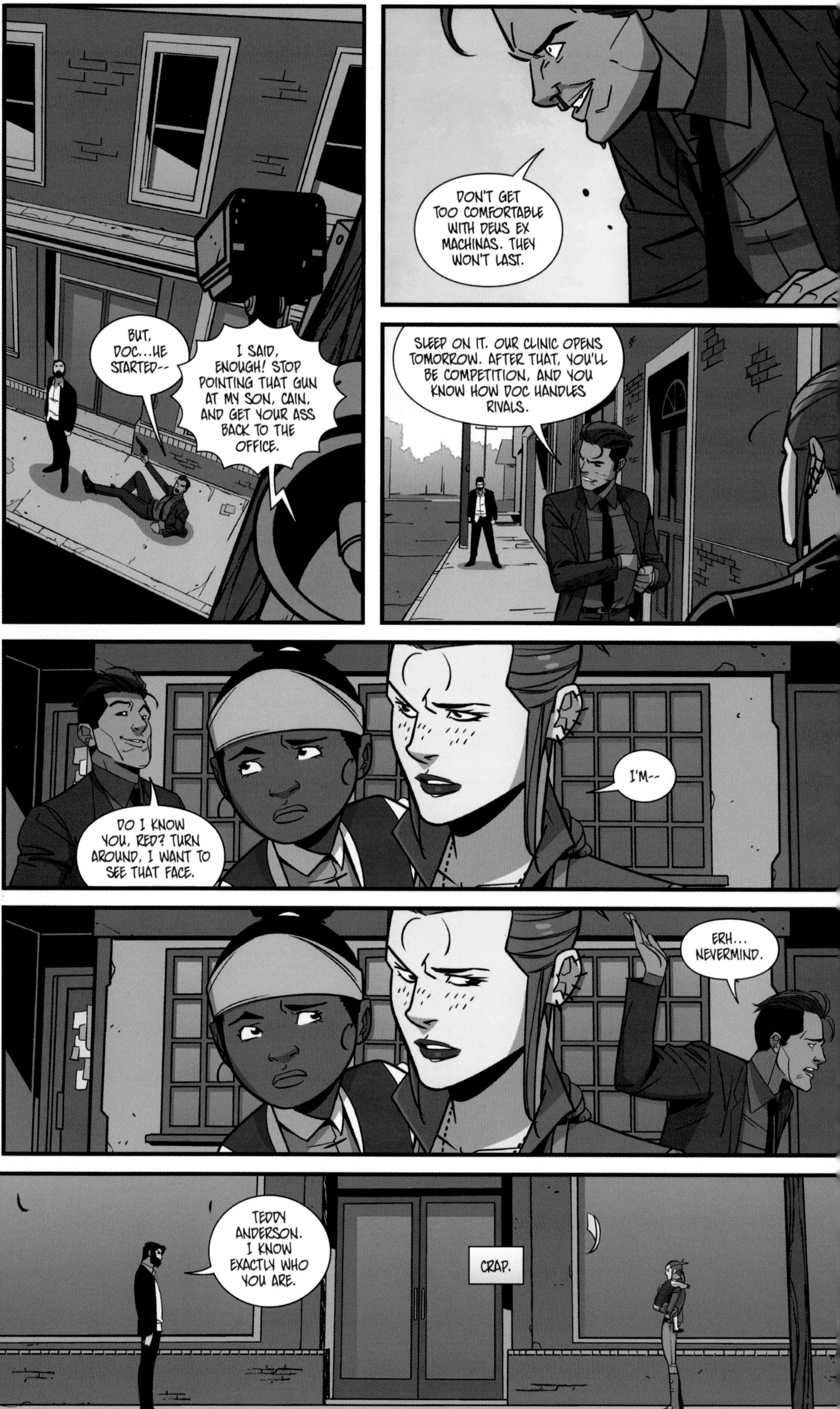
BUT, DOC...HE STARTED--
I SAID, ENOUGH! STOP POINTING THAT GUN AT MY SON, CAIN, AND GET YOUR ASS BACK TO THE OFFICE.
DON'T GET TOO COMFORTABLE WITH DEUS EX MACHINAS. THEY WON'T LAST.
SLEEP ON IT. OUR CLINIC OPENS TOMORROW. AFTER THAT, YOU'LL BE COMPETITION, AND YOU KNOW HOW DOC HANDLES RIVALS.
DO I KNOW YOU, RED? TURN AROUND, I WANT TO SEE THAT FACE.
I'M--
ERH... NEVERMIND.
TEDDY ANDERSON. I KNOW EXACTLY WHO YOU ARE.
CRAP.

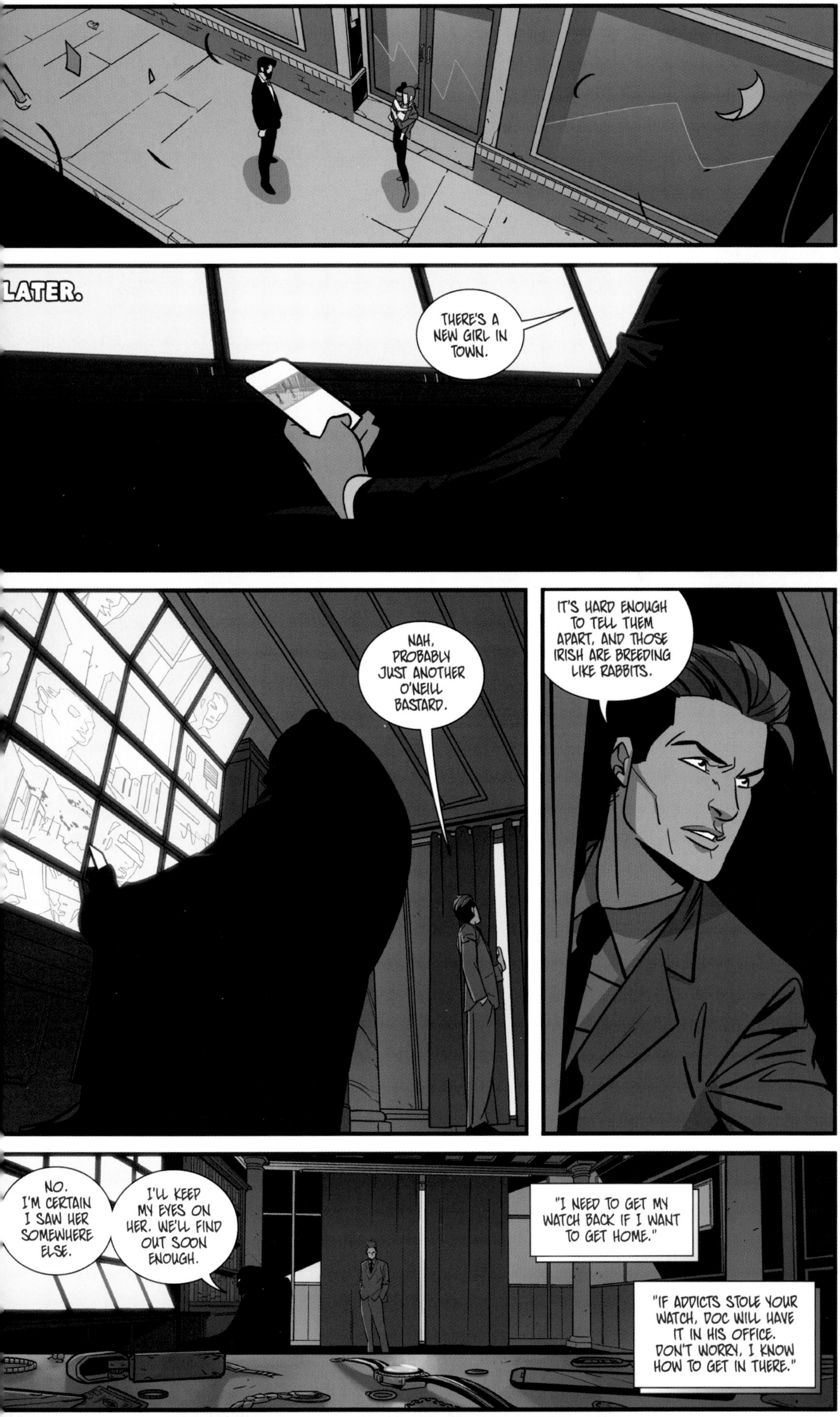
LATER.
THERE'S A NEW GIRL IN TOWN.
NAH, PROBABLY JUST ANOTHER O'NEILL BASTARD.
IT'S HARD ENOUGH TO TELL THEM APART, AND THOSE IRISH ARE BREEDING LIKE RABBITS.
NO. I'M CERTAIN I SAW HER SOMEWHERE ELSE.
I'LL KEEP MY EYES ON HER. WE'LL FIND OUT SOON ENOUGH.
"I NEED TO GET MY WATCH BACK IF I WANT TO GET HOME."
"IF ADDICTS STOLE YOUR WATCH, DOC WILL HAVE IT IN HIS OFFICE. DON'T WORRY, I KNOW HOW TO GET IN THERE."

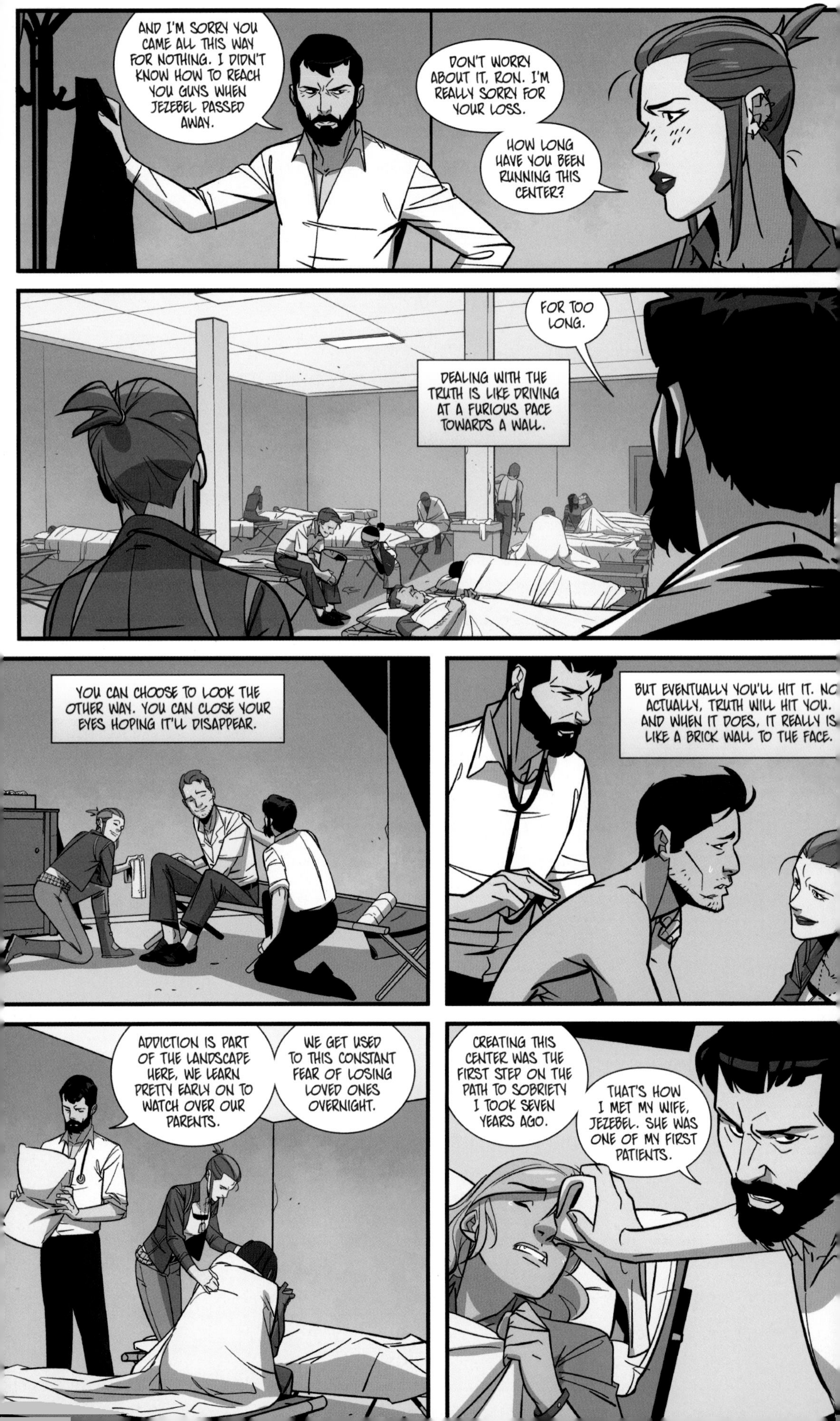
AND I'M SORRY YOU CAME ALL THIS WAY FOR NOTHING. I DIDN'T KNOW HOW TO REACH YOU GUYS WHEN JEZEBEL PASSED AWAY.
DON'T WORRY ABOUT IT, RON. I'M REALLY SORRY FOR YOUR LOSS.
HOW LONG HAVE YOU BEEN RUNNING THIS CENTER?
DEALING WITH THE TRUTH IS LIKE DRIVING AT A FURIOUS PACE TOWARDS A WALL.
FOR TOO LONG.
YOU CAN CHOOSE TO LOOK THE OTHER WAY. YOU CAN CLOSE YOUR EYES HOPING IT'LL DISAPPEAR.
BUT EVENTUALLY YOU'LL HIT IT. NO ACTUALLY, TRUTH WILL HIT YOU. AND WHEN IT DOES, IT REALLY IS LIKE A BRICK WALL TO THE FACE.
ADDICTION IS PART OF THE LANDSCAPE HERE, WE LEARN PRETTY EARLY ON TO WATCH OVER OUR PARENTS.
WE GET USED TO THIS CONSTANT FEAR OF LOSING LOVED ONES OVERNIGHT.
CREATING THIS CENTER WAS THE FIRST STEP ON THE PATH TO SOBRIETY I TOOK SEVEN YEARS AGO.
THAT'S HOW I MET MY WIFE, JEZEBEL. SHE WAS ONE OF MY FIRST PATIENTS.

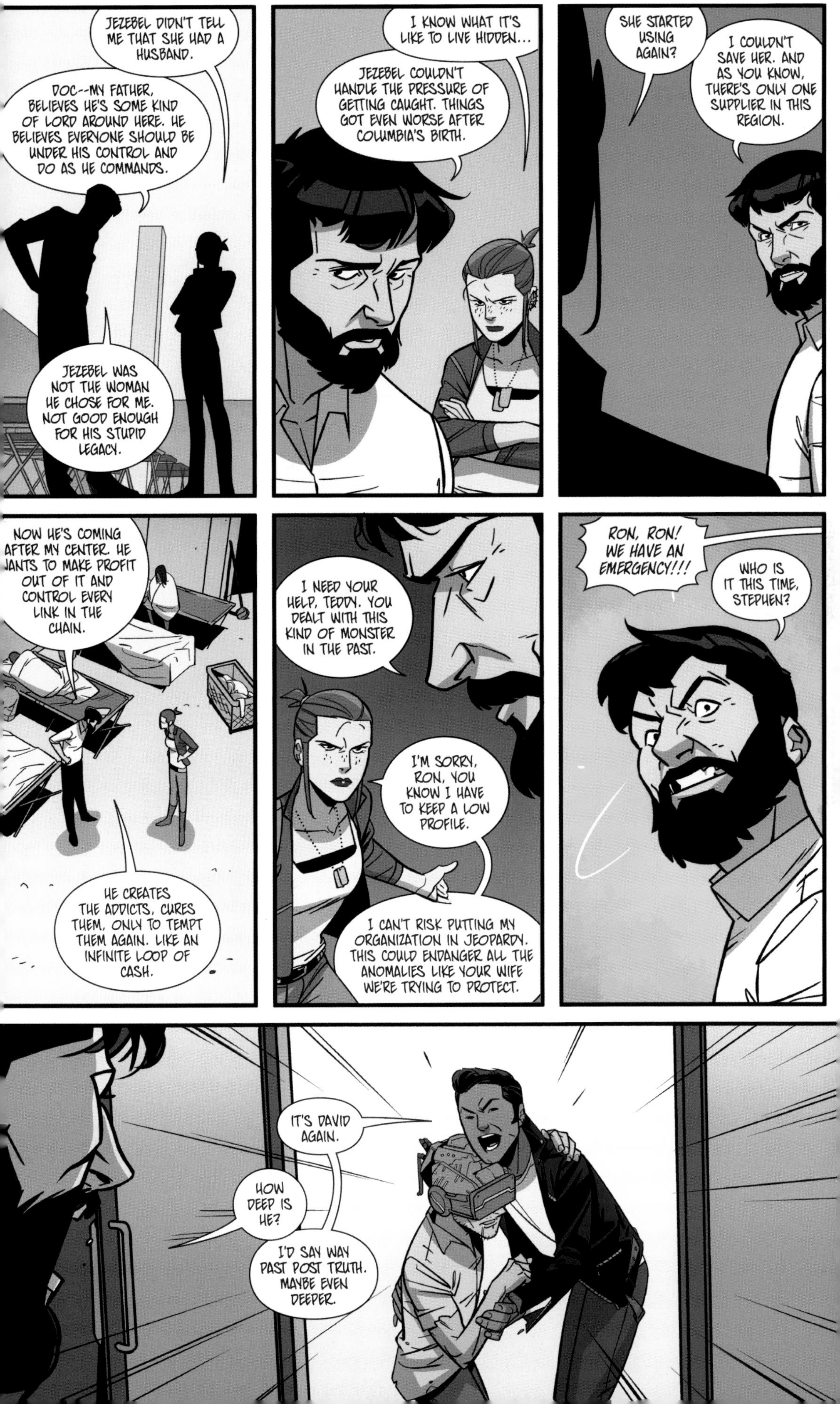
JEZEBEL DIDN'T TELL ME THAT SHE HAD A HUSBAND.
DOC--MY FATHER, BELIEVES HE'S SOME KIND OF LORD AROUND HERE. HE BELIEVES EVERYONE SHOULD BE UNDER HIS CONTROL AND DO AS HE COMMANDS.
JEZEBEL WAS NOT THE WOMAN HE CHOSE FOR ME. NOT GOOD ENOUGH FOR HIS STUPID LEGACY.
I KNOW WHAT IT'S LIKE TO LIVE HIDDEN...
JEZEBEL COULDN'T HANDLE THE PRESSURE OF GETTING CAUGHT. THINGS GOT EVEN WORSE AFTER COLUMBIA'S BIRTH.
SHE STARTED USING AGAIN?
I COULDN'T SAVE HER. AND AS YOU KNOW, THERE'S ONLY ONE SUPPLIER IN THIS REGION.
NOW HE'S COMING AFTER MY CENTER. HE WANTS TO MAKE PROFIT OUT OF IT AND CONTROL EVERY LINK IN THE CHAIN.
HE CREATES THE ADDICTS, CURES THEM, ONLY TO TEMPT THEM AGAIN. LIKE AN INFINITE LOOP OF CASH.
I NEED YOUR HELP, TEDDY. YOU DEALT WITH THIS KIND OF MONSTER IN THE PAST.
I'M SORRY, RON. YOU KNOW I HAVE TO KEEP A LOW PROFILE.
I CAN'T RISK PUTTING MY ORGANIZATION IN JEOPARDY. THIS COULD ENDANGER ALL THE ANOMALIES LIKE YOUR WIFE WE'RE TRYING TO PROTECT.
RON, RON! WE HAVE AN EMERGENCY!!!
WHO IS IT THIS TIME, STEPHEN?
IT'S DAVID AGAIN.
HOW DEEP IS HE?
I'D SAY WAY PAST POST TRUTH. MAYBE EVEN DEEPER.

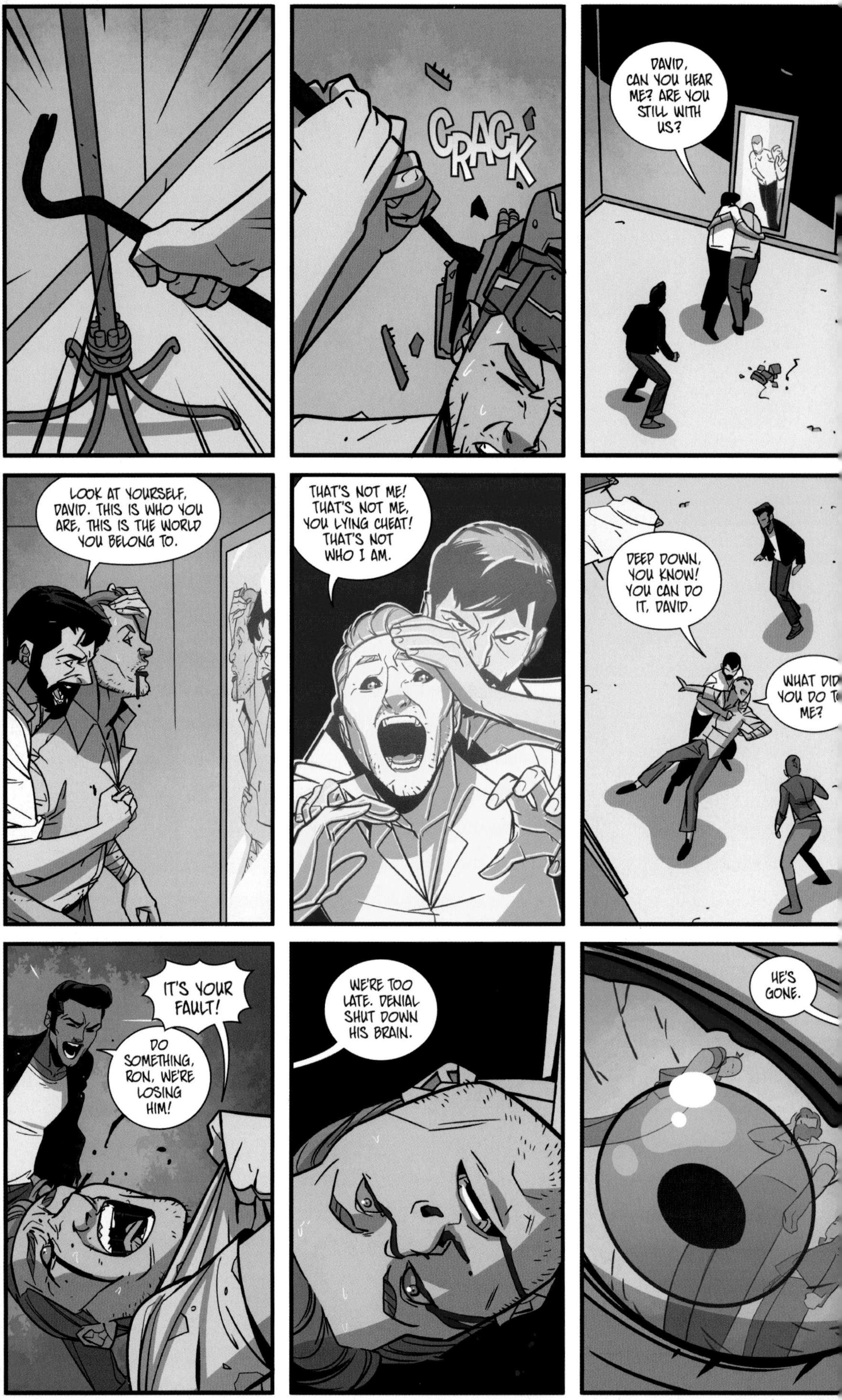
CRACK
DAVID, CAN YOU HEAR ME? ARE YOU STILL WITH US?
LOOK AT YOURSELF, DAVID. THIS IS WHO YOU ARE, THIS IS THE WORLD YOU BELONG TO.
THAT'S NOT ME! THAT'S NOT ME, YOU LYING CHEAT! THAT'S NOT WHO I AM.
DEEP DOWN, YOU KNOW! YOU CAN DO IT, DAVID.
WHAT DID YOU DO TO ME?
IT'S YOUR FAULT!
DO SOMETHING, RON, WE'RE LOSING HIM!
WE'RE TOO LATE. DENIAL SHUT DOWN HIS BRAIN.
HE'S GONE.

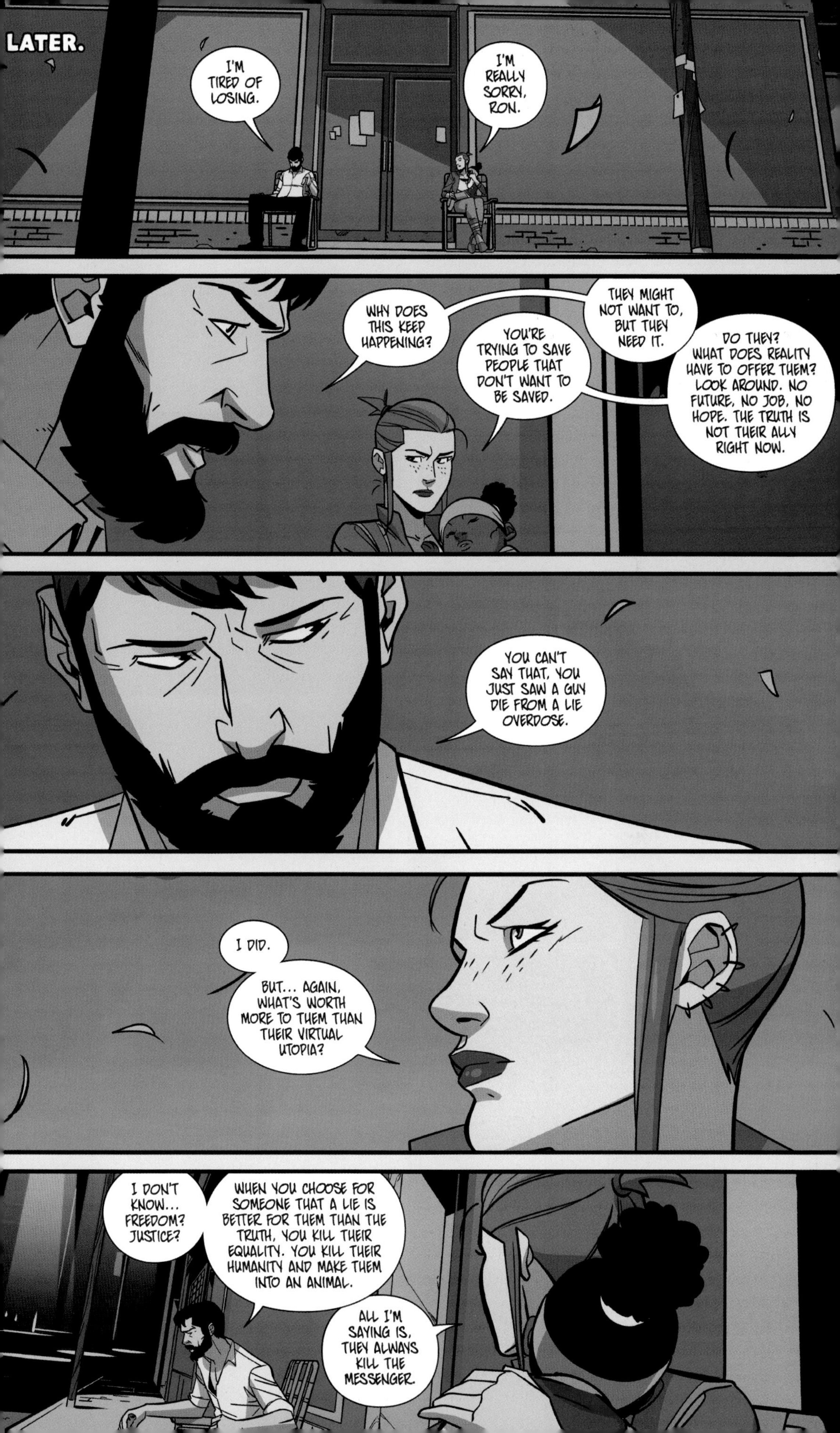
LATER.
I'M TIRED OF LOSING.
I'M REALLY SORRY, RON.
WHY DOES THIS KEEP HAPPENING?
YOU'RE TRYING TO SAVE PEOPLE THAT DON'T WANT TO BE SAVED.
THEY MIGHT NOT WANT TO, BUT THEY NEED IT.
DO THEY? WHAT DOES REALITY HAVE TO OFFER THEM? LOOK AROUND. NO FUTURE, NO JOB, NO HOPE. THE TRUTH IS NOT THEIR ALLY RIGHT NOW.
YOU CAN'T SAY THAT, YOU JUST SAW A GUY DIE FROM A LIE OVERDOSE.
I DID.
BUT... AGAIN, WHAT'S WORTH MORE TO THEM THAN THEIR VIRTUAL UTOPIA?
I DON'T KNOW... FREEDOM? JUSTICE?
WHEN YOU CHOOSE FOR SOMEONE THAT A LIE IS BETTER FOR THEM THAN THE TRUTH, YOU KILL THEIR EQUALITY. YOU KILL THEIR HUMANITY AND MAKE THEM INTO AN ANIMAL.
ALL I'M SAYING IS, THEY ALWAYS KILL THE MESSENGER.

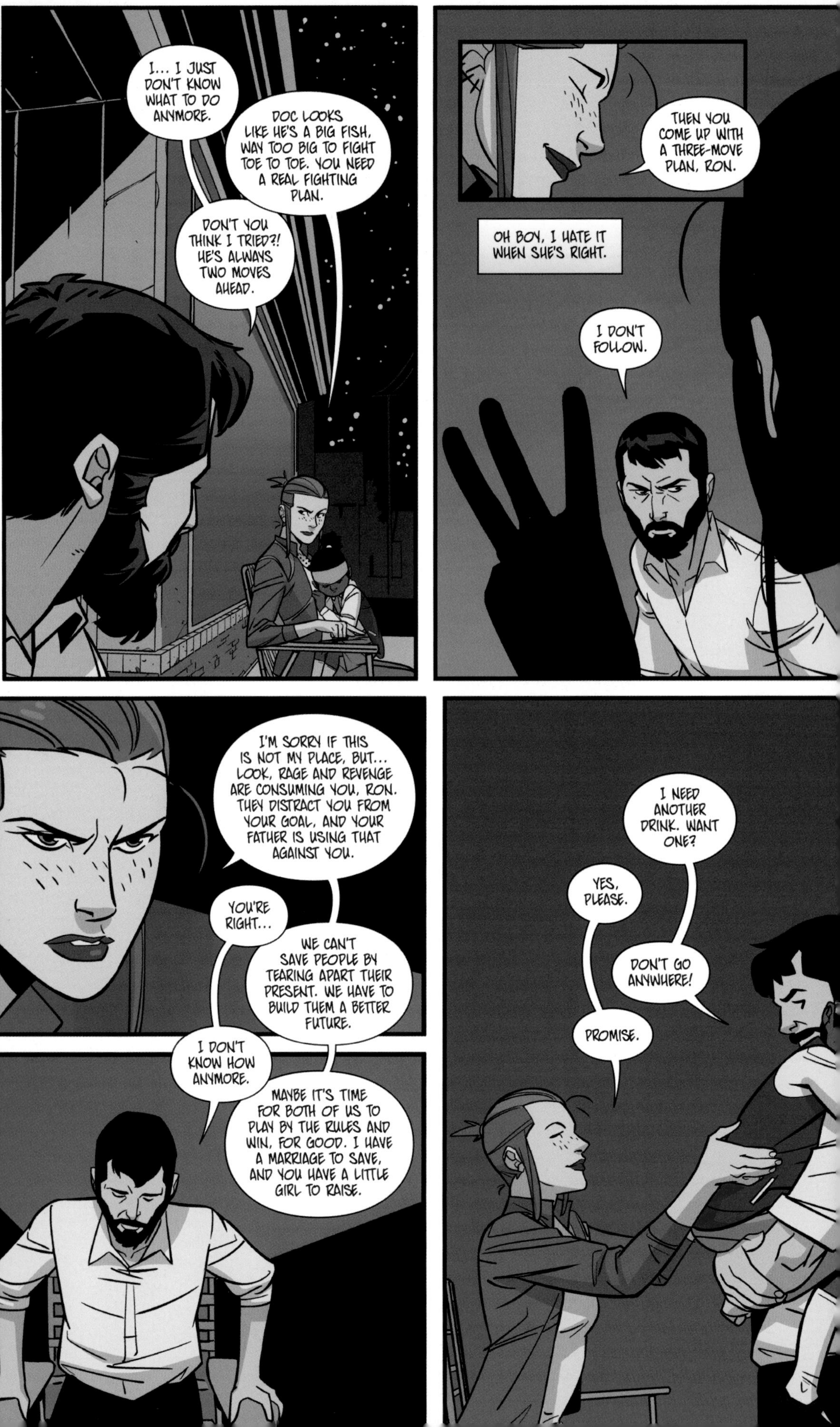
I... I JUST DON'T KNOW WHAT TO DO ANYMORE.
DOC LOOKS LIKE HE'S A BIG FISH, WAY TOO BIG TO FIGHT TOE TO TOE. YOU NEED A REAL FIGHTING PLAN.
DON'T YOU THINK I TRIED?! HE'S ALWAYS TWO MOVES AHEAD.
THEN YOU COME UP WITH A THREE-MOVE PLAN, RON.
OH BOY, I HATE IT WHEN SHE'S RIGHT.
I DON'T FOLLOW.
I'M SORRY IF THIS IS NOT MY PLACE, BUT... LOOK, RAGE AND REVENGE ARE CONSUMING YOU, RON. THEY DISTRACT YOU FROM YOUR GOAL, AND YOUR FATHER IS USING THAT AGAINST YOU.
YOU'RE RIGHT...
WE CAN'T SAVE PEOPLE BY TEARING APART THEIR PRESENT. WE HAVE TO BUILD THEM A BETTER FUTURE.
I DON'T KNOW HOW ANYMORE.
MAYBE IT'S TIME FOR BOTH OF US TO PLAY BY THE RULES AND WIN, FOR GOOD. I HAVE A MARRIAGE TO SAVE, AND YOU HAVE A LITTLE GIRL TO RAISE.
I NEED ANOTHER DRINK. WANT ONE?
YES, PLEASE.
DON'T GO ANYWHERE!
PROMISE.

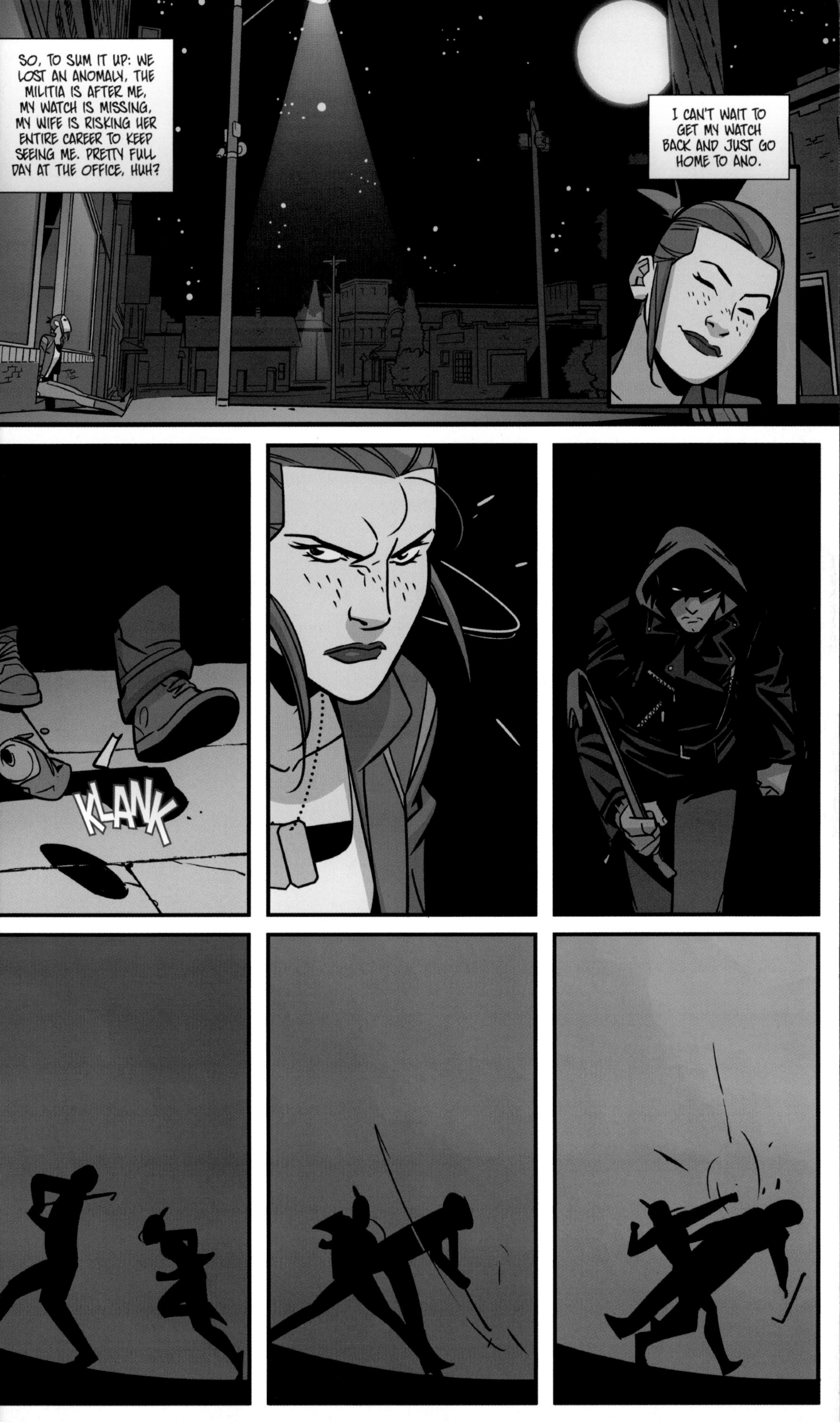
SO, TO SUM IT UP: WE LOST AN ANOMALY, THE MILITIA IS AFTER ME, MY WATCH IS MISSING, MY WIFE IS RISKING HER ENTIRE CAREER TO KEEP SEEING ME. PRETTY FULL DAY AT THE OFFICE, HUH?
I CAN'T WAIT TO GET MY WATCH BACK AND JUST GO HOME TO ANO.
KLANK

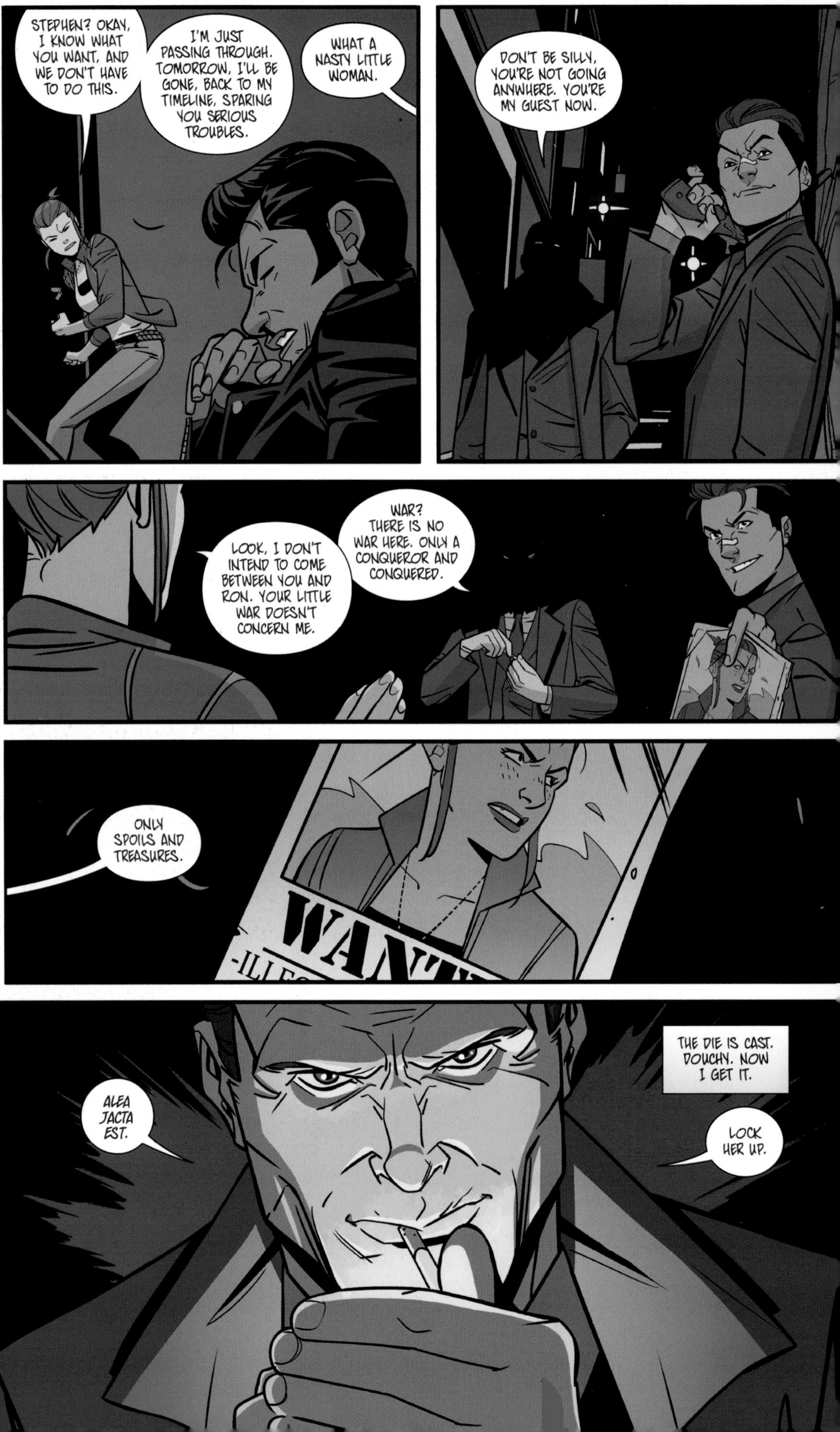
STEPHEN? OKAY, I KNOW WHAT YOU WANT, AND WE DON'T HAVE TO DO THIS.
I'M JUST PASSING THROUGH. TOMORROW, I'LL BE GONE, BACK TO MY TIMELINE, SPARING YOU SERIOUS TROUBLES.
WHAT A NASTY LITTLE WOMAN.
DON'T BE SILLY, YOU'RE NOT GOING ANYWHERE. YOU'RE MY GUEST NOW.
LOOK, I DON'T INTEND TO COME BETWEEN YOU AND RON. YOUR LITTLE WAR DOESN'T CONCERN ME.
WAR? THERE IS NO WAR HERE. ONLY A CONQUEROR AND CONQUERED.
ONLY SPOILS AND TREASURES.
ALEA JACTA EST.
THE DIE IS CAST. DOUCHY. NOW I GET IT.
LOCK HER UP.

Art by CLIFF CHIANG

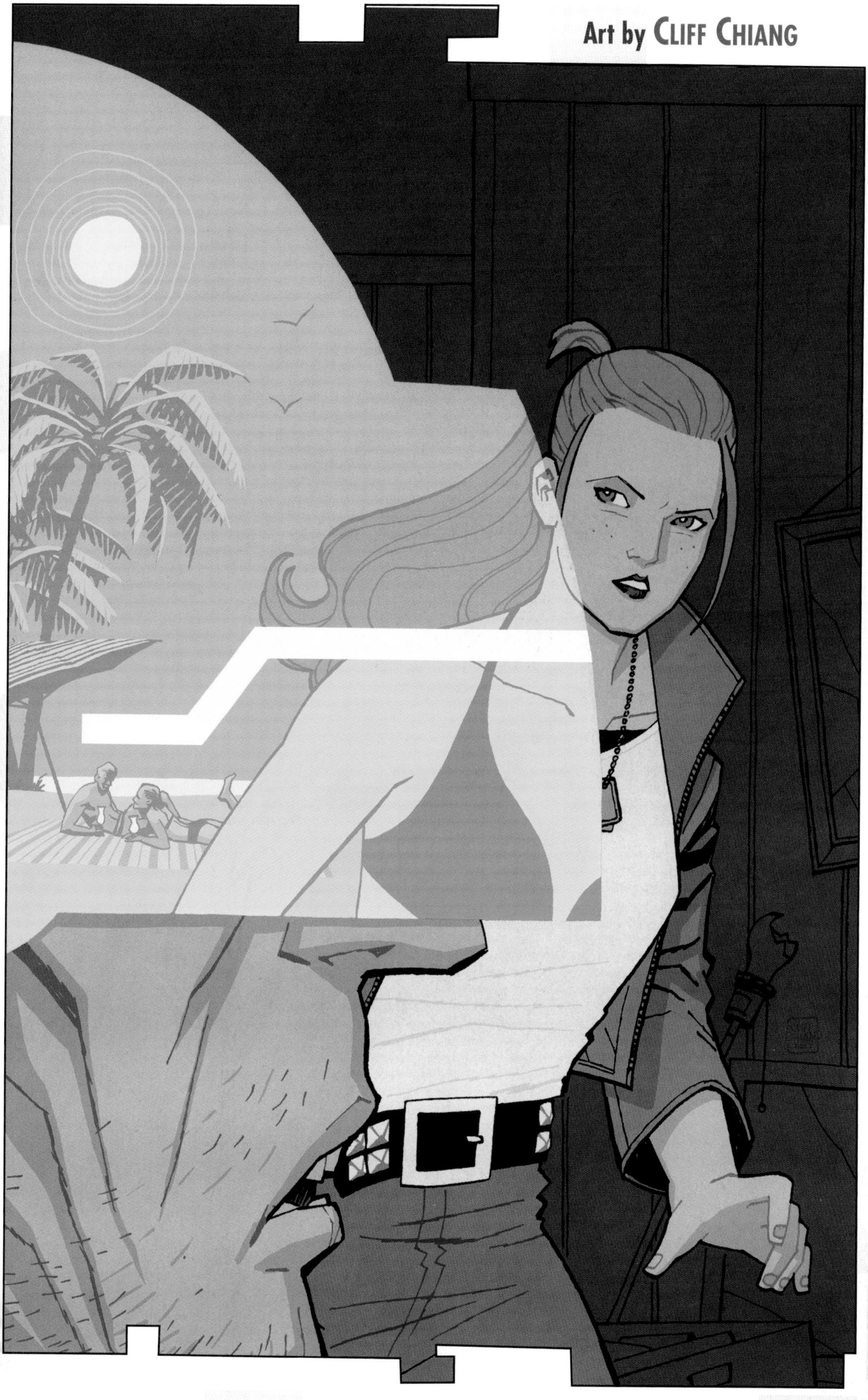

Art by
ELSA CHARRETIER

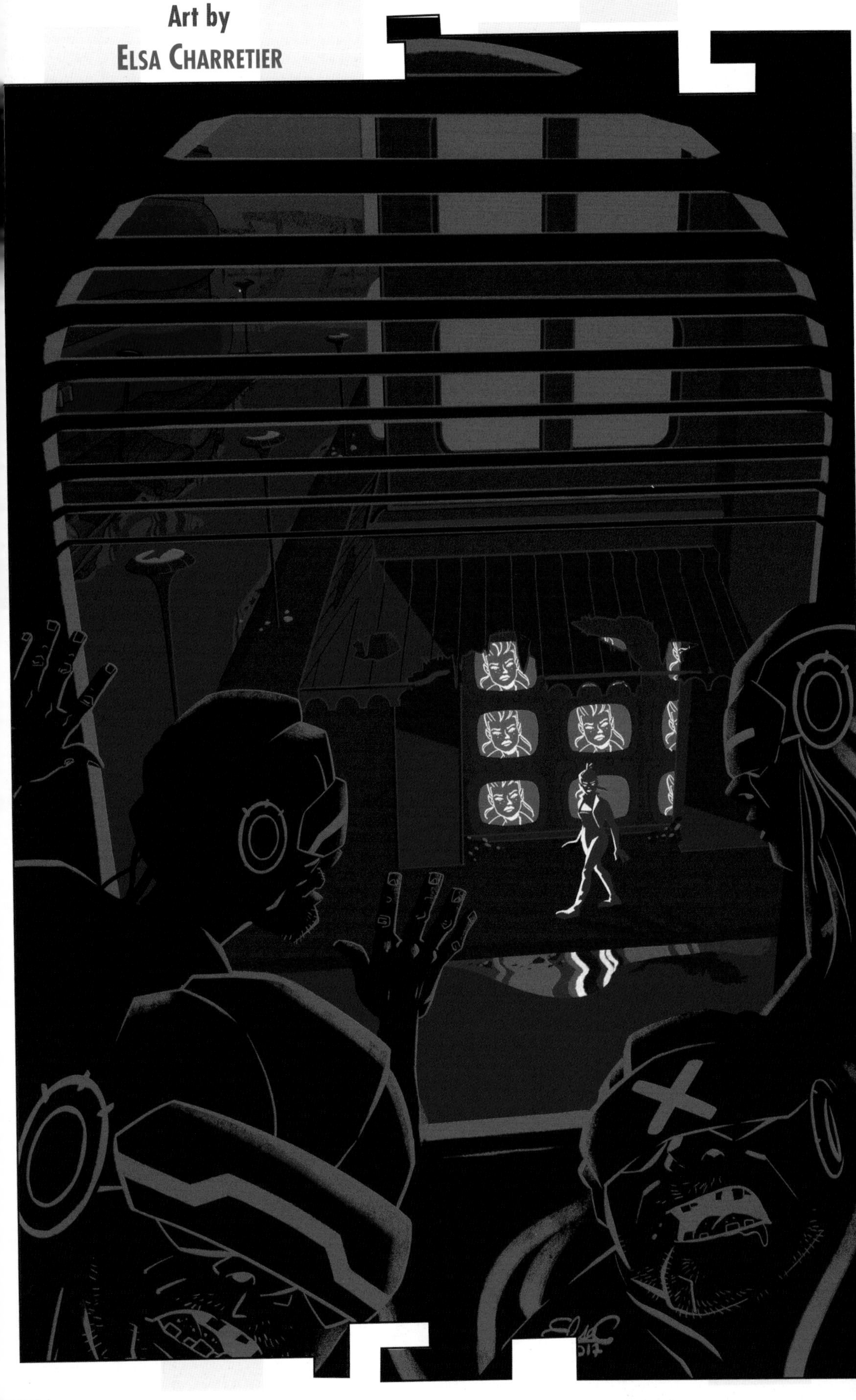

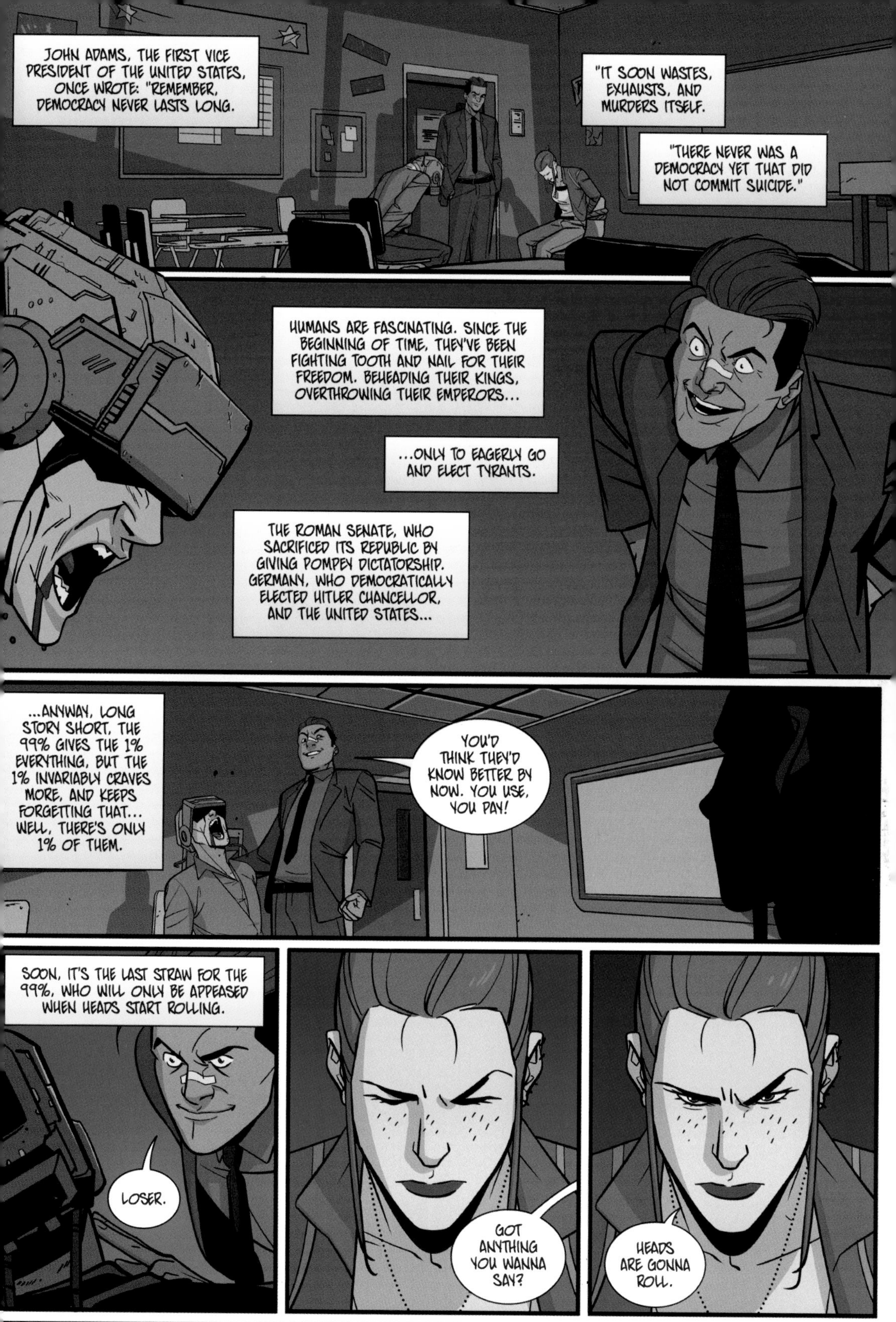
JOHN ADAMS, THE FIRST VICE PRESIDENT OF THE UNITED STATES, ONCE WROTE: "REMEMBER, DEMOCRACY NEVER LASTS LONG.
"IT SOON WASTES, EXHAUSTS, AND MURDERS ITSELF.
"THERE NEVER WAS A DEMOCRACY YET THAT DID NOT COMMIT SUICIDE."
HUMANS ARE FASCINATING. SINCE THE BEGINNING OF TIME, THEY'VE BEEN FIGHTING TOOTH AND NAIL FOR THEIR FREEDOM. BEHEADING THEIR KINGS, OVERTHROWING THEIR EMPERORS...
...ONLY TO EAGERLY GO AND ELECT TYRANTS.
THE ROMAN SENATE, WHO SACRIFICED ITS REPUBLIC BY GIVING POMPEY DICTATORSHIP. GERMANY, WHO DEMOCRATICALLY ELECTED HITLER CHANCELLOR, AND THE UNITED STATES...
...ANYWAY, LONG STORY SHORT, THE 99% GIVES THE 1% EVERYTHING, BUT THE 1% INVARIABLY CRAVES MORE, AND KEEPS FORGETTING THAT... WELL, THERE'S ONLY 1% OF THEM.
YOU'D THINK THEY'D KNOW BETTER BY NOW. YOU USE, YOU PAY!
SOON, IT'S THE LAST STRAW FOR THE 99%, WHO WILL ONLY BE APPEASED WHEN HEADS START ROLLING.
LOSER.
GOT ANYTHING YOU WANNA SAY?
HEADS ARE GONNA ROLL.

THE INFINITE LOOP

2. GOOD MAN, MADMAN

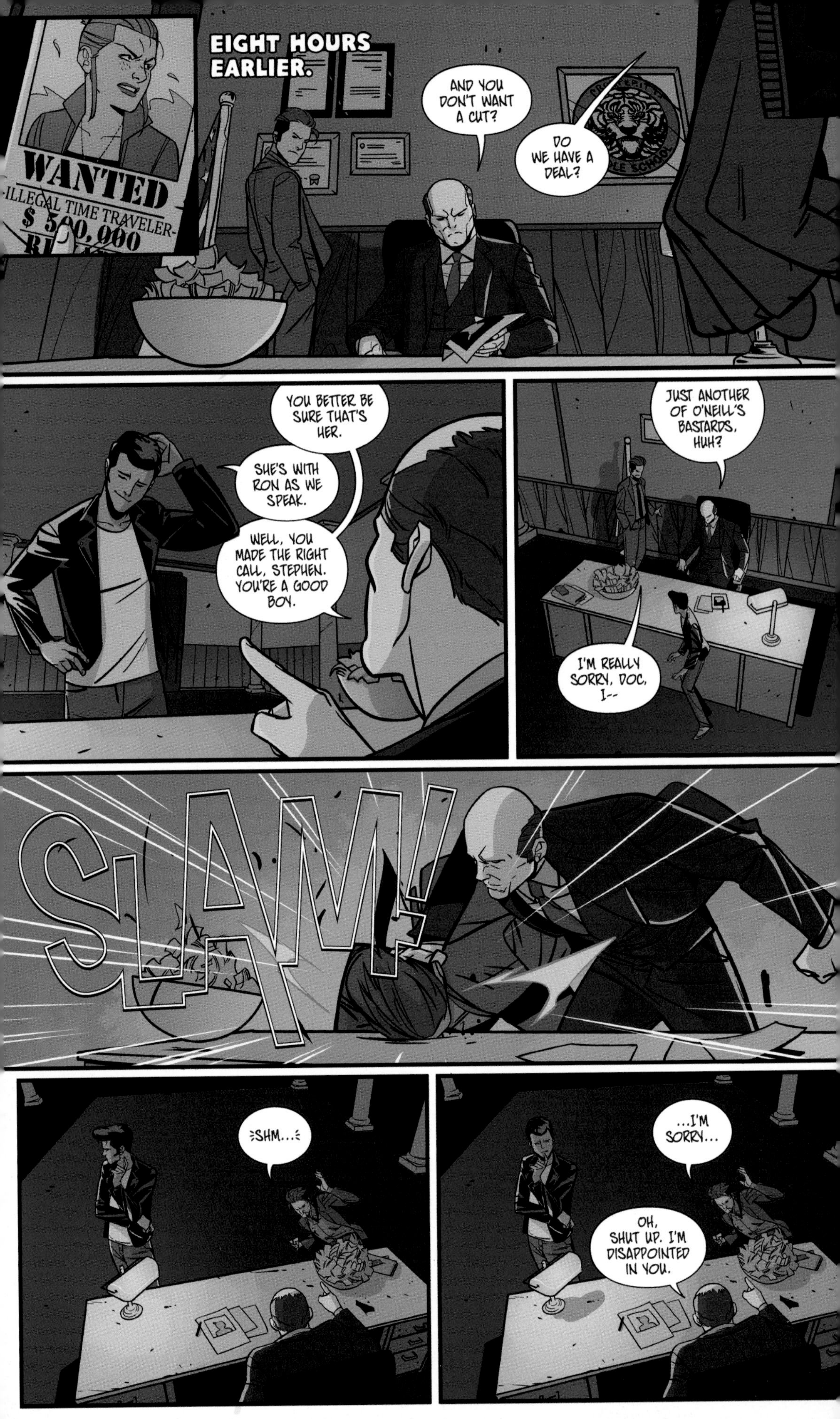
EIGHT HOURS EARLIER.
WANTED
-ILLEGAL TIME TRAVELER-
$ 500,000
AND YOU DON'T WANT A CUT?
DO WE HAVE A DEAL?
YOU BETTER BE SURE THAT'S HER.
SHE'S WITH RON AS WE SPEAK.
WELL, YOU MADE THE RIGHT CALL, STEPHEN. YOU'RE A GOOD BOY.
JUST ANOTHER OF O'NEILL'S BASTARDS, HUH?
I'M REALLY SORRY, DOC, I--
SLAM!
SHM...
...I'M SORRY...
OH, SHUT UP. I'M DISAPPOINTED IN YOU.

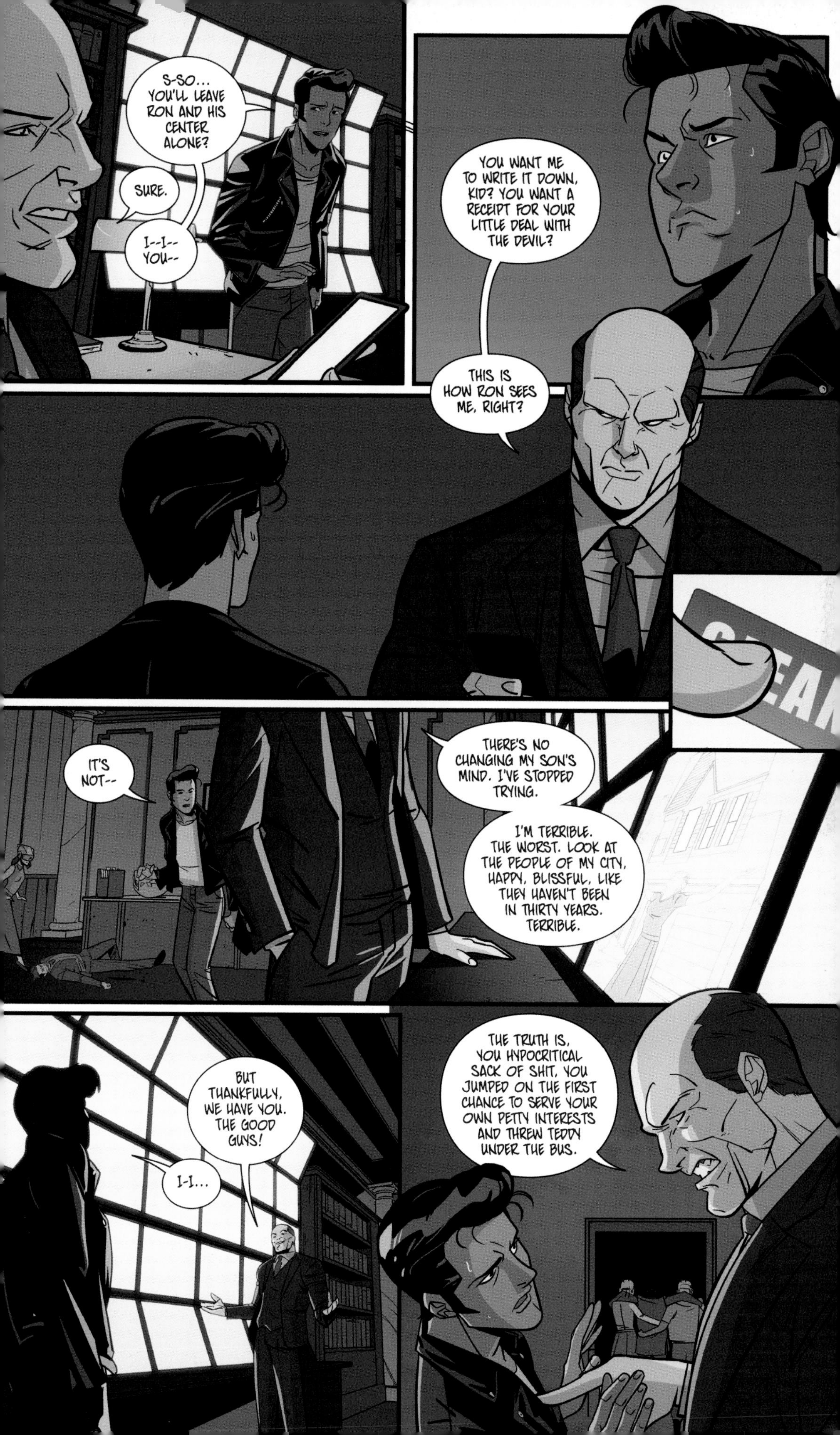
S-SO... YOU'LL LEAVE RON AND HIS CENTER ALONE?
SURE.
I--I-- YOU--
YOU WANT ME TO WRITE IT DOWN, KID? YOU WANT A RECEIPT FOR YOUR LITTLE DEAL WITH THE DEVIL?
THIS IS HOW RON SEES ME, RIGHT?
IT'S NOT--
THERE'S NO CHANGING MY SON'S MIND. I'VE STOPPED TRYING.
I'M TERRIBLE. THE WORST. LOOK AT THE PEOPLE OF MY CITY, HAPPY, BLISSFUL, LIKE THEY HAVEN'T BEEN IN THIRTY YEARS. TERRIBLE.
BUT THANKFULLY, WE HAVE YOU. THE GOOD GUYS!
I-I...
THE TRUTH IS, YOU HYPOCRITICAL SACK OF SHIT, YOU JUMPED ON THE FIRST CHANCE TO SERVE YOUR OWN PETTY INTERESTS AND THREW TEDDY UNDER THE BUS.

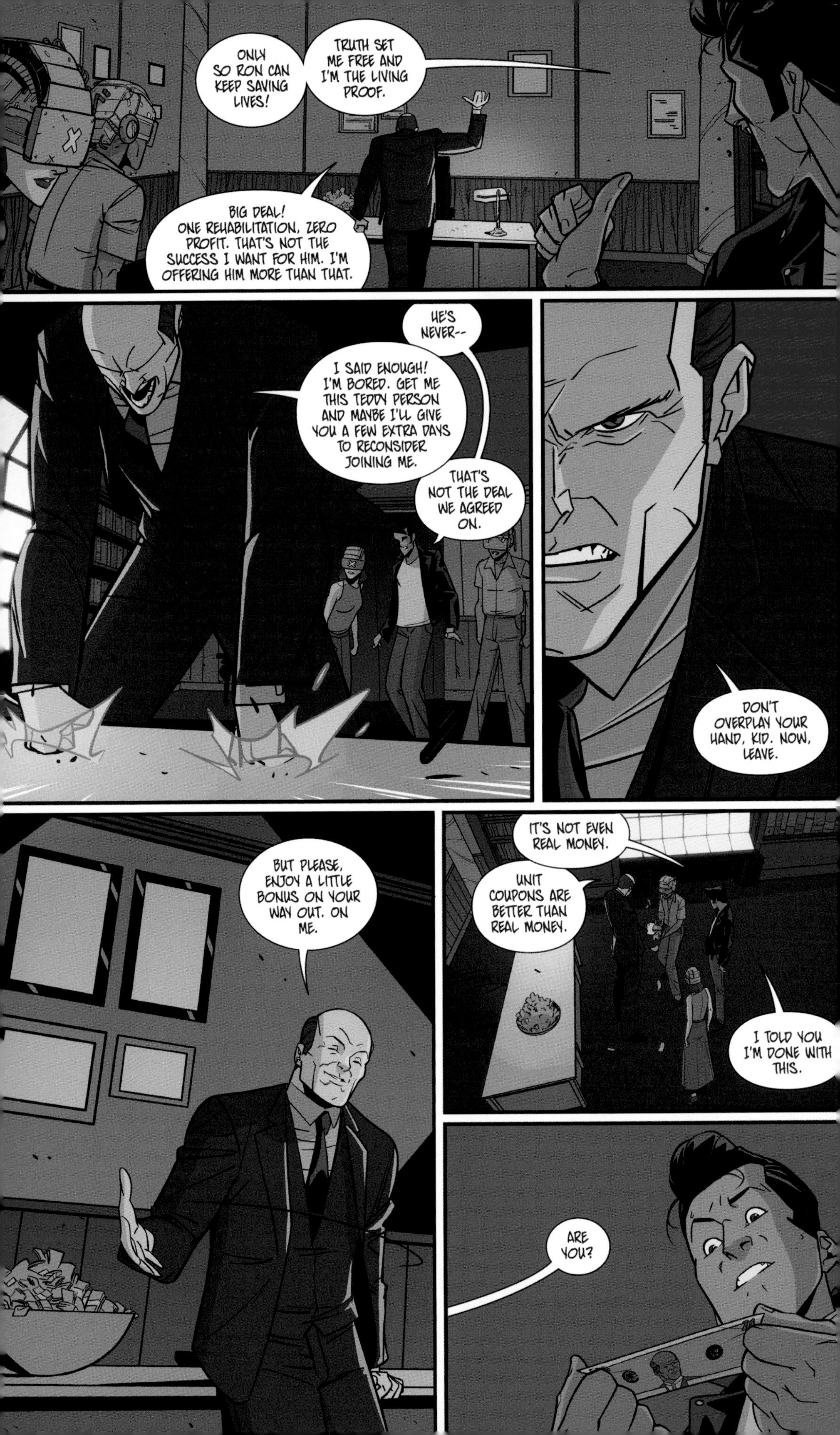
ONLY SO RON CAN KEEP SAVING LIVES!
TRUTH SET ME FREE AND I'M THE LIVING PROOF.
BIG DEAL! ONE REHABILITATION, ZERO PROFIT. THAT'S NOT THE SUCCESS I WANT FOR HIM. I'M OFFERING HIM MORE THAN THAT.
HE'S NEVER--
I SAID ENOUGH! I'M BORED. GET ME THIS TEDDY PERSON AND MAYBE I'LL GIVE YOU A FEW EXTRA DAYS TO RECONSIDER JOINING ME.
THAT'S NOT THE DEAL WE AGREED ON.
DON'T OVERPLAY YOUR HAND, KID. NOW, LEAVE.
BUT PLEASE, ENJOY A LITTLE BONUS ON YOUR WAY OUT. ON ME.
IT'S NOT EVEN REAL MONEY.
UNIT COUPONS ARE BETTER THAN REAL MONEY.
I TOLD YOU I'M DONE WITH THIS.
ARE YOU?

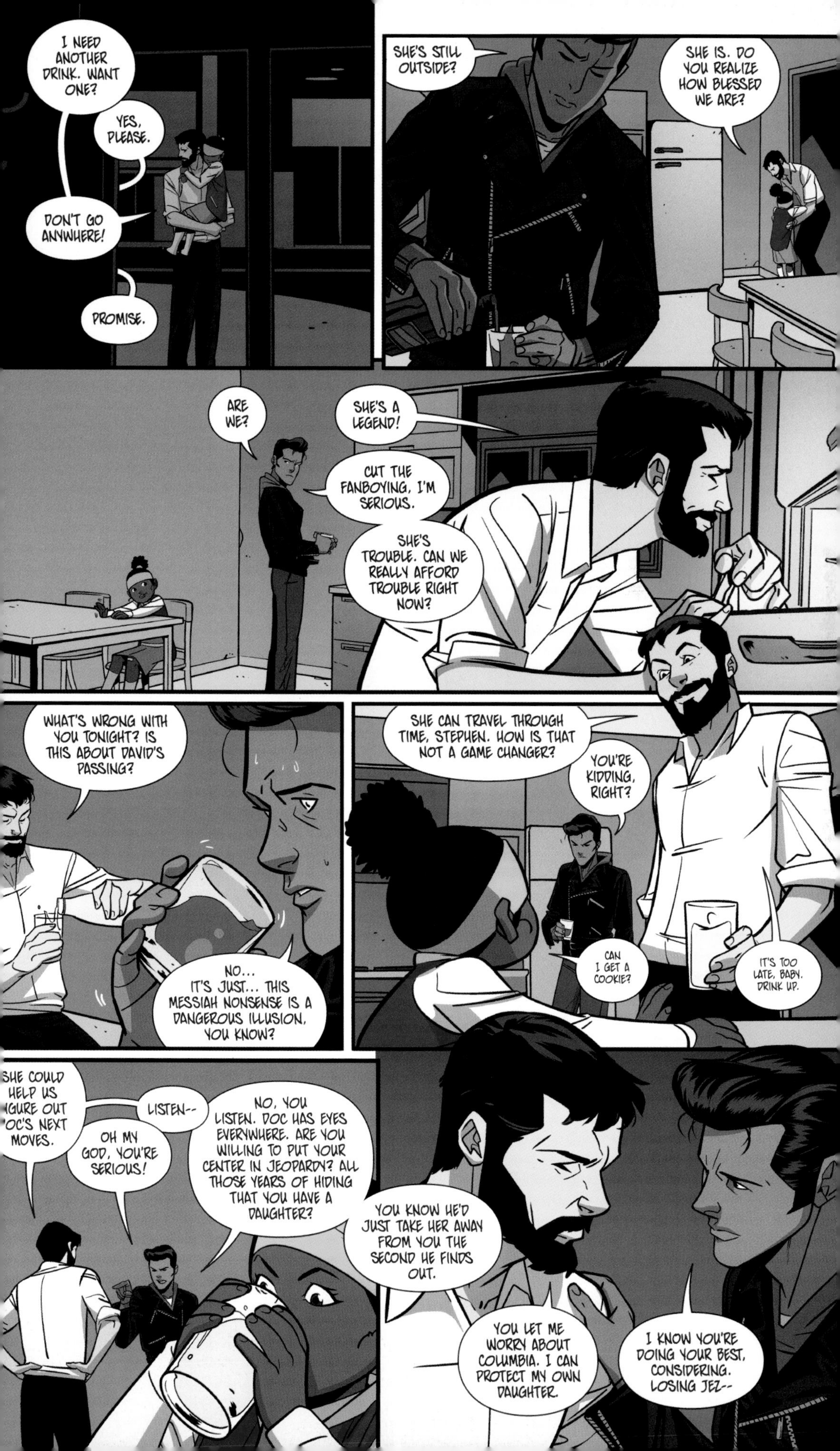

I NEED ANOTHER DRINK. WANT ONE?
YES, PLEASE.
DON'T GO ANYWHERE!
PROMISE.
SHE'S STILL OUTSIDE?
SHE IS. DO YOU REALIZE HOW BLESSED WE ARE?
ARE WE?
SHE'S A LEGEND!
CUT THE FANBOYING, I'M SERIOUS.
SHE'S TROUBLE. CAN WE REALLY AFFORD TROUBLE RIGHT NOW?
WHAT'S WRONG WITH YOU TONIGHT? IS THIS ABOUT DAVID'S PASSING?
NO... IT'S JUST... THIS MESSIAH NONSENSE IS A DANGEROUS ILLUSION, YOU KNOW?
SHE CAN TRAVEL THROUGH TIME, STEPHEN. HOW IS THAT NOT A GAME CHANGER?
YOU'RE KIDDING, RIGHT?
CAN I GET A COOKIE?
IT'S TOO LATE, BABY. DRINK UP.
SHE COULD HELP US IGURE OUT OC'S NEXT MOVES.
LISTEN--
OH MY GOD, YOU'RE SERIOUS!
NO, YOU LISTEN. DOC HAS EYES EVERYWHERE. ARE YOU WILLING TO PUT YOUR CENTER IN JEOPARDY? ALL THOSE YEARS OF HIDING THAT YOU HAVE A DAUGHTER?
YOU KNOW HE'D JUST TAKE HER AWAY FROM YOU THE SECOND HE FINDS OUT.
YOU LET ME WORRY ABOUT COLUMBIA. I CAN PROTECT MY OWN DAUGHTER.
I KNOW YOU'RE DOING YOUR BEST, CONSIDERING. LOSING JEZ--

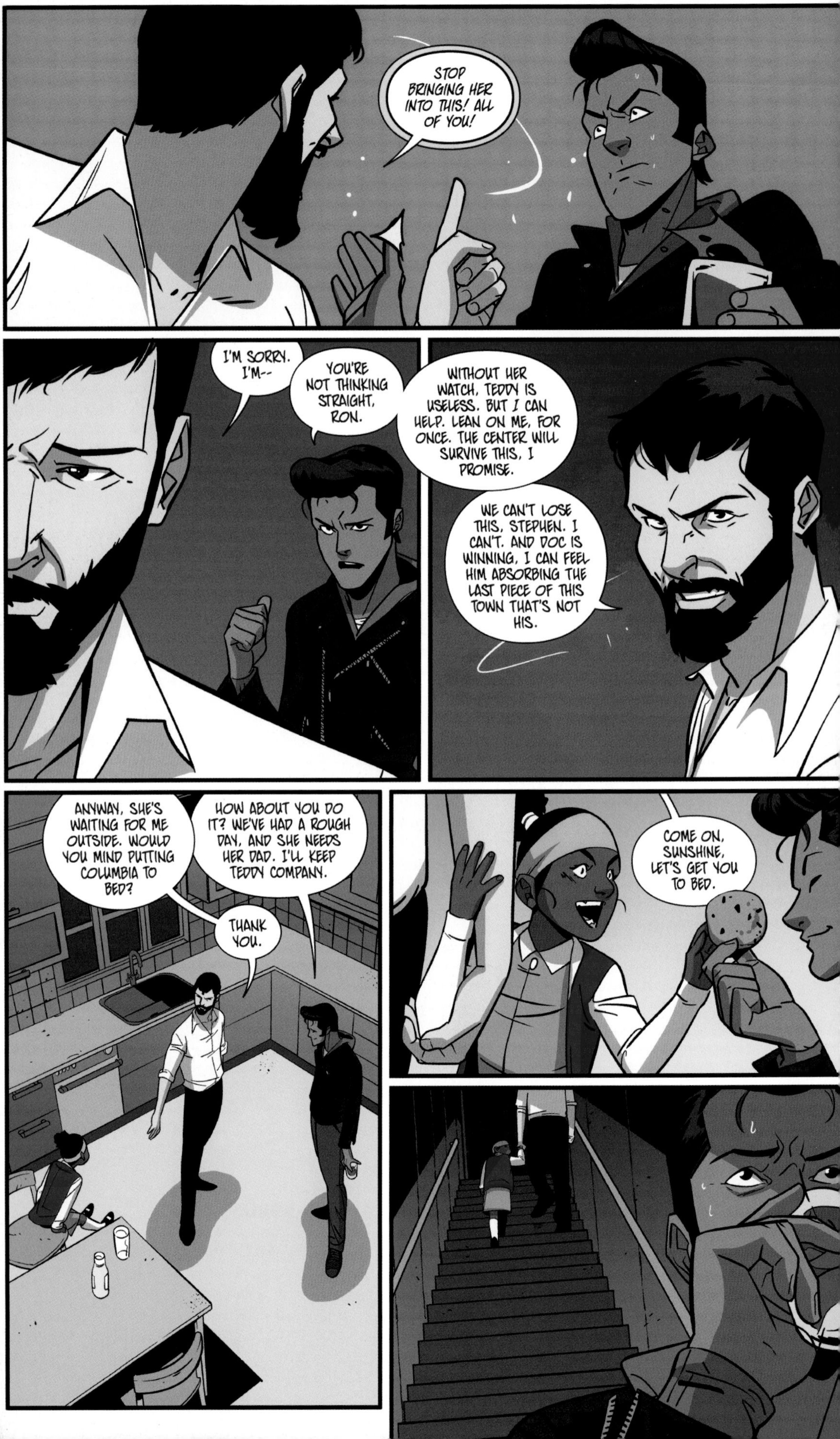
STOP BRINGING HER INTO THIS! ALL OF YOU!
I'M SORRY. I'M--
YOU'RE NOT THINKING STRAIGHT, RON.
WITHOUT HER WATCH, TEDDY IS USELESS. BUT I CAN HELP. LEAN ON ME, FOR ONCE. THE CENTER WILL SURVIVE THIS, I PROMISE.
WE CAN'T LOSE THIS, STEPHEN. I CAN'T. AND DOC IS WINNING, I CAN FEEL HIM ABSORBING THE LAST PIECE OF THIS TOWN THAT'S NOT HIS.
ANYWAY, SHE'S WAITING FOR ME OUTSIDE. WOULD YOU MIND PUTTING COLUMBIA TO BED?
HOW ABOUT YOU DO IT? WE'VE HAD A ROUGH DAY, AND SHE NEEDS HER DAD. I'LL KEEP TEDDY COMPANY.
THANK YOU.
COME ON, SUNSHINE, LET'S GET YOU TO BED.

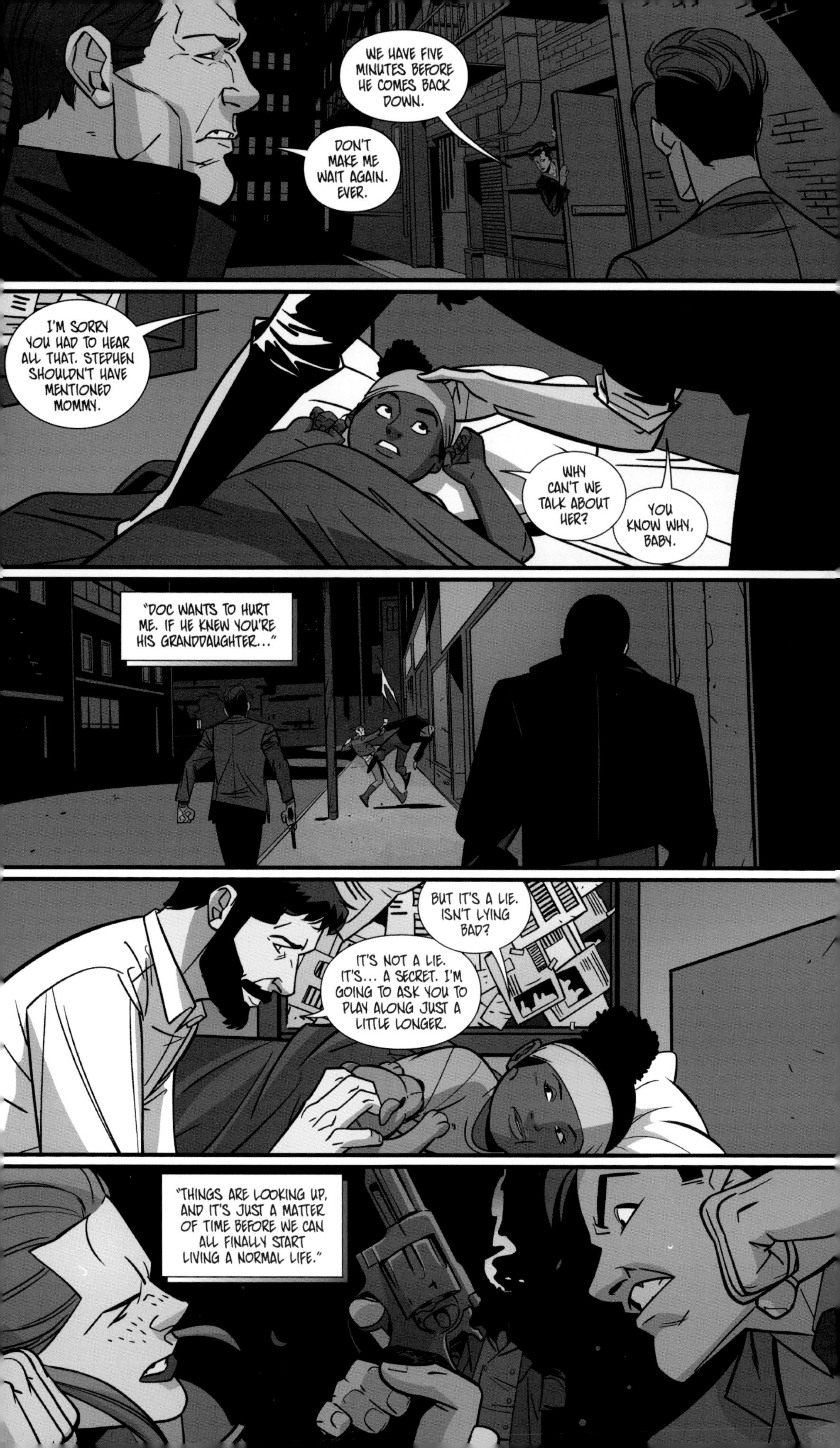

DON'T MAKE ME WAIT AGAIN. EVER.
WE HAVE FIVE MINUTES BEFORE HE COMES BACK DOWN.
I'M SORRY YOU HAD TO HEAR ALL THAT. STEPHEN SHOULDN'T HAVE MENTIONED MOMMY.
WHY CAN'T WE TALK ABOUT HER?
YOU KNOW WHY, BABY.
"DOC WANTS TO HURT ME. IF HE KNEW YOU'RE HIS GRANDDAUGHTER..."
BUT IT'S A LIE. ISN'T LYING BAD?
IT'S NOT A LIE. IT'S... A SECRET. I'M GOING TO ASK YOU TO PLAY ALONG JUST A LITTLE LONGER.
"THINGS ARE LOOKING UP, AND IT'S JUST A MATTER OF TIME BEFORE WE CAN ALL FINALLY START LIVING A NORMAL LIFE."

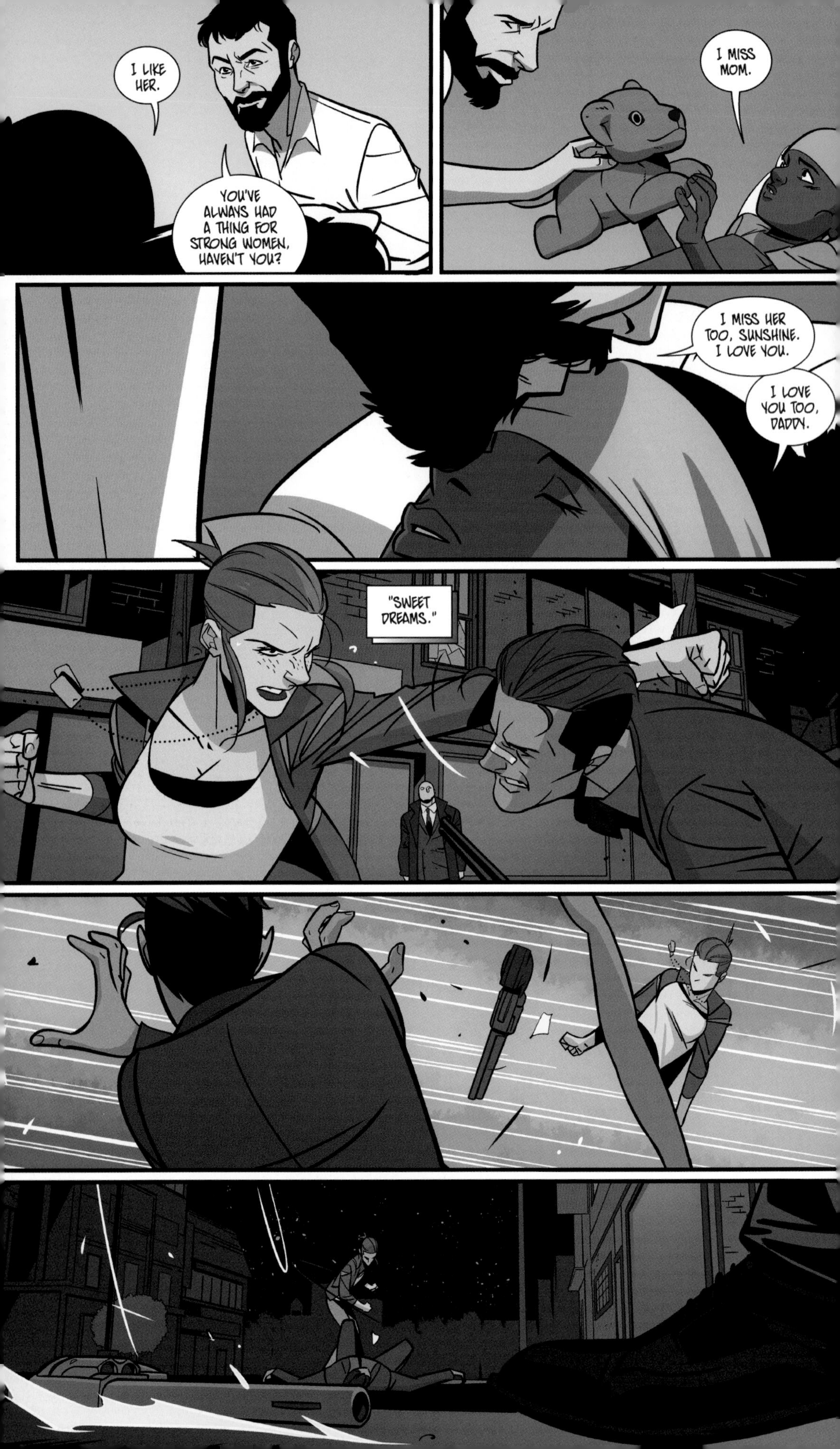
I LIKE HER.
YOU'VE ALWAYS HAD A THING FOR STRONG WOMEN, HAVEN'T YOU?
I MISS MOM.
I MISS HER TOO, SUNSHINE. I LOVE YOU.
I LOVE YOU TOO, DADDY.
"SWEET DREAMS."

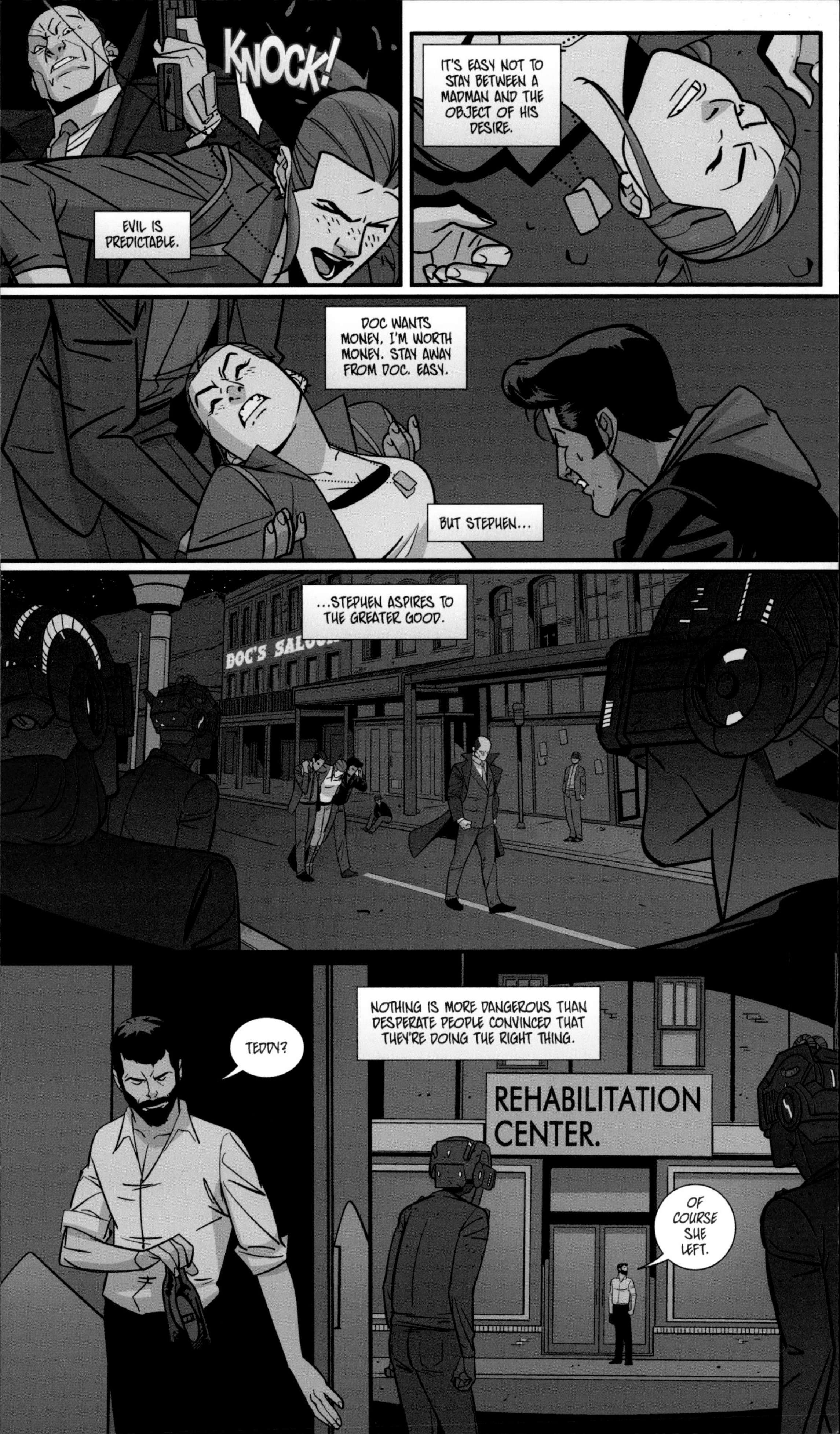
KNOCK!
EVIL IS PREDICTABLE.
IT'S EASY NOT TO STAY BETWEEN A MADMAN AND THE OBJECT OF HIS DESIRE.
DOC WANTS MONEY. I'M WORTH MONEY. STAY AWAY FROM DOC. EASY.
BUT STEPHEN...
...STEPHEN ASPIRES TO THE GREATER GOOD.
DOC'S SALOO
NOTHING IS MORE DANGEROUS THAN DESPERATE PEOPLE CONVINCED THAT THEY'RE DOING THE RIGHT THING.
TEDDY?
REHABILITATION CENTER.
OF COURSE SHE LEFT.

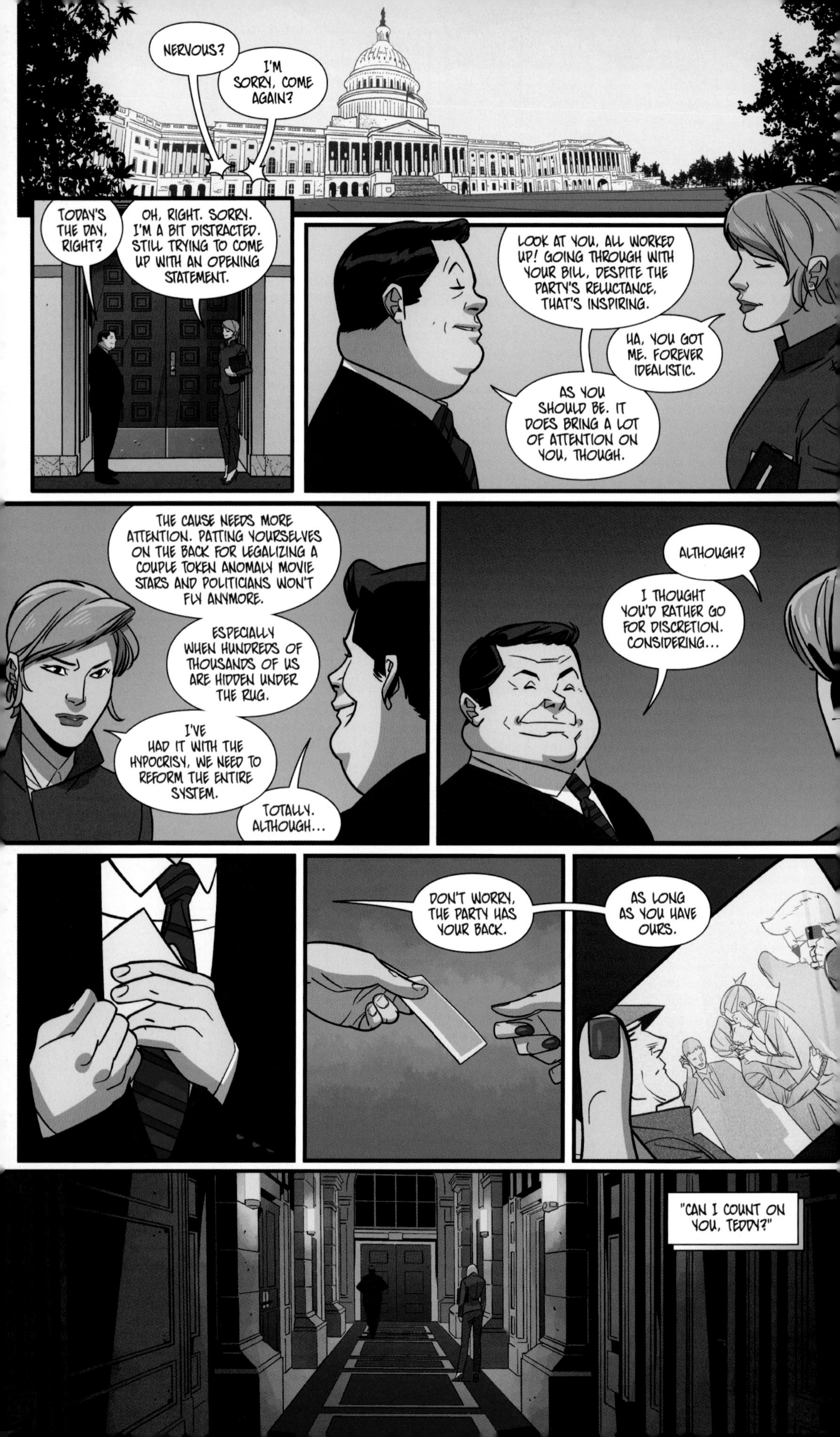
NERVOUS?
I'M SORRY, COME AGAIN?
TODAY'S THE DAY, RIGHT?
OH, RIGHT. SORRY. I'M A BIT DISTRACTED. STILL TRYING TO COME UP WITH AN OPENING STATEMENT.
LOOK AT YOU, ALL WORKED UP! GOING THROUGH WITH YOUR BILL, DESPITE THE PARTY'S RELUCTANCE, THAT'S INSPIRING.
HA, YOU GOT ME. FOREVER IDEALISTIC.
AS YOU SHOULD BE. IT DOES BRING A LOT OF ATTENTION ON YOU, THOUGH.
THE CAUSE NEEDS MORE ATTENTION. PATTING YOURSELVES ON THE BACK FOR LEGALIZING A COUPLE TOKEN ANOMALY MOVIE STARS AND POLITICIANS WON'T FLY ANYMORE.
ESPECIALLY WHEN HUNDREDS OF THOUSANDS OF US ARE HIDDEN UNDER THE RUG.
I'VE HAD IT WITH THE HYPOCRISY, WE NEED TO REFORM THE ENTIRE SYSTEM.
TOTALLY. ALTHOUGH...
ALTHOUGH?
I THOUGHT YOU'D RATHER GO FOR DISCRETION. CONSIDERING...
DON'T WORRY, THE PARTY HAS YOUR BACK.
AS LONG AS YOU HAVE OURS.
"CAN I COUNT ON YOU, TEDDY?"

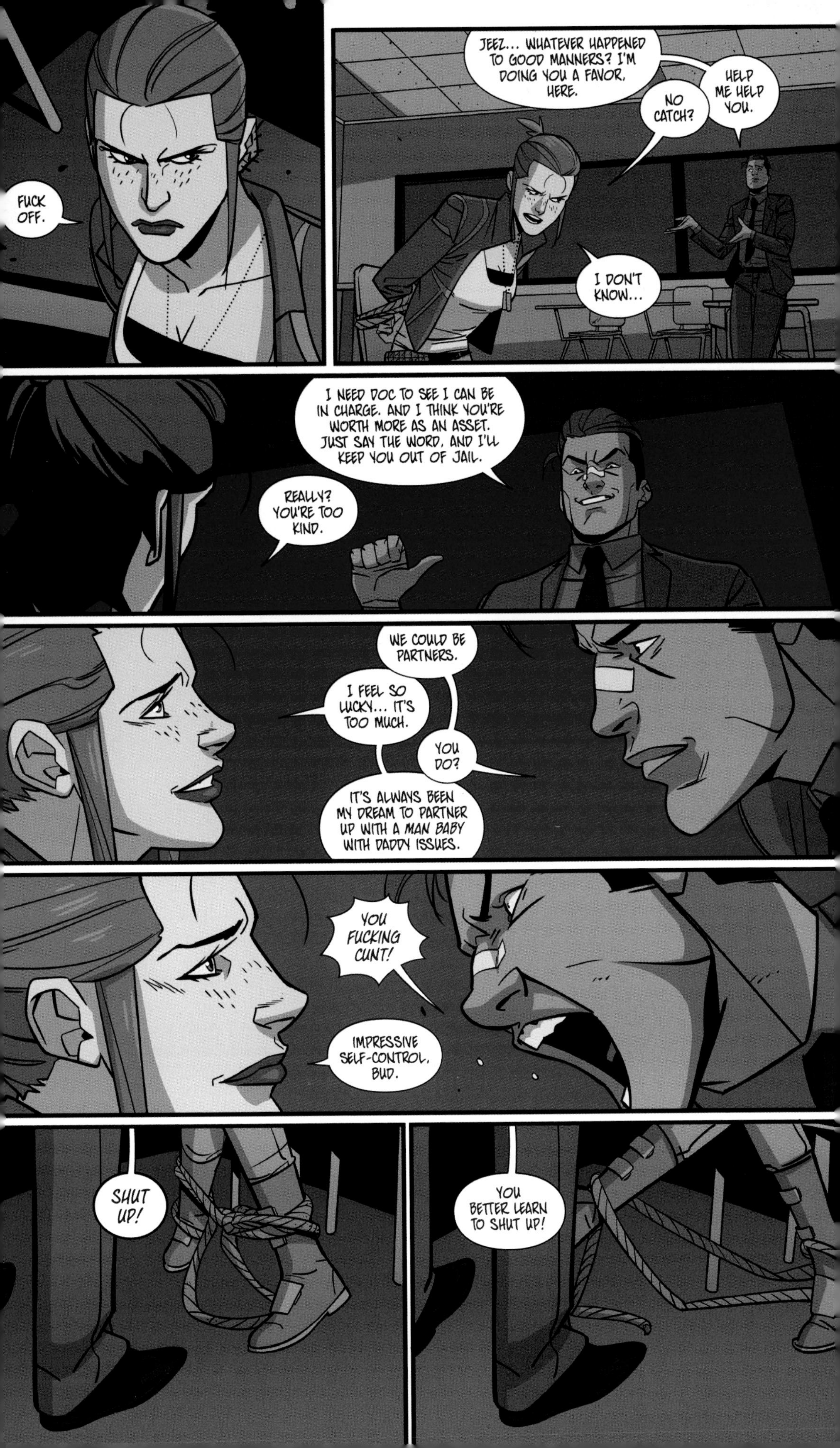
FUCK OFF.
JEEZ... WHATEVER HAPPENED TO GOOD MANNERS? I'M DOING YOU A FAVOR, HERE.
HELP ME HELP YOU.
NO CATCH?
I DON'T KNOW...
I NEED DOC TO SEE I CAN BE IN CHARGE. AND I THINK YOU'RE WORTH MORE AS AN ASSET. JUST SAY THE WORD, AND I'LL KEEP YOU OUT OF JAIL.
REALLY? YOU'RE TOO KIND.
WE COULD BE PARTNERS.
I FEEL SO LUCKY... IT'S TOO MUCH.
YOU DO?
IT'S ALWAYS BEEN MY DREAM TO PARTNER UP WITH A *MAN BABY* WITH DADDY ISSUES.
YOU *FUCKING CUNT!*
IMPRESSIVE SELF-CONTROL, BUD.
SHUT UP!
YOU BETTER LEARN TO SHUT UP!

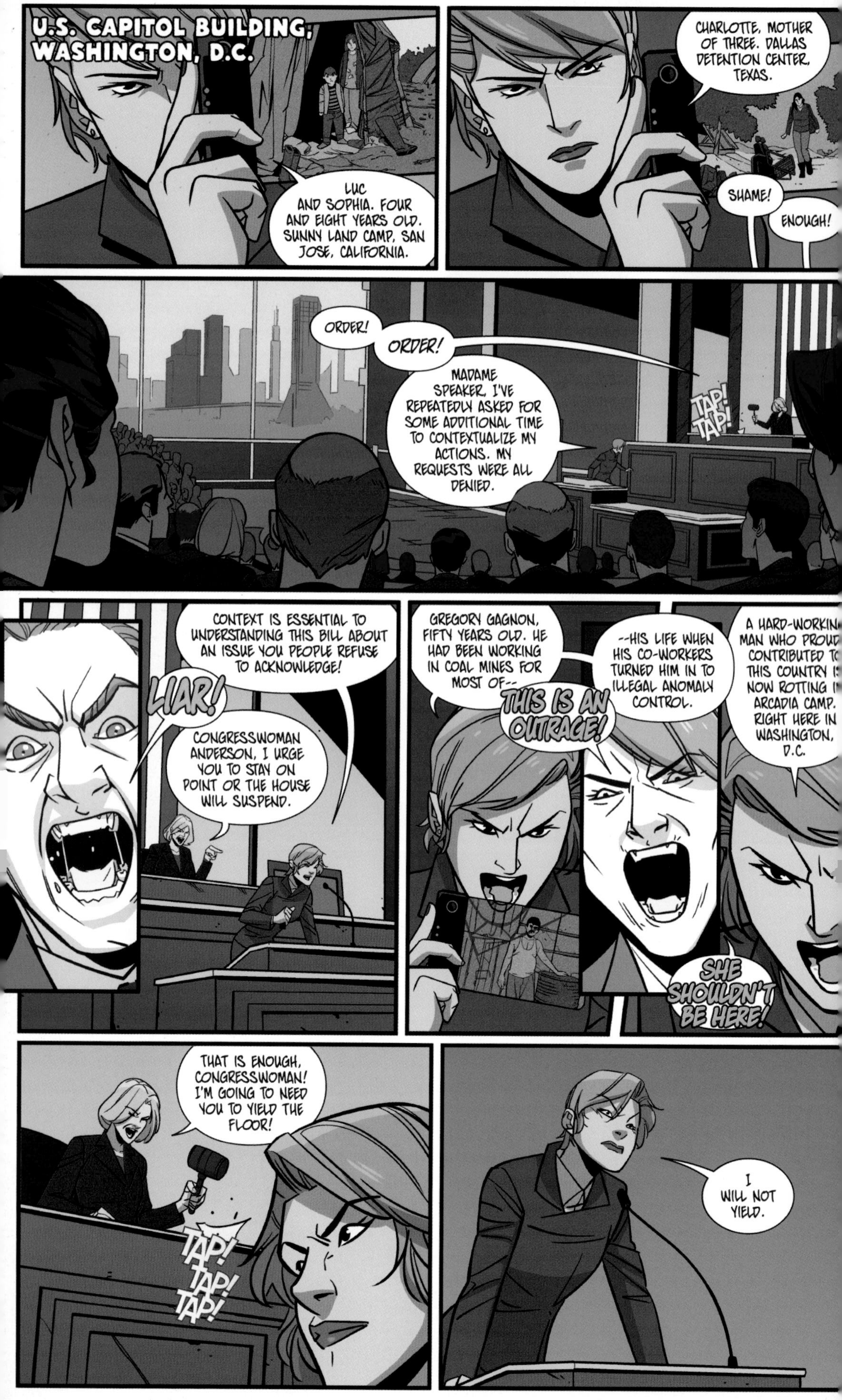
U.S. CAPITOL BUILDING, WASHINGTON, D.C.
LUC AND SOPHIA. FOUR AND EIGHT YEARS OLD. SUNNY LAND CAMP, SAN JOSE, CALIFORNIA.
CHARLOTTE, MOTHER OF THREE. DALLAS DETENTION CENTER, TEXAS.
SHAME!
ENOUGH!
ORDER!
ORDER!
MADAME SPEAKER, I'VE REPEATEDLY ASKED FOR SOME ADDITIONAL TIME TO CONTEXTUALIZE MY ACTIONS. MY REQUESTS WERE ALL DENIED.
TAP! TAP!
CONTEXT IS ESSENTIAL TO UNDERSTANDING THIS BILL ABOUT AN ISSUE YOU PEOPLE REFUSE TO ACKNOWLEDGE!
LIAR!
CONGRESSWOMAN ANDERSON, I URGE YOU TO STAY ON POINT OR THE HOUSE WILL SUSPEND.
GREGORY GAGNON, FIFTY YEARS OLD. HE HAD BEEN WORKING IN COAL MINES FOR MOST OF--
THIS IS AN OUTRAGE!
--HIS LIFE WHEN HIS CO-WORKERS TURNED HIM IN TO ILLEGAL ANOMALY CONTROL.
A HARD-WORKIN MAN WHO PROUD CONTRIBUTED TO THIS COUNTRY I NOW ROTTING I ARCADIA CAMP. RIGHT HERE IN WASHINGTON, D.C.
SHE SHOULDN'T BE HERE!
THAT IS ENOUGH, CONGRESSWOMAN! I'M GOING TO NEED YOU TO YIELD THE FLOOR!
TAP! TAP! TAP!
I WILL NOT YIELD.

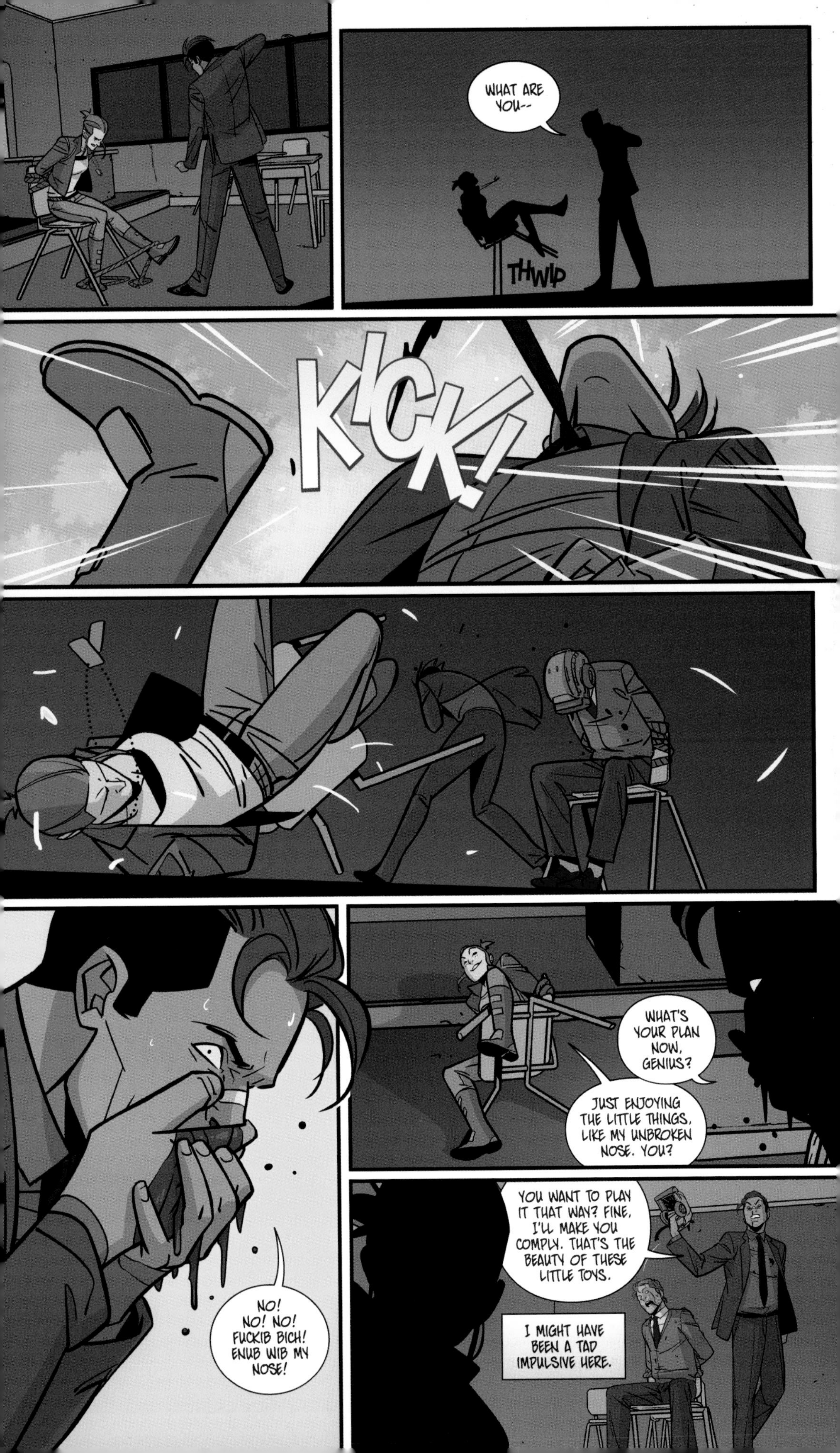
WHAT ARE YOU--
THWIP
KICK!
NO! NO! NO! FUCKIB BICH! ENUB WIB MY NOSE!
WHAT'S YOUR PLAN NOW, GENIUS?
JUST ENJOYING THE LITTLE THINGS, LIKE MY UNBROKEN NOSE. YOU?
YOU WANT TO PLAY IT THAT WAY? FINE. I'LL MAKE YOU COMPLY. THAT'S THE BEAUTY OF THESE LITTLE TOYS.
I MIGHT HAVE BEEN A TAD IMPULSIVE HERE.

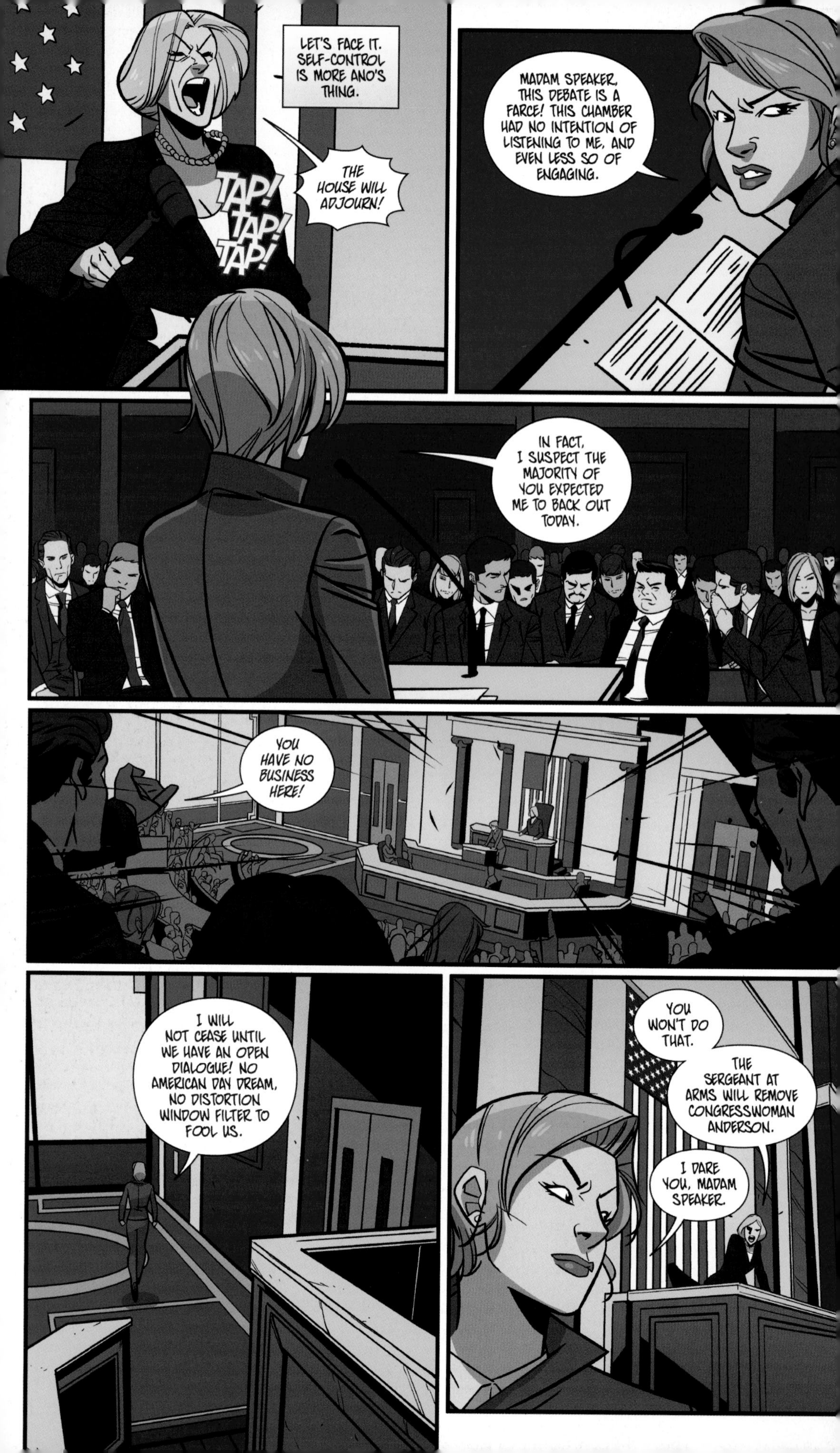
LET'S FACE IT. SELF-CONTROL IS MORE ANO'S THING.
THE HOUSE WILL ADJOURN!
TAP! TAP! TAP!
MADAM SPEAKER, THIS DEBATE IS A FARCE! THIS CHAMBER HAD NO INTENTION OF LISTENING TO ME, AND EVEN LESS SO OF ENGAGING.
IN FACT, I SUSPECT THE MAJORITY OF YOU EXPECTED ME TO BACK OUT TODAY.
YOU HAVE NO BUSINESS HERE!
I WILL NOT CEASE UNTIL WE HAVE AN OPEN DIALOGUE! NO AMERICAN DAY DREAM, NO DISTORTION WINDOW FILTER TO FOOL US.
YOU WON'T DO THAT.
THE SERGEANT AT ARMS WILL REMOVE CONGRESSWOMAN ANDERSON.
I DARE YOU, MADAM SPEAKER.

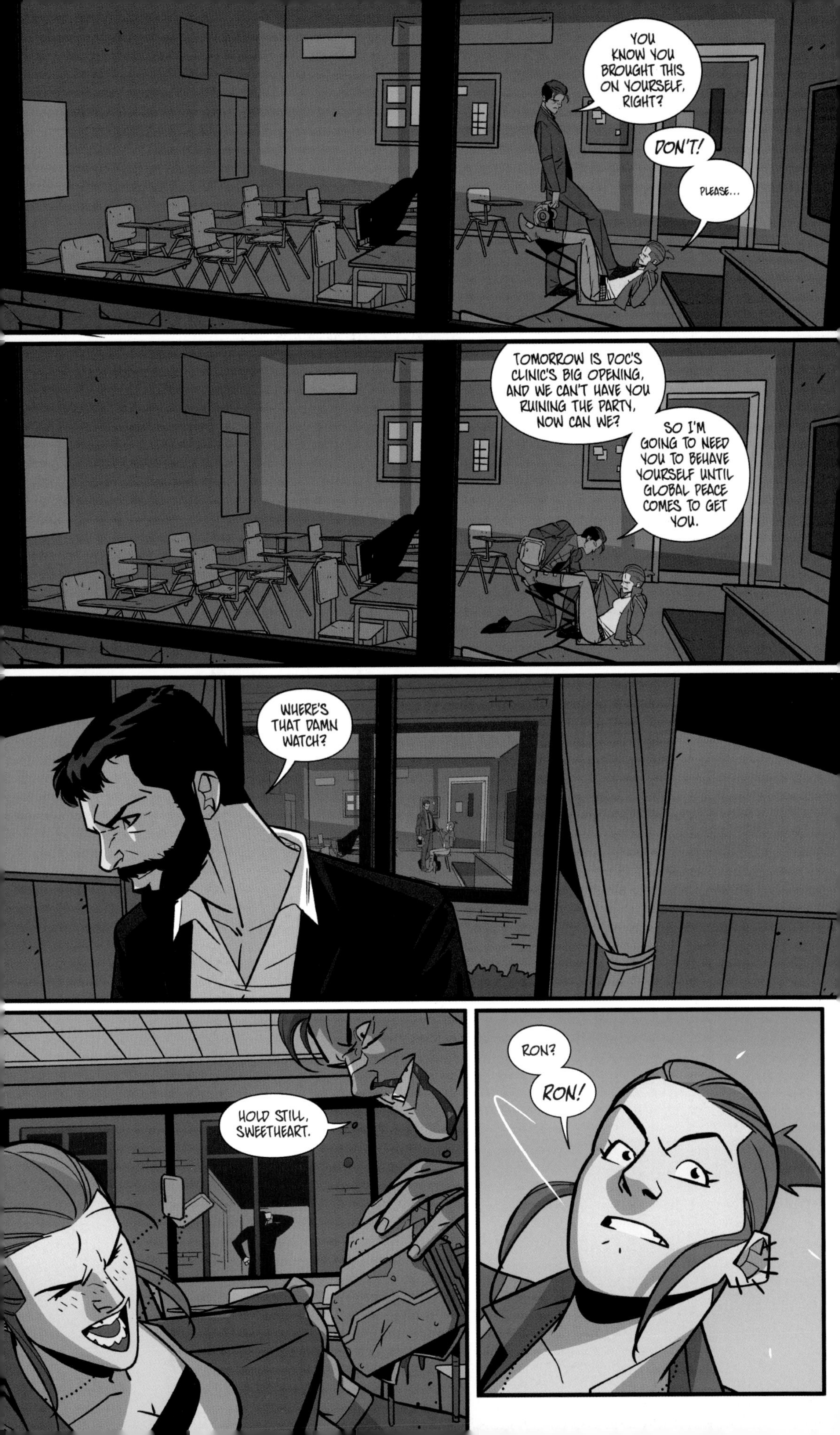
YOU KNOW YOU BROUGHT THIS ON YOURSELF, RIGHT?
DON'T!
PLEASE...
TOMORROW IS DOC'S CLINIC'S BIG OPENING, AND WE CAN'T HAVE YOU RUINING THE PARTY, NOW CAN WE?
SO I'M GOING TO NEED YOU TO BEHAVE YOURSELF UNTIL GLOBAL PEACE COMES TO GET YOU.
WHERE'S THAT DAMN WATCH?
HOLD STILL, SWEETHEART.
RON?
RON!

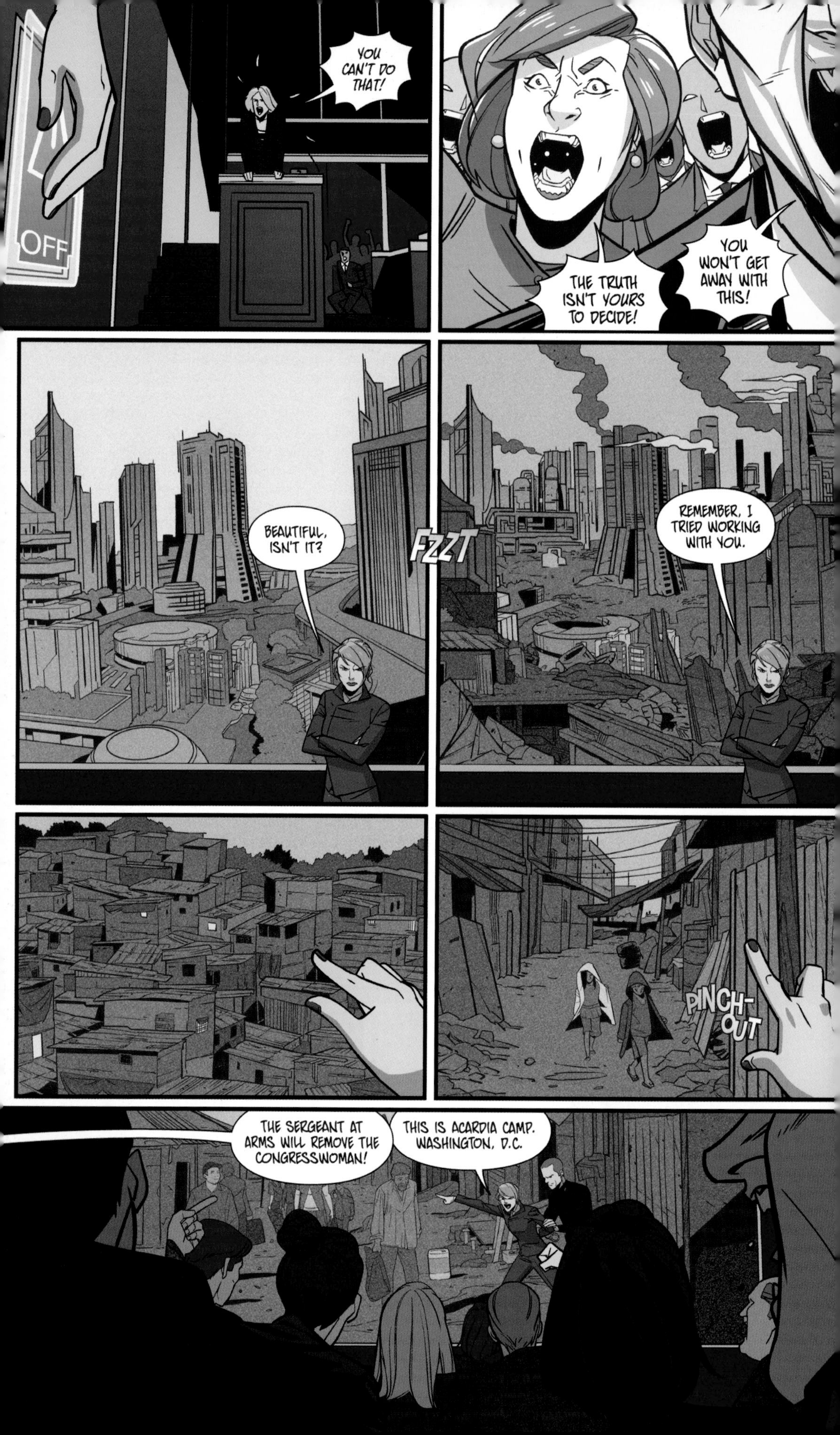
OFF
YOU CAN'T DO THAT!
THE TRUTH ISN'T YOURS TO DECIDE!
YOU WON'T GET AWAY WITH THIS!
BEAUTIFUL, ISN'T IT?
FZZT
REMEMBER, I TRIED WORKING WITH YOU.
PINCH-OUT
THE SERGEANT AT ARMS WILL REMOVE THE CONGRESSWOMAN!
THIS IS ACARDIA CAMP. WASHINGTON, D.C.

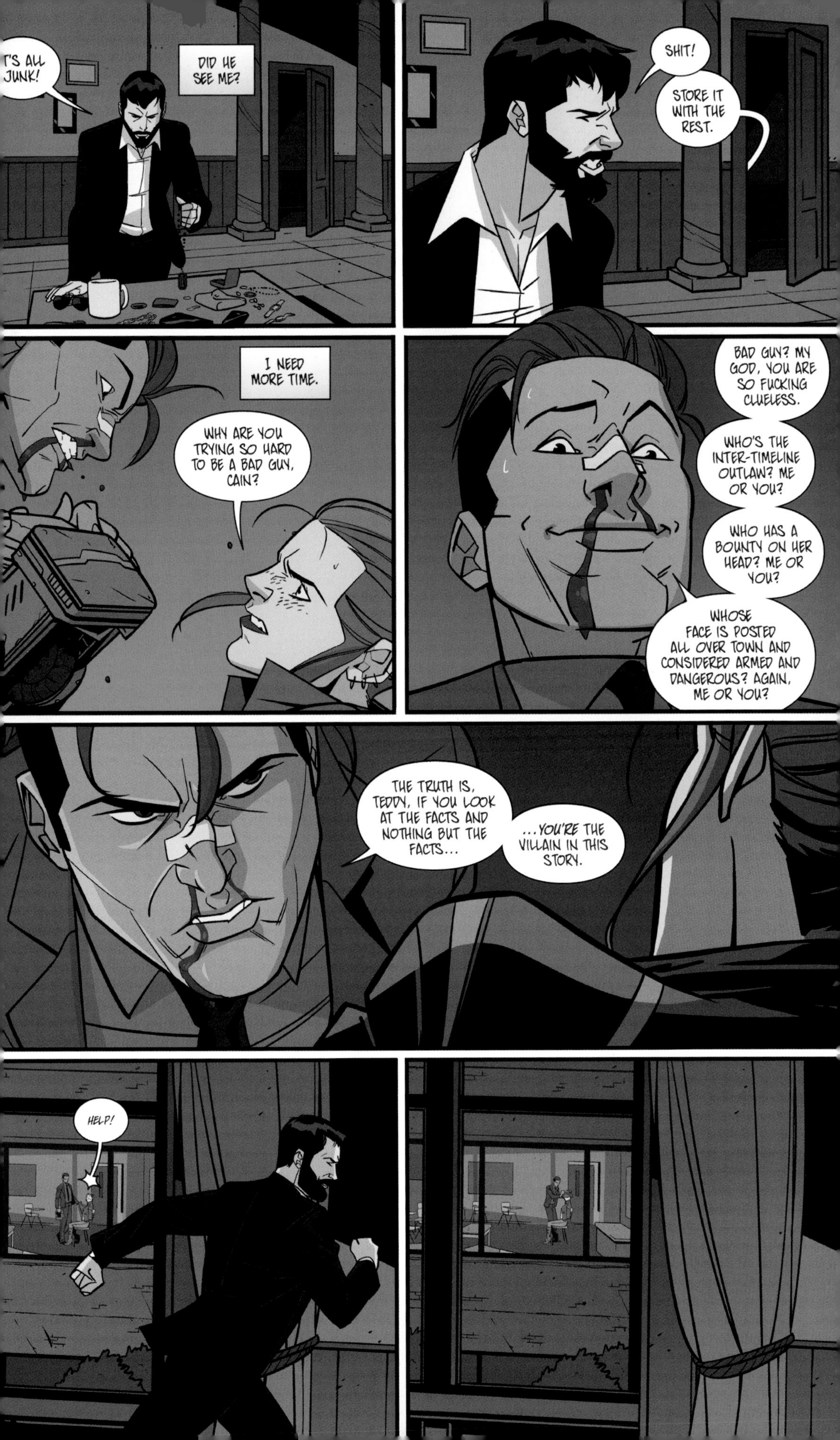

'T'S ALL JUNK!
DID HE SEE ME?
SHIT!
STORE IT WITH THE REST.
I NEED MORE TIME.
WHY ARE YOU TRYING SO HARD TO BE A BAD GUY, CAIN?
BAD GUY? MY GOD, YOU ARE SO FUCKING CLUELESS.
WHO'S THE INTER-TIMELINE OUTLAW? ME OR YOU?
WHO HAS A BOUNTY ON HER HEAD? ME OR YOU?
WHOSE FACE IS POSTED ALL OVER TOWN AND CONSIDERED ARMED AND DANGEROUS? AGAIN, ME OR YOU?
THE TRUTH IS, TEDDY, IF YOU LOOK AT THE FACTS AND NOTHING BUT THE FACTS...
...YOU'RE THE VILLAIN IN THIS STORY.
HELP!

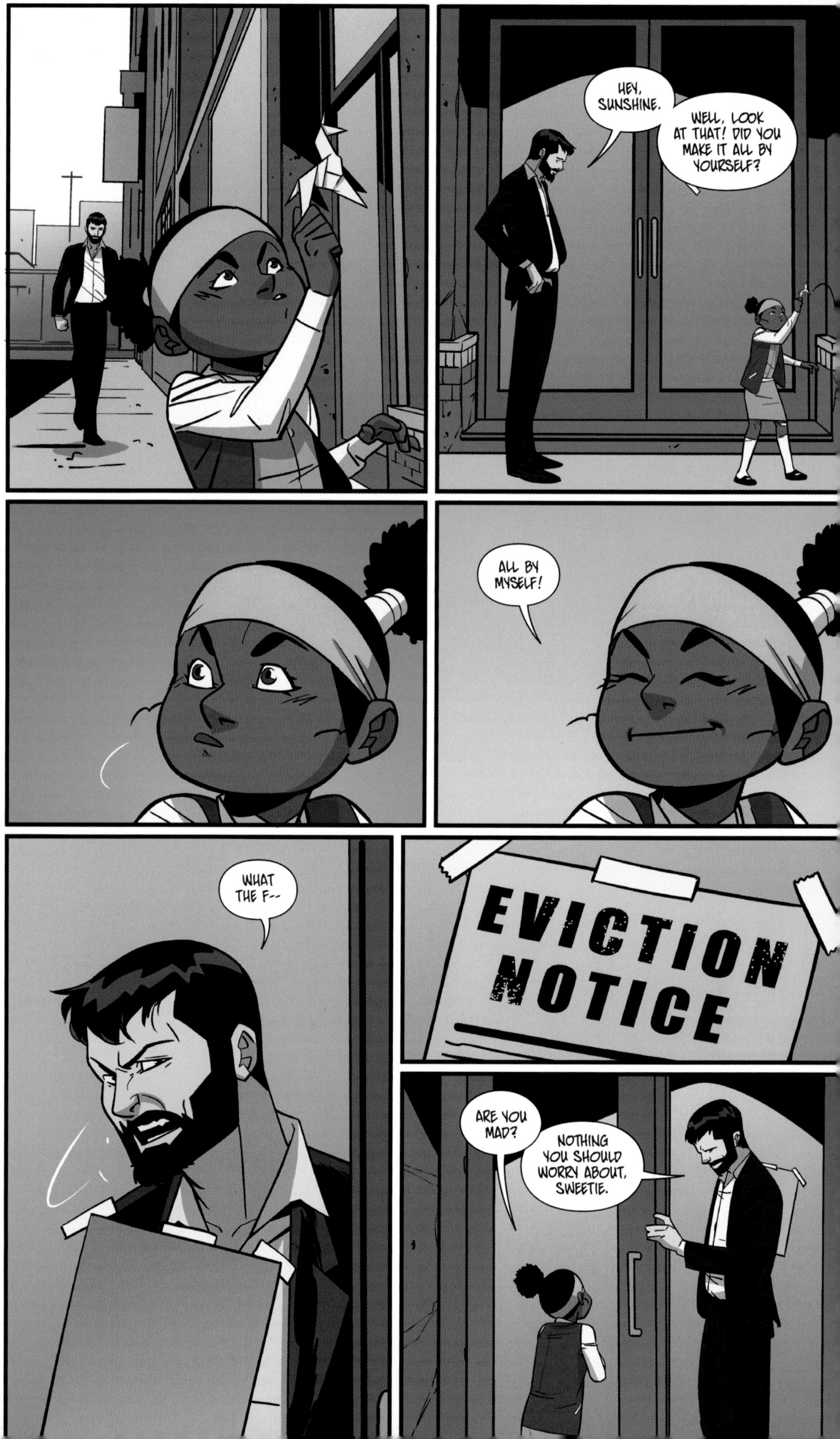
HEY, SUNSHINE.
WELL, LOOK AT THAT! DID YOU MAKE IT ALL BY YOURSELF?
ALL BY MYSELF!
WHAT THE F--
EVICTION NOTICE
ARE YOU MAD?
NOTHING YOU SHOULD WORRY ABOUT, SWEETIE.

HOW DID HE TAKE IT?

YOU'RE RIGHT, STRANGER DANGER. GOOD GIRL.

IT'S SAD IT HAD TO COME TO THIS. ALL I WANTED WAS TO HELP HIM DO A BETTER JOB.

BUT I GUESS SOME PEOPLE JUST DON'T KNOW WHAT'S GOOD FOR THEM. TRUST ME, I KNOW, I'M A DOCTOR.

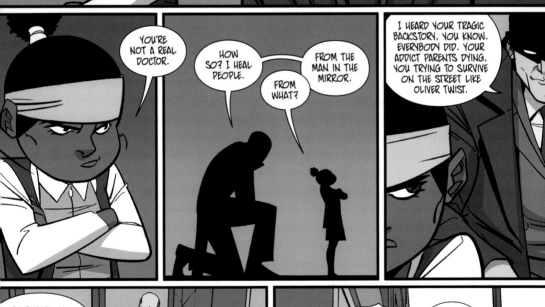

YOU'RE NOT A REAL DOCTOR.

HOW SO? I HEAL PEOPLE.

FROM WHAT?

FROM THE MAN IN THE MIRROR.

I HEARD YOUR TRAGIC BACKSTORY, YOU KNOW. EVERYBODY DID. YOUR ADDICT PARENTS DYING, YOU TRYING TO SURVIVE ON THE STREET LIKE OLIVER TWIST.

TEAR-JERKING, REALLY. BUT NOT AS SAD AS RON TRYING TO PUSH THIS CHEAP NARRATIVE.

AND I HAVE TO SAY, YOU SMELL PRETTY NICE FOR A DICKENS CHARACTER RIPOFF.

YOU'RE A LIAR!

AREN'T WE ALL, COLUMBIA? AREN'T WE ALL?

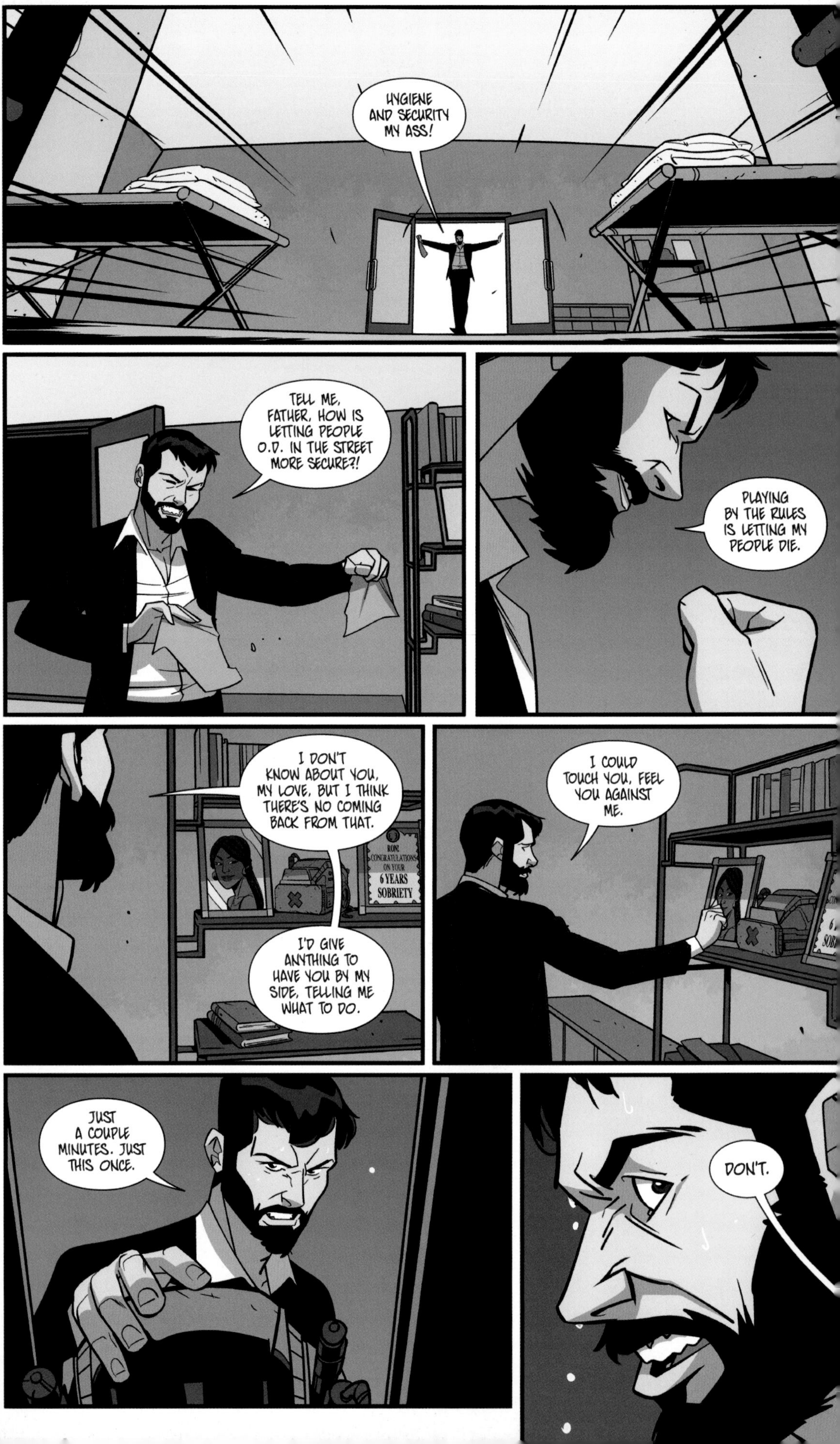

HYGIENE AND SECURITY MY ASS!
TELL ME, FATHER, HOW IS LETTING PEOPLE O.D. IN THE STREET MORE SECURE?!
PLAYING BY THE RULES IS LETTING MY PEOPLE DIE.
I DON'T KNOW ABOUT YOU, MY LOVE, BUT I THINK THERE'S NO COMING BACK FROM THAT.
RON: CONGRATULATIONS ON YOUR 6 YEARS SOBRIETY
I'D GIVE ANYTHING TO HAVE YOU BY MY SIDE, TELLING ME WHAT TO DO.
I COULD TOUCH YOU, FEEL YOU AGAINST ME.
JUST A COUPLE MINUTES. JUST THIS ONCE.
DON'T.

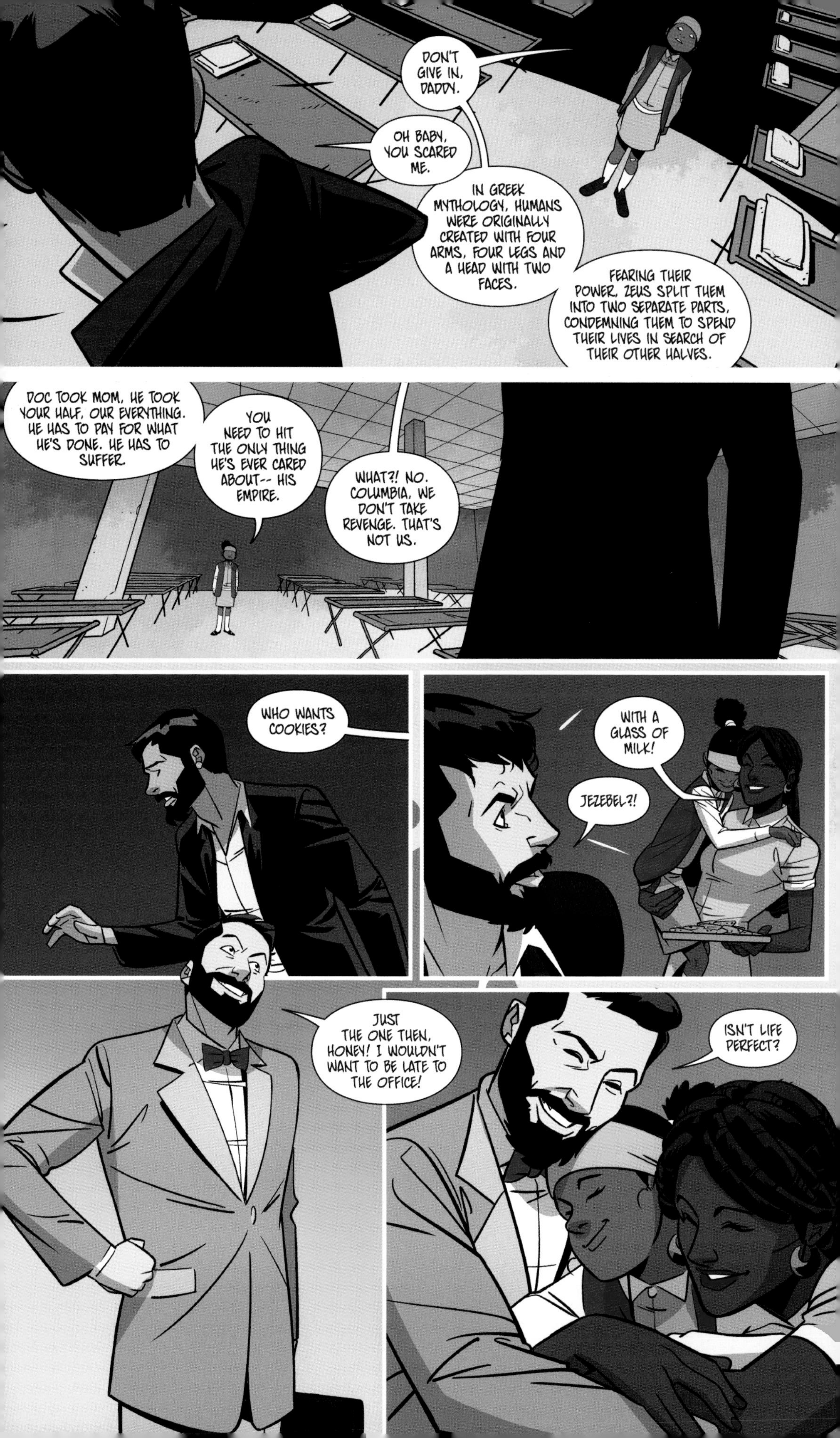
DON'T GIVE IN, DADDY.
OH BABY, YOU SCARED ME.
IN GREEK MYTHOLOGY, HUMANS WERE ORIGINALLY CREATED WITH FOUR ARMS, FOUR LEGS AND A HEAD WITH TWO FACES.
FEARING THEIR POWER, ZEUS SPLIT THEM INTO TWO SEPARATE PARTS, CONDEMNING THEM TO SPEND THEIR LIVES IN SEARCH OF THEIR OTHER HALVES.
DOC TOOK MOM, HE TOOK YOUR HALF, OUR EVERYTHING. HE HAS TO PAY FOR WHAT HE'S DONE. HE HAS TO SUFFER.
YOU NEED TO HIT THE ONLY THING HE'S EVER CARED ABOUT-- HIS EMPIRE.
WHAT?! NO. COLUMBIA, WE DON'T TAKE REVENGE. THAT'S NOT US.
WHO WANTS COOKIES?
WITH A GLASS OF MILK!
JEZEBEL?!
JUST THE ONE THEN, HONEY! I WOULDN'T WANT TO BE LATE TO THE OFFICE!
ISN'T LIFE PERFECT?

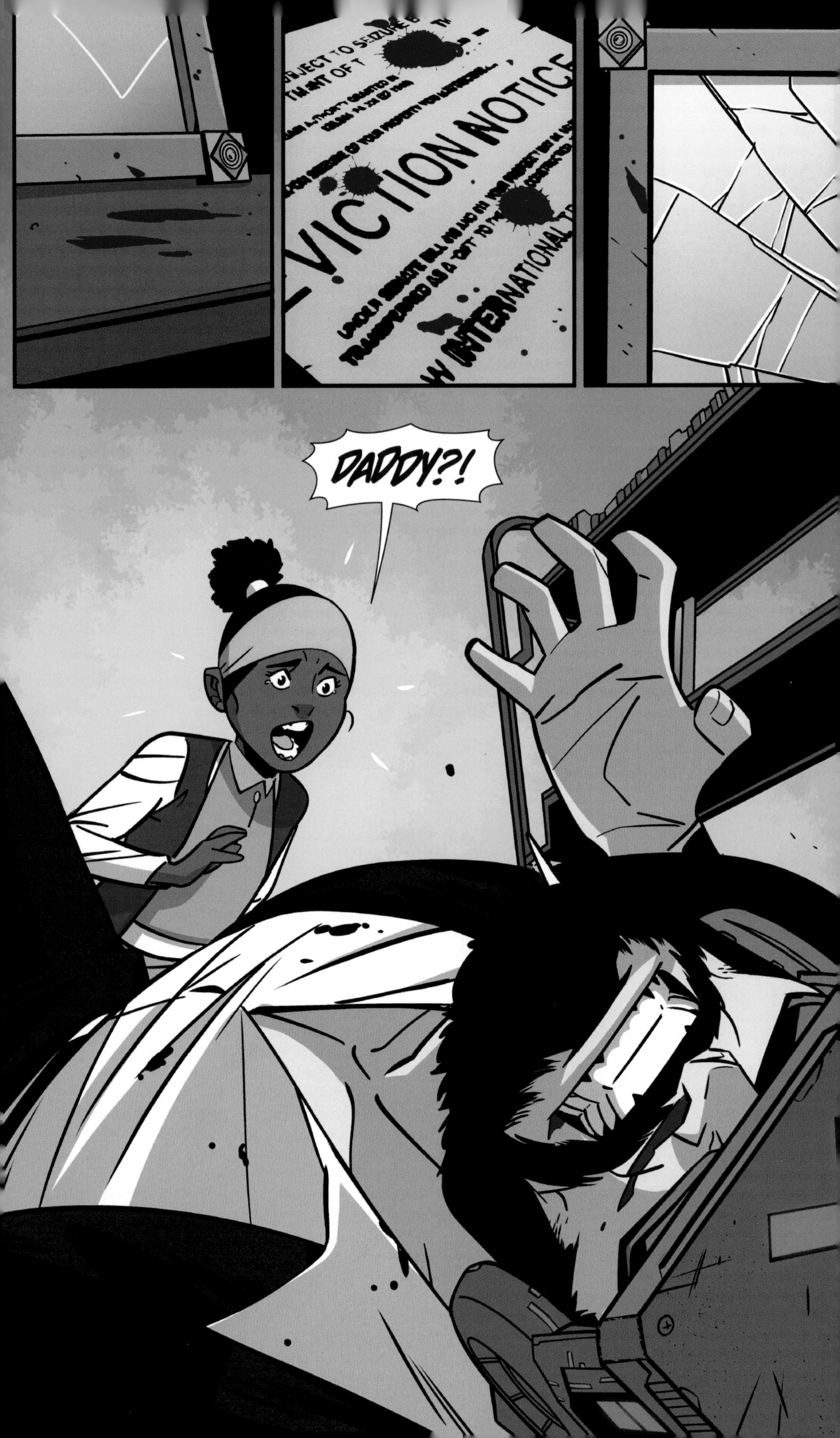
VICTION NOTICE
INTERNATIONAL
DADDY?!

Art by RAFAEL ALBUQUERQUE

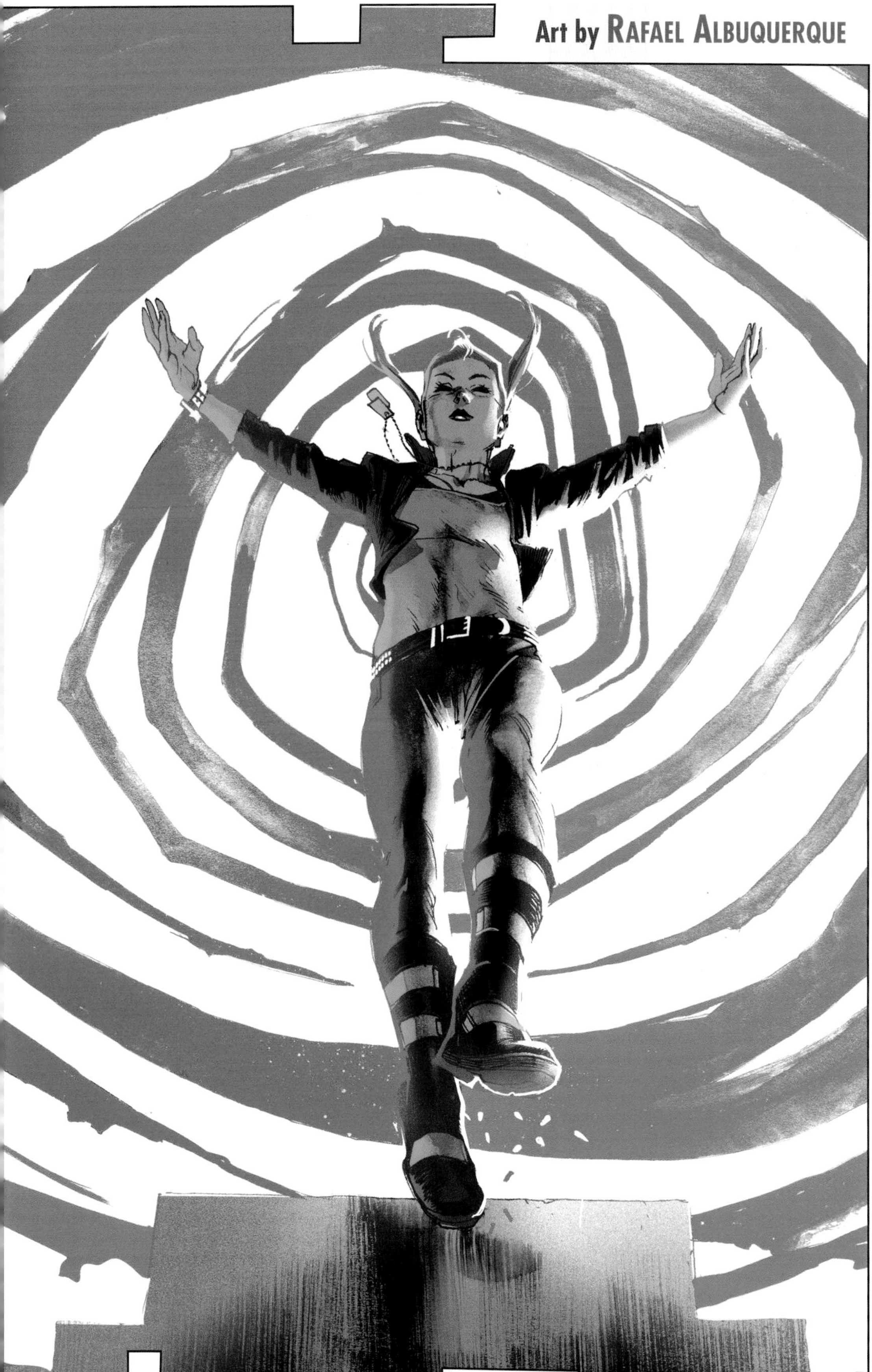

Art by
ELSA CHARRETIER

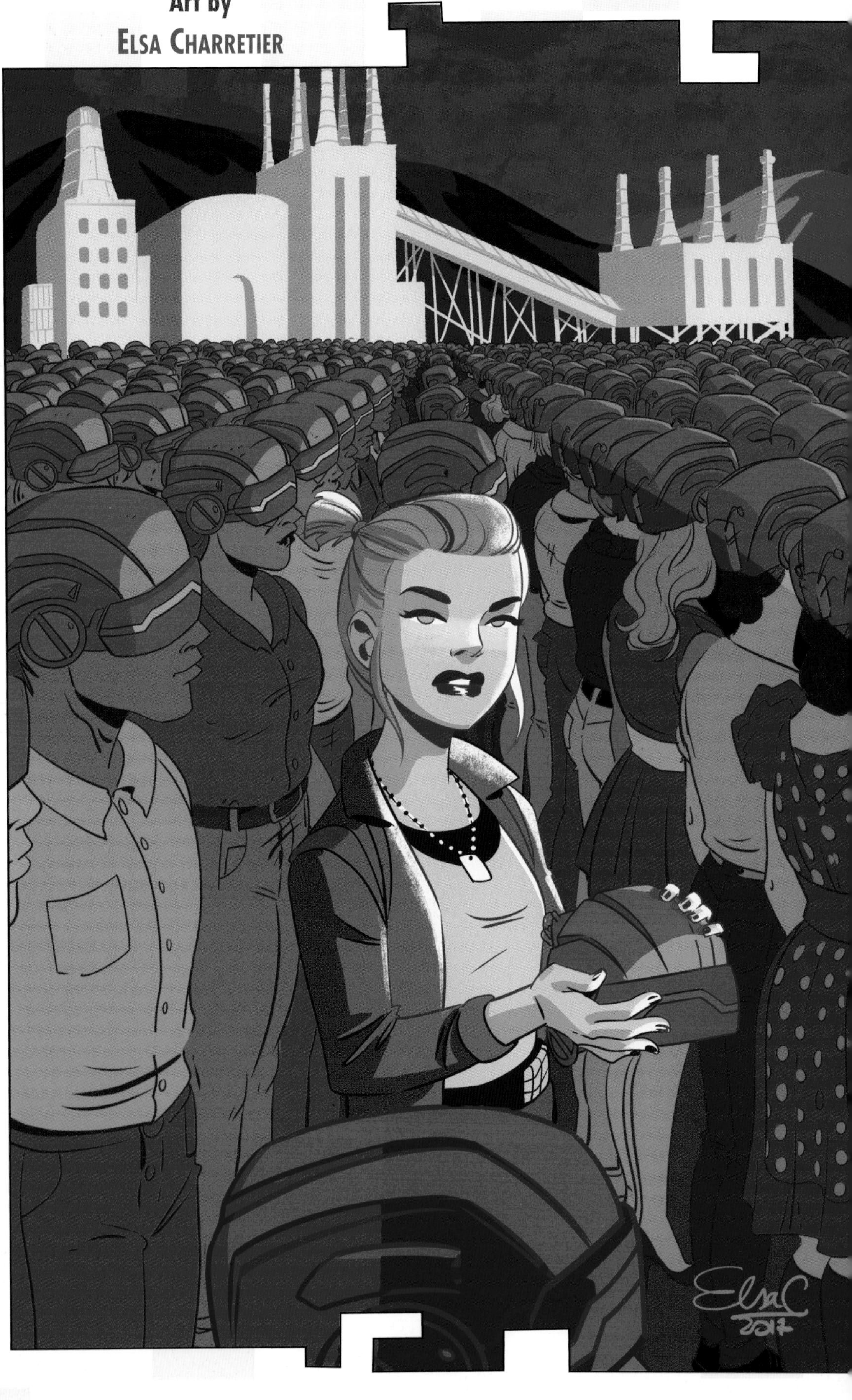

ElsaC
2017

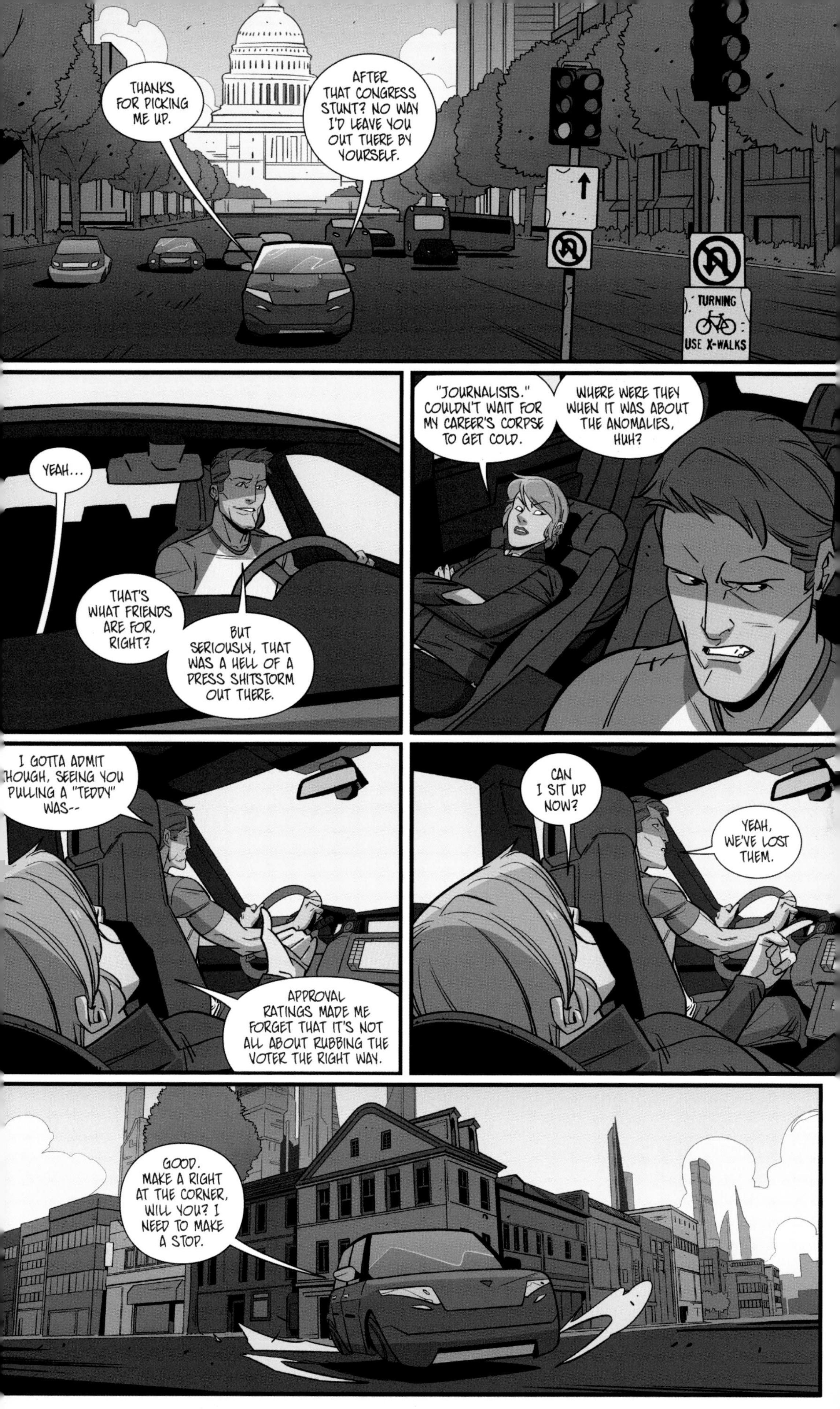
THANKS FOR PICKING ME UP.
AFTER THAT CONGRESS STUNT? NO WAY I'D LEAVE YOU OUT THERE BY YOURSELF.
TURNING
USE X-WALKS
YEAH...
THAT'S WHAT FRIENDS ARE FOR, RIGHT?
BUT SERIOUSLY, THAT WAS A HELL OF A PRESS SHITSTORM OUT THERE.
"JOURNALISTS." COULDN'T WAIT FOR MY CAREER'S CORPSE TO GET COLD.
WHERE WERE THEY WHEN IT WAS ABOUT THE ANOMALIES, HUH?
I GOTTA ADMIT THOUGH, SEEING YOU PULLING A "TEDDY" WAS--
APPROVAL RATINGS MADE ME FORGET THAT IT'S NOT ALL ABOUT RUBBING THE VOTER THE RIGHT WAY.
CAN I SIT UP NOW?
YEAH, WE'VE LOST THEM.
GOOD. MAKE A RIGHT AT THE CORNER, WILL YOU? I NEED TO MAKE A STOP.

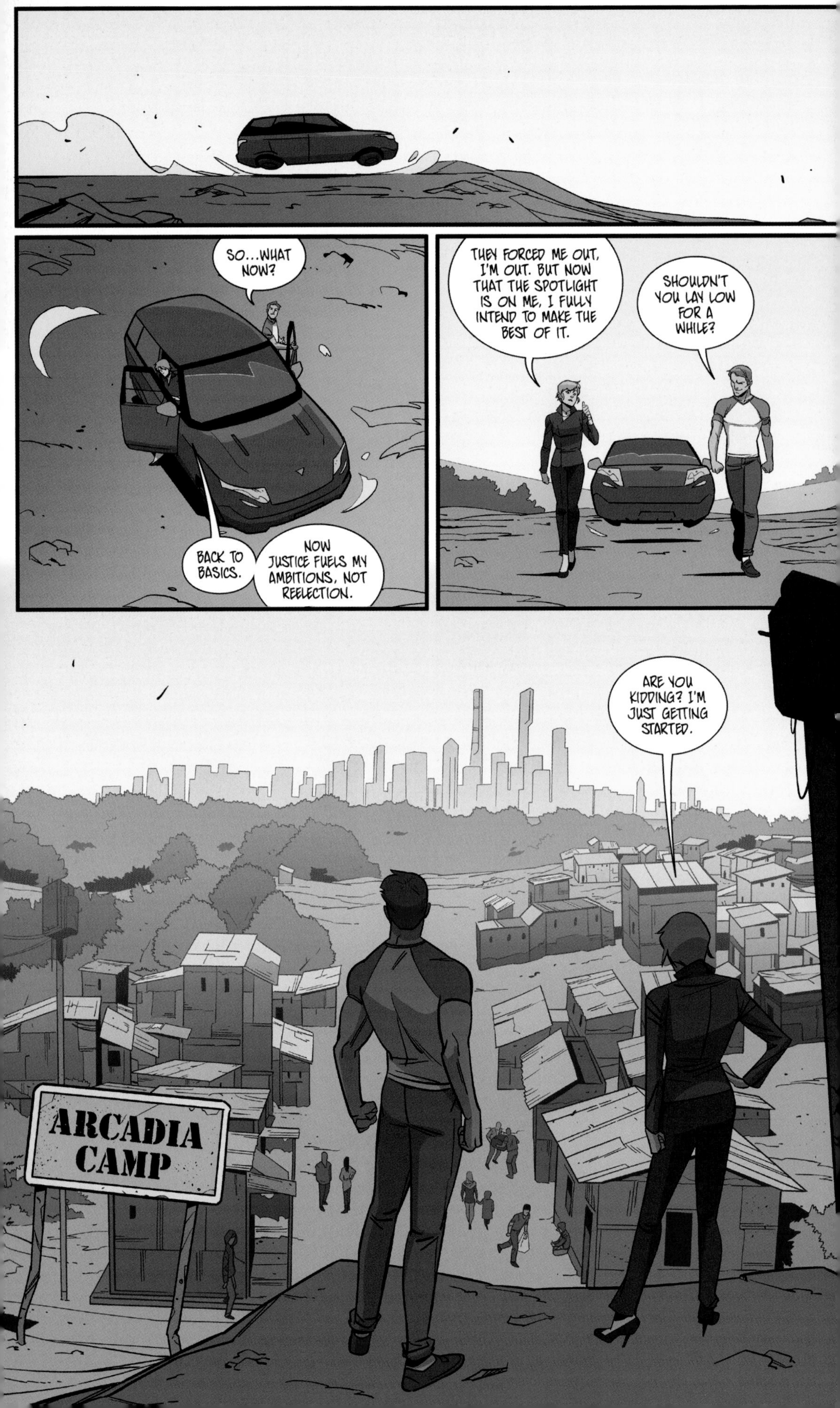
SO...WHAT NOW?
BACK TO BASICS.
NOW JUSTICE FUELS MY AMBITIONS, NOT REELECTION.
THEY FORCED ME OUT, I'M OUT. BUT NOW THAT THE SPOTLIGHT IS ON ME, I FULLY INTEND TO MAKE THE BEST OF IT.
SHOULDN'T YOU LAY LOW FOR A WHILE?
ARE YOU KIDDING? I'M JUST GETTING STARTED.
ARCADIA CAMP

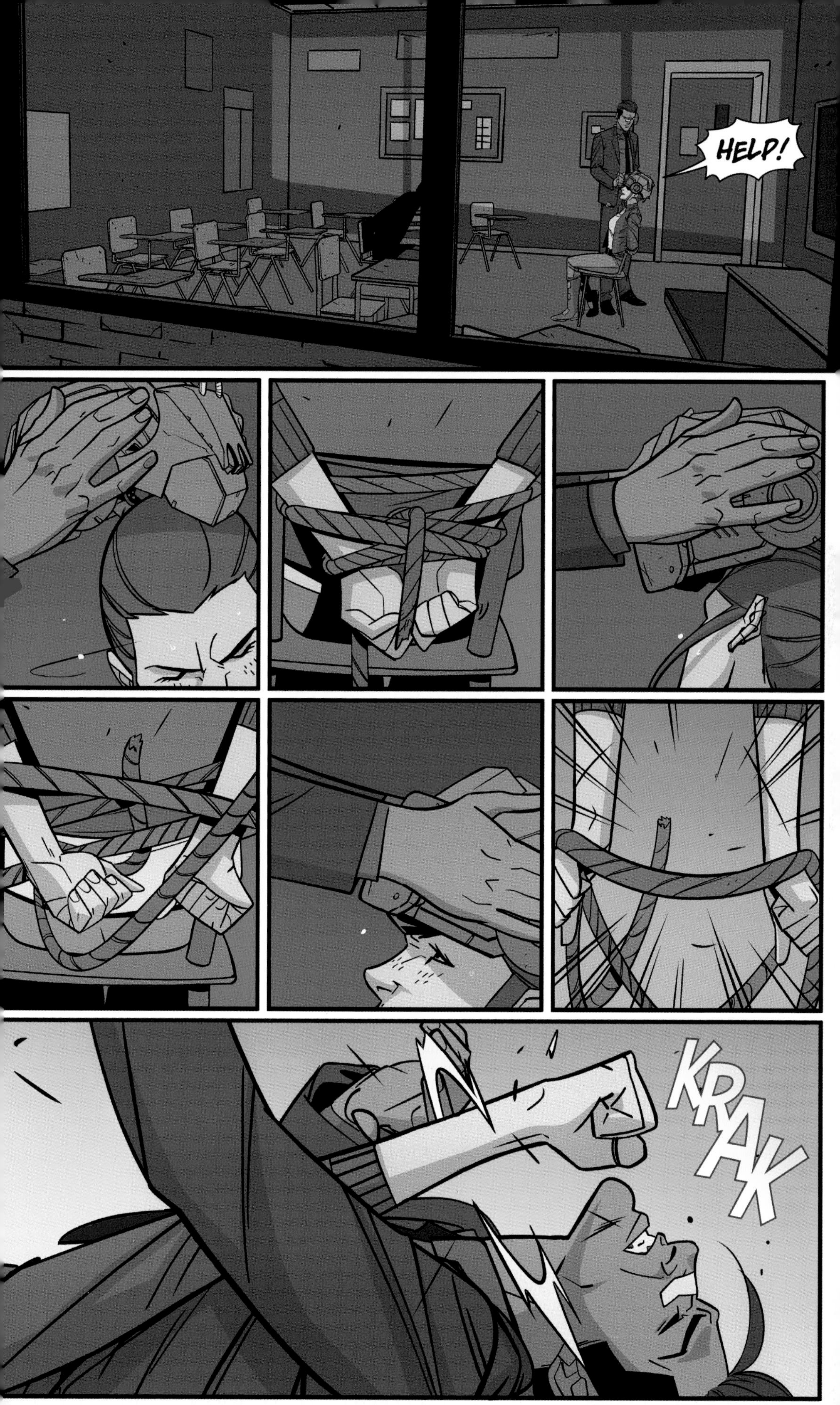
HELP!
KRAK

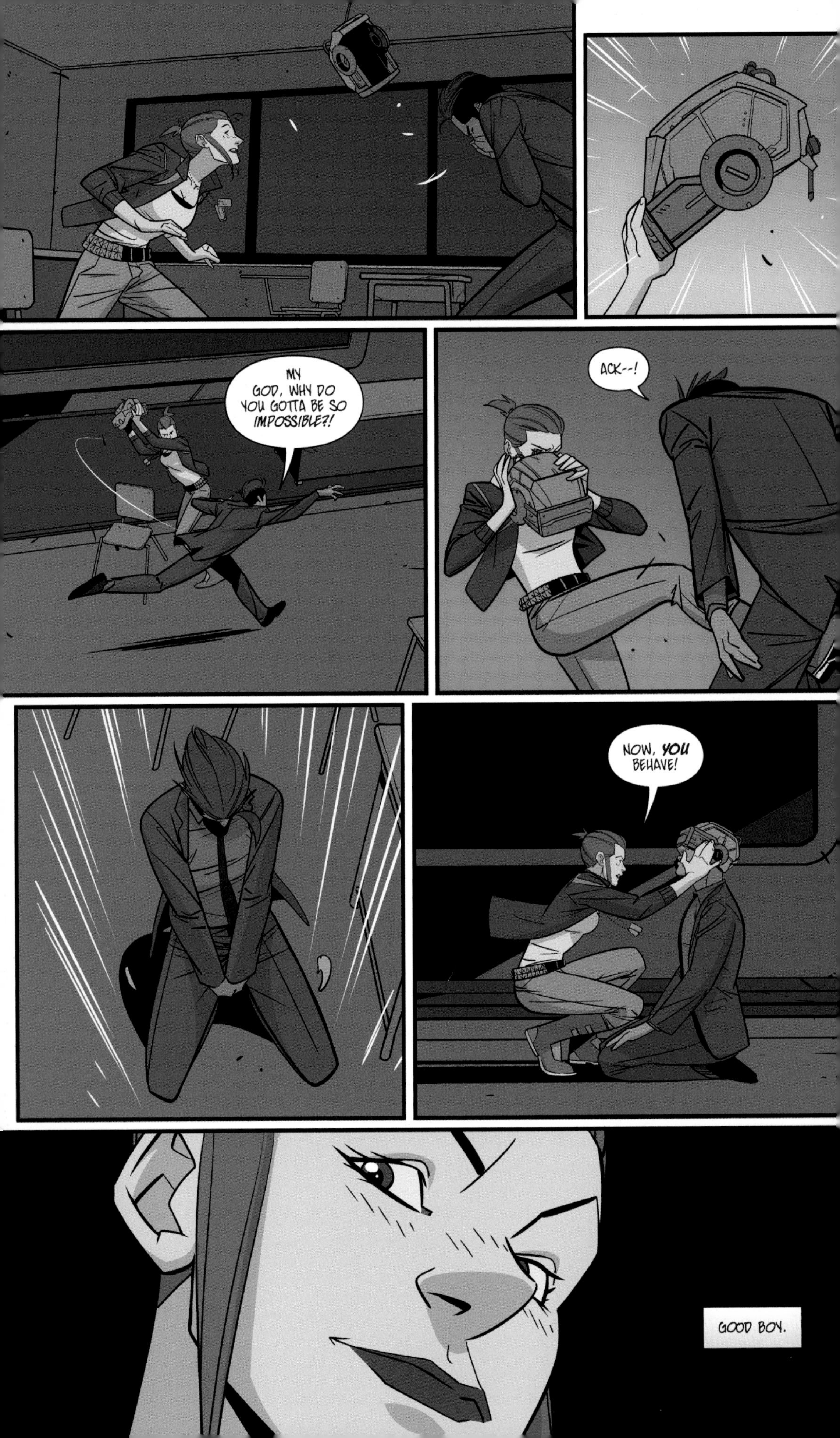
MY GOD, WHY DO YOU GOTTA BE SO IMPOSSIBLE?!
ACK--!
NOW, YOU BEHAVE!
GOOD BOY.

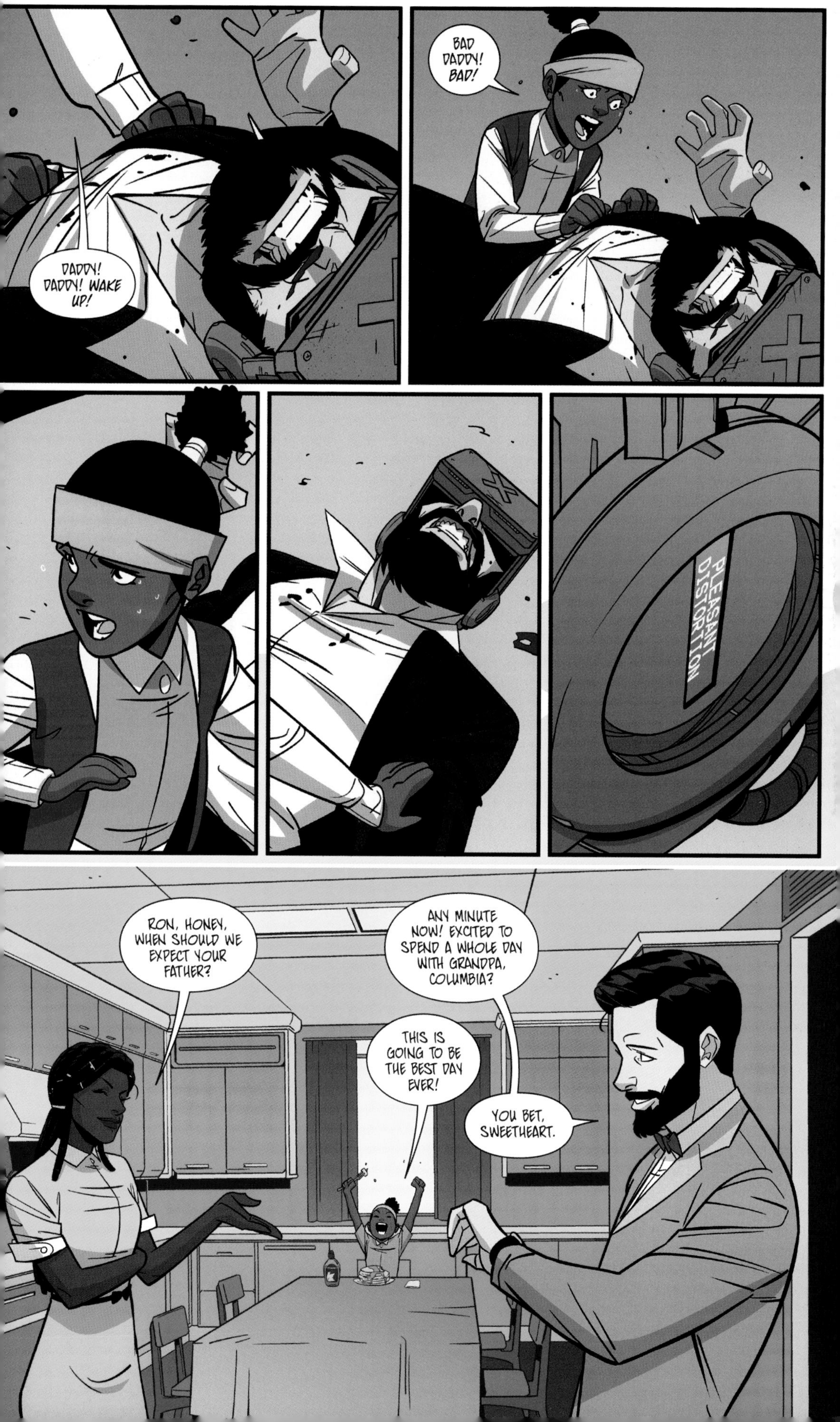
DADDY! DADDY! WAKE UP!
BAD DADDY! BAD!
PLEASANT DISTORTION
RON, HONEY, WHEN SHOULD WE EXPECT YOUR FATHER?
ANY MINUTE NOW! EXCITED TO SPEND A WHOLE DAY WITH GRANDPA, COLUMBIA?
THIS IS GOING TO BE THE BEST DAY EVER!
YOU BET, SWEETHEART.

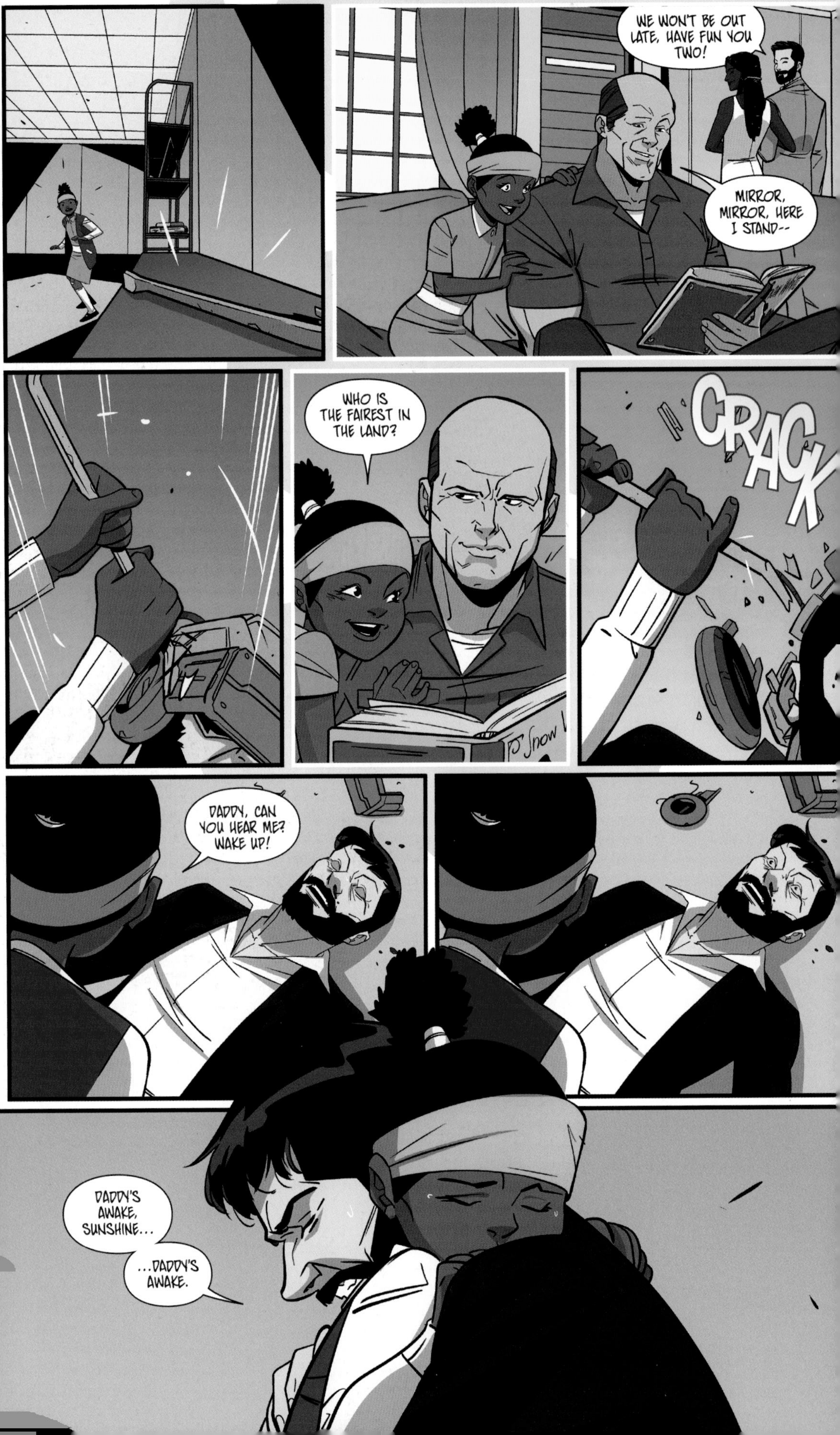
WE WON'T BE OUT LATE, HAVE FUN YOU TWO!
MIRROR, MIRROR, HERE I STAND--
WHO IS THE FAIREST IN THE LAND?
CRACK
DADDY, CAN YOU HEAR ME? WAKE UP!
DADDY'S AWAKE, SUNSHINE...
...DADDY'S AWAKE.

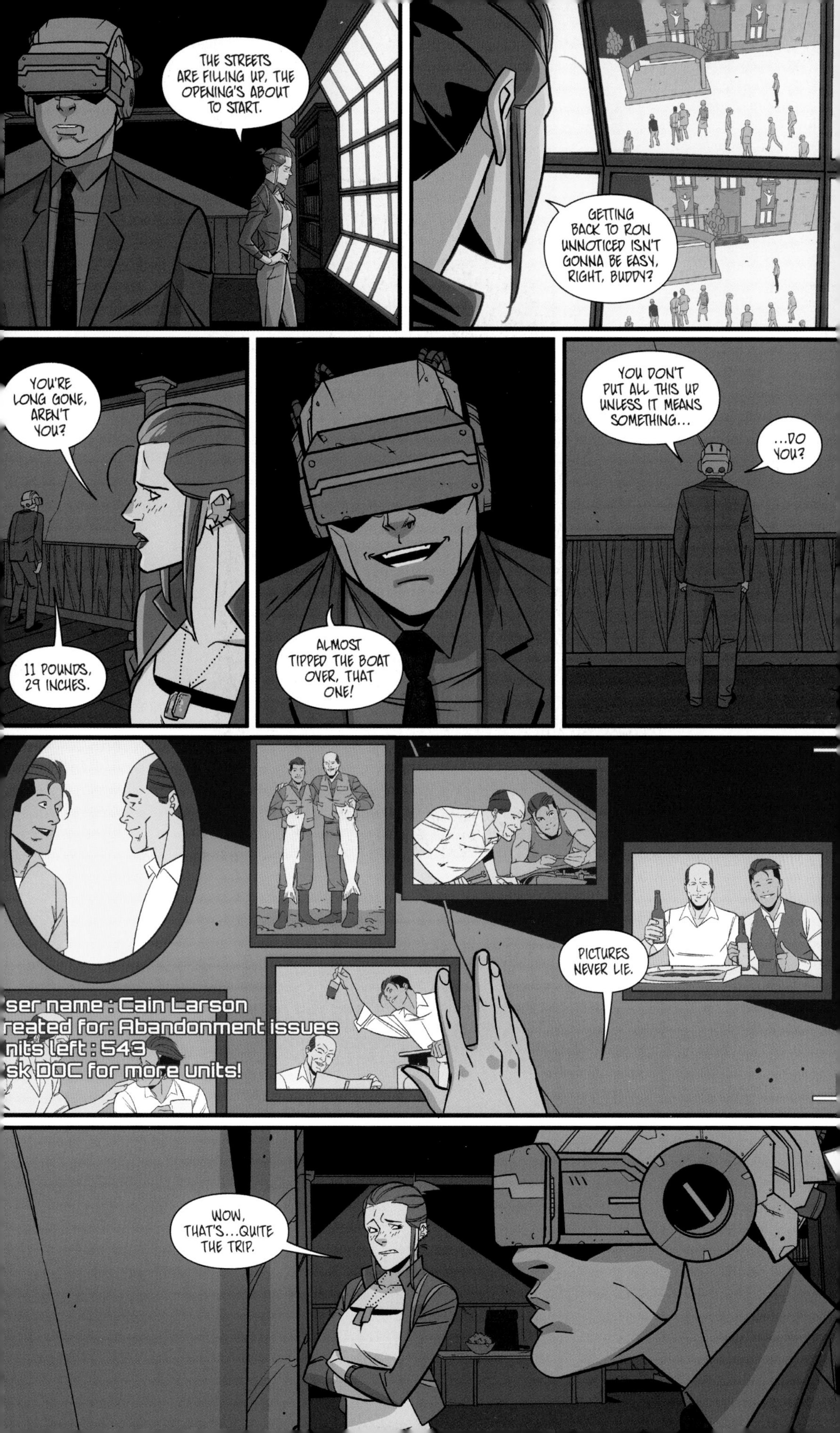
THE STREETS ARE FILLING UP, THE OPENING'S ABOUT TO START.
GETTING BACK TO RON UNNOTICED ISN'T GONNA BE EASY, RIGHT, BUDDY?
YOU'RE LONG GONE, AREN'T YOU?
11 POUNDS, 29 INCHES.
ALMOST TIPPED THE BOAT OVER, THAT ONE!
YOU DON'T PUT ALL THIS UP UNLESS IT MEANS SOMETHING...
...DO YOU?
ser name : Cain Larson
reated for: Abandonment issues
nits left : 543
sk DOC for more units!
PICTURES NEVER LIE.
WOW, THAT'S...QUITE THE TRIP.

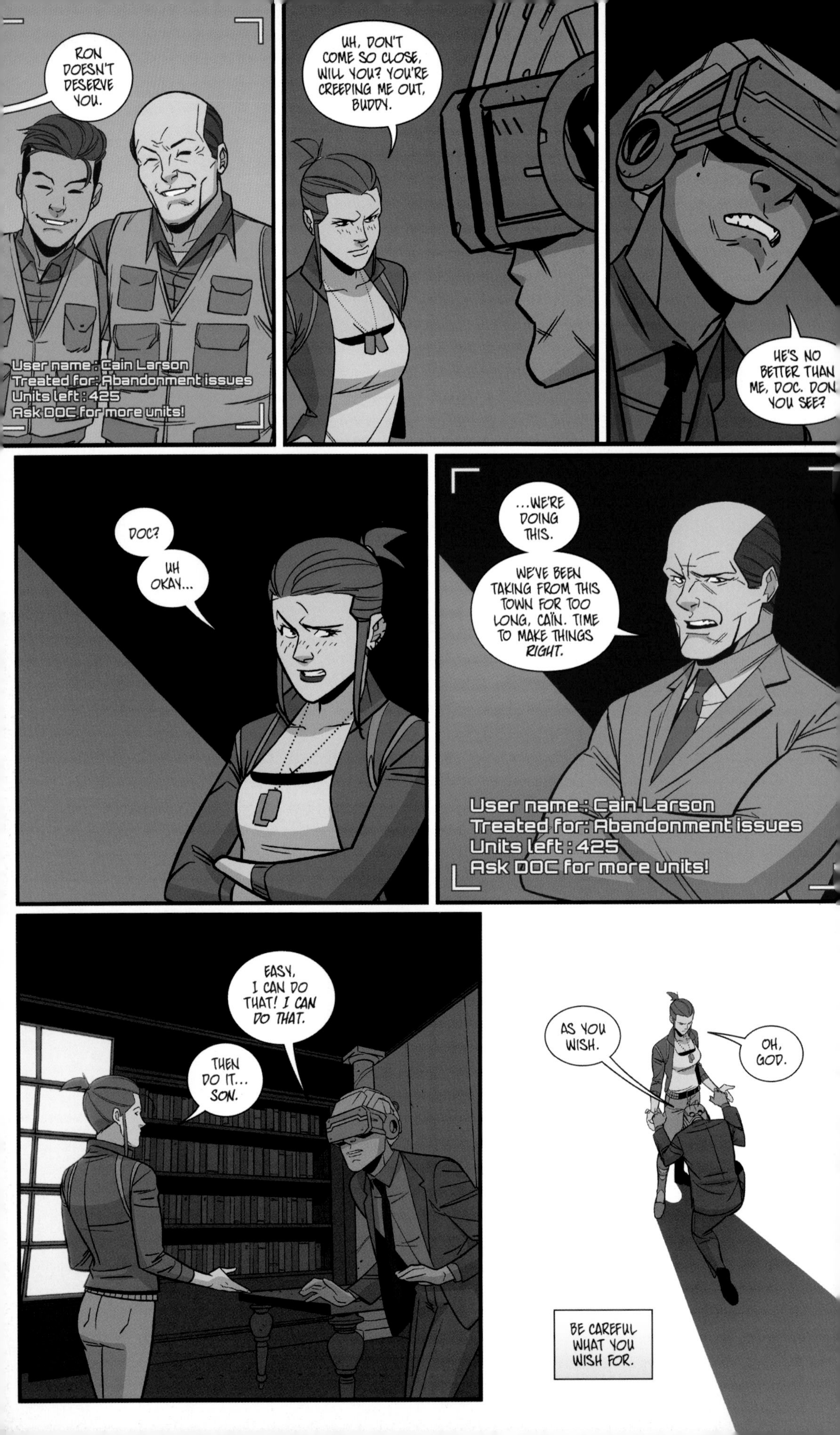
RON DOESN'T DESERVE YOU.
User name : Cain Larson
Treated for: Abandonment issues
Units left : 425
Ask DOC for more units!
UH, DON'T COME SO CLOSE, WILL YOU? YOU'RE CREEPING ME OUT, BUDDY.
HE'S NO BETTER THAN ME, DOC. DON YOU SEE?
DOC?
UH OKAY...
...WE'RE DOING THIS.
WE'VE BEEN TAKING FROM THIS TOWN FOR TOO LONG, CAÏN. TIME TO MAKE THINGS RIGHT.
User name : Cain Larson
Treated for: Abandonment issues
Units left : 425
Ask DOC for more units!
EASY, I CAN DO THAT! I CAN DO THAT.
THEN DO IT... SON.
AS YOU WISH.
OH, GOD.
BE CAREFUL WHAT YOU WISH FOR.

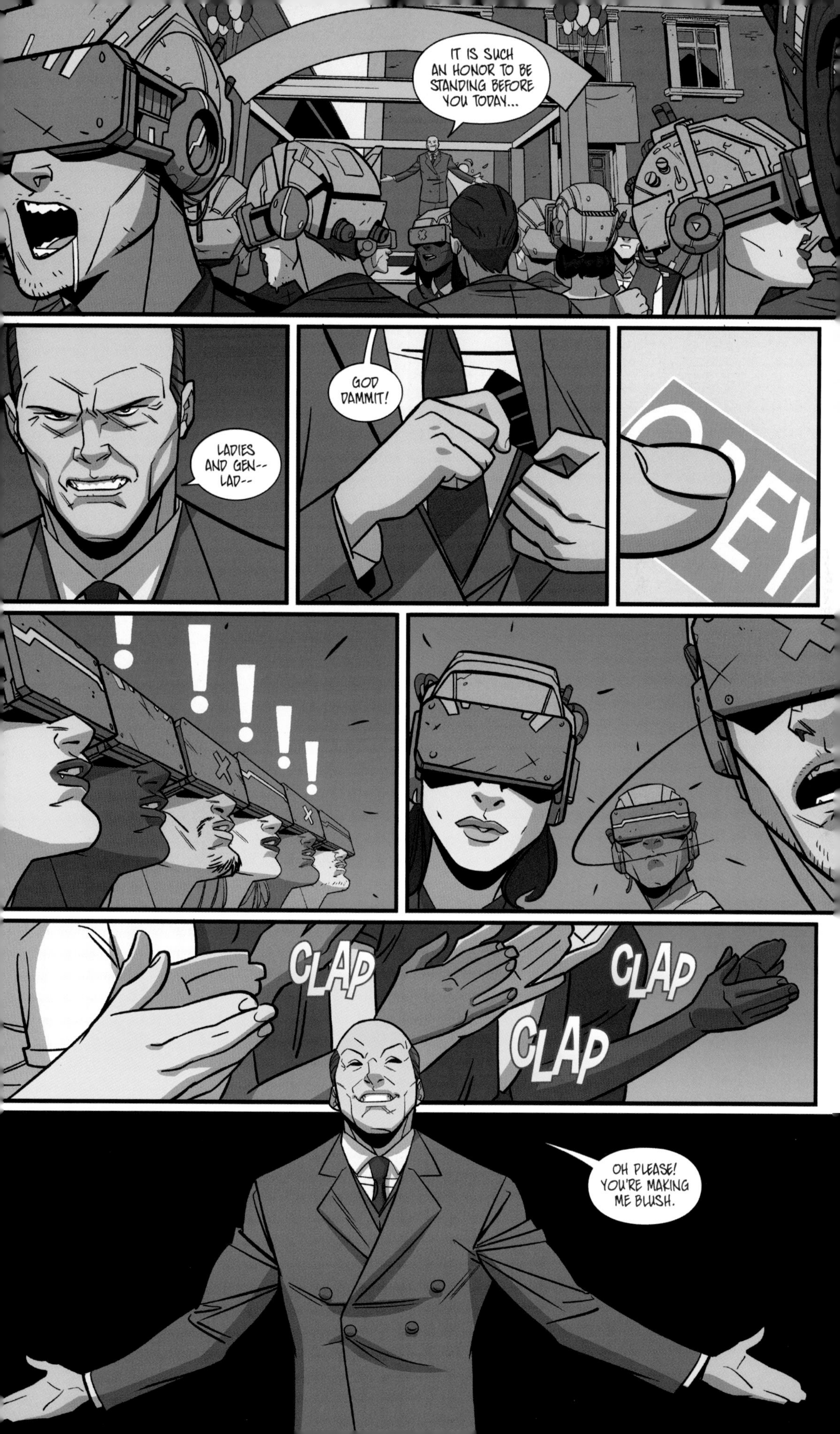
IT IS SUCH AN HONOR TO BE STANDING BEFORE YOU TODAY...
LADIES AND GEN-- LAD--
GOD DAMMIT!
CLAP
CLAP
CLAP
OH PLEASE! YOU'RE MAKING ME BLUSH.

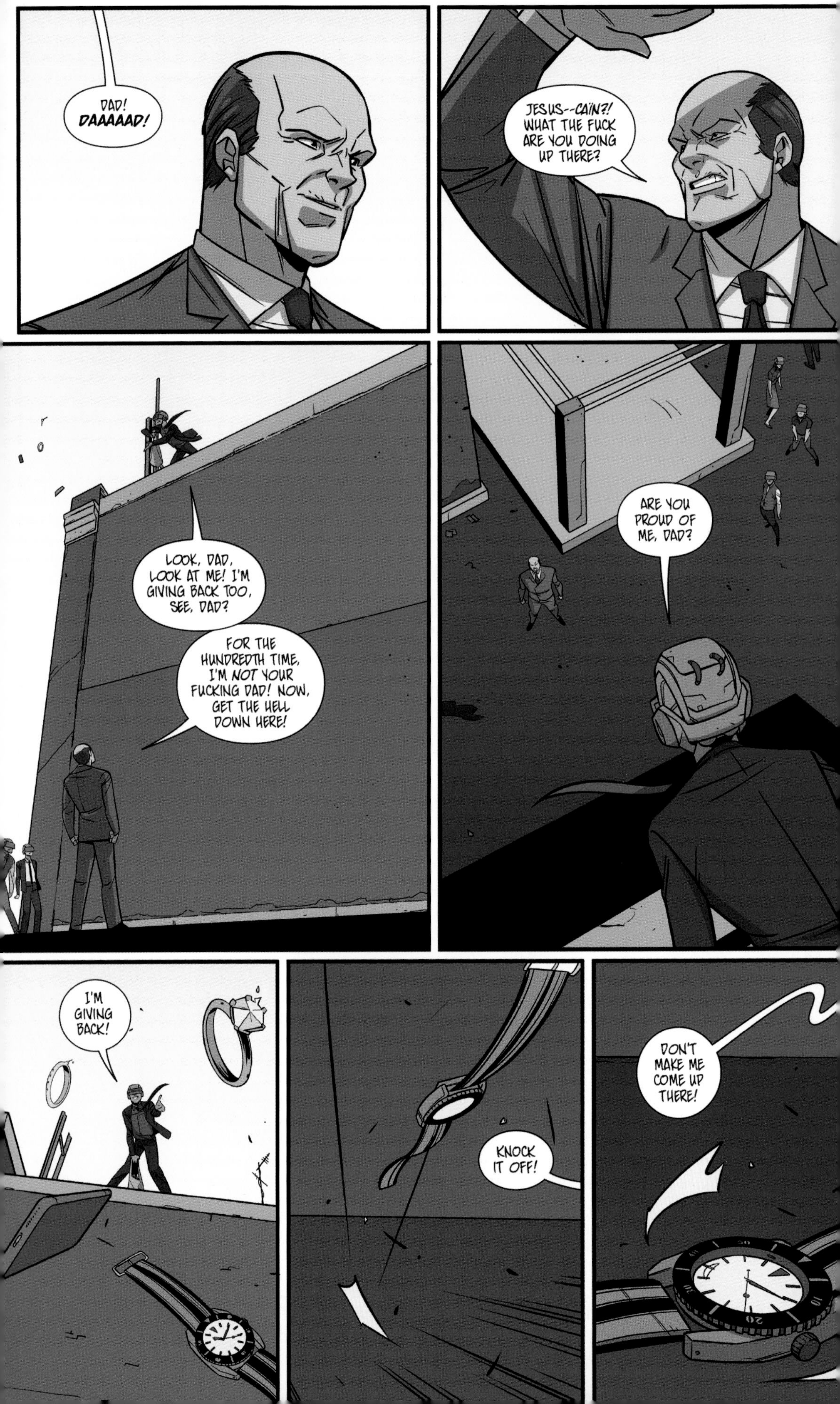
DAD! DAAAAAD!
JESUS--CAIN?! WHAT THE FUCK ARE YOU DOING UP THERE?
LOOK, DAD, LOOK AT ME! I'M GIVING BACK TOO, SEE, DAD?
FOR THE HUNDREDTH TIME, I'M NOT YOUR FUCKING DAD! NOW, GET THE HELL DOWN HERE!
ARE YOU PROUD OF ME, DAD?
I'M GIVING BACK!
KNOCK IT OFF!
DON'T MAKE ME COME UP THERE!

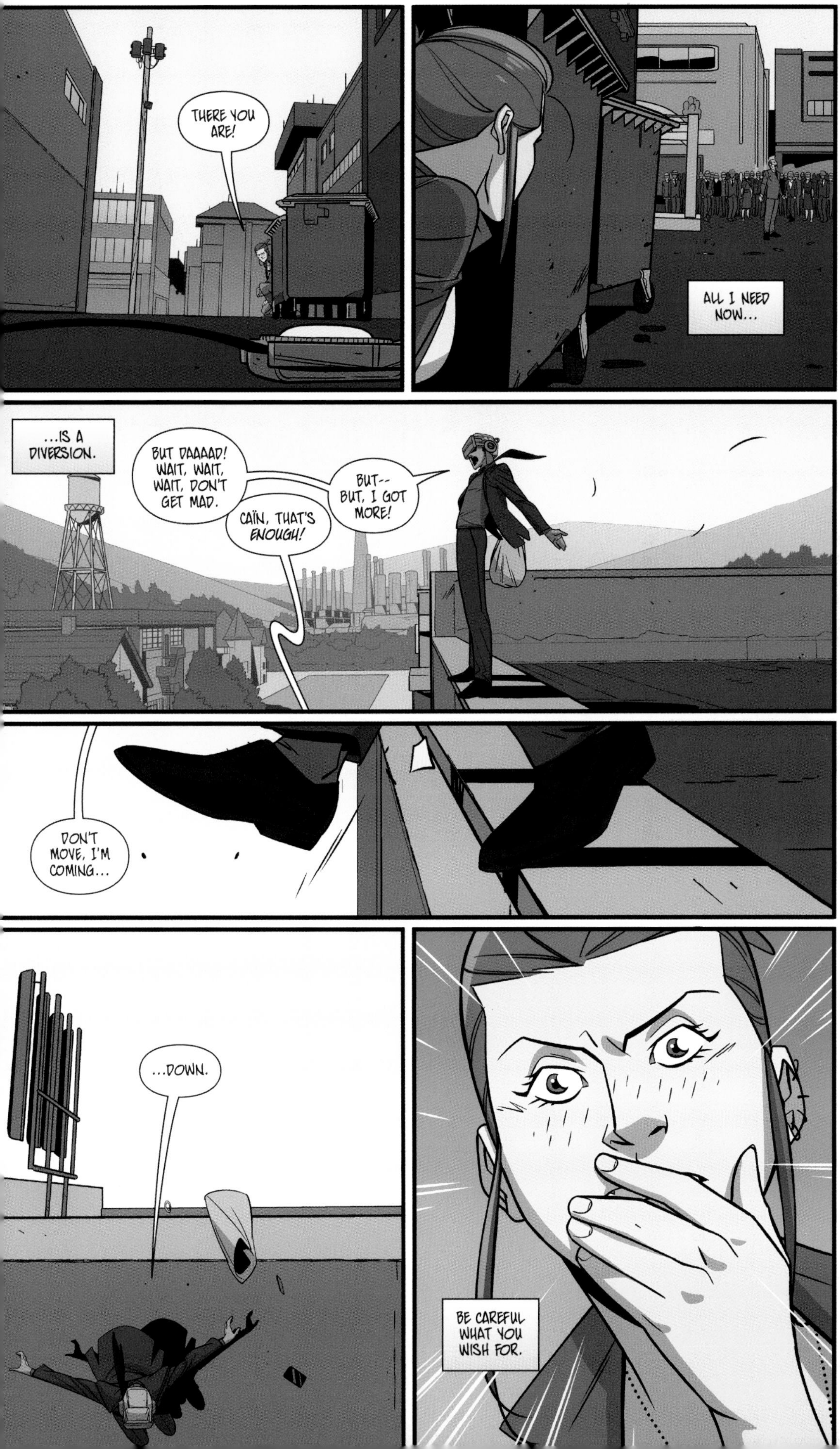
THERE YOU ARE!
ALL I NEED NOW...
...IS A DIVERSION.
BUT DAAAAD! WAIT, WAIT, WAIT, DON'T GET MAD.
CAÏN, THAT'S ENOUGH!
BUT-- BUT, I GOT MORE!
DON'T MOVE, I'M COMING...
...DOWN.
BE CAREFUL WHAT YOU WISH FOR.

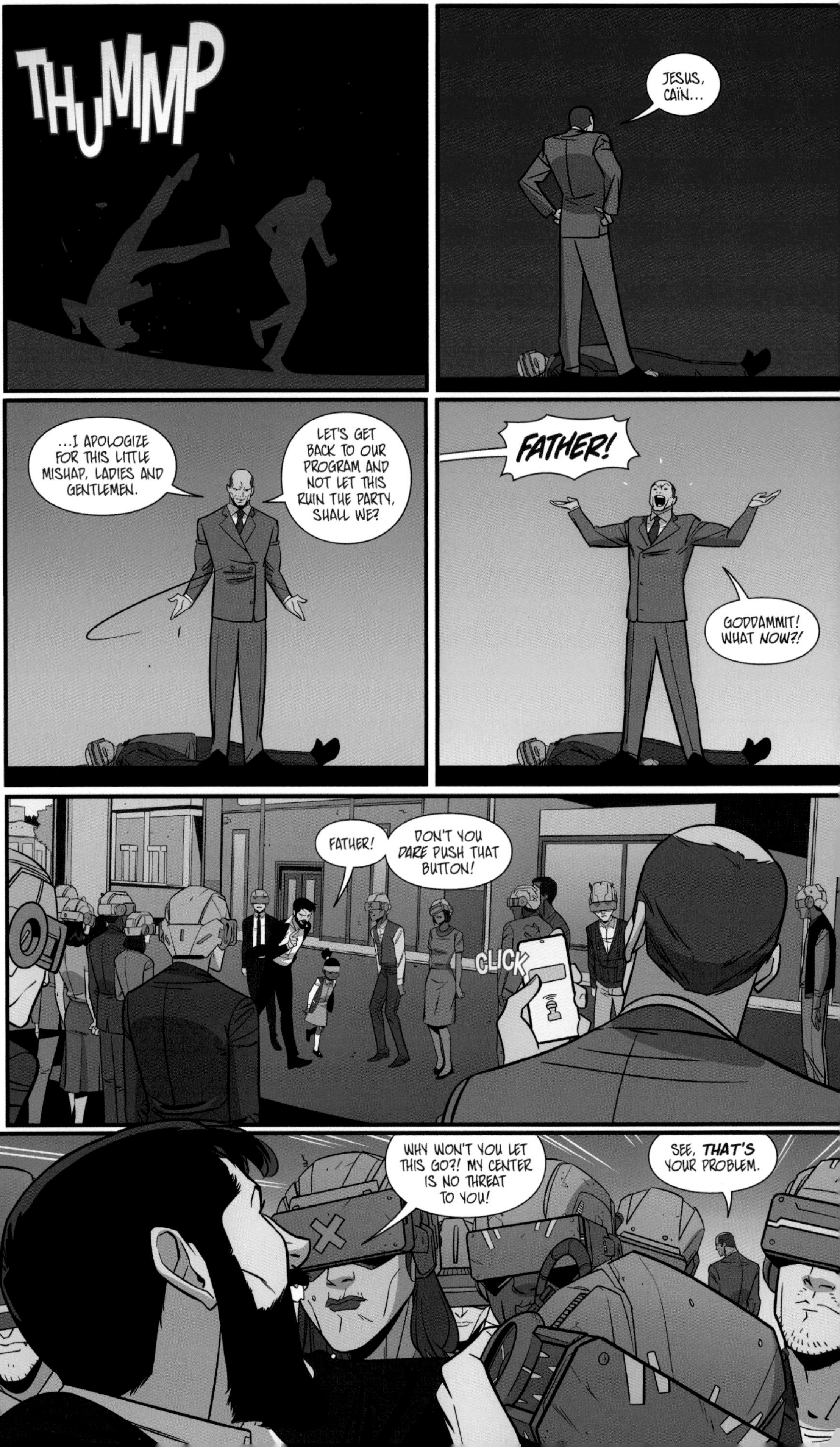
THUMMP
JESUS, CAÏN...
...I APOLOGIZE FOR THIS LITTLE MISHAP, LADIES AND GENTLEMEN.
LET'S GET BACK TO OUR PROGRAM AND NOT LET THIS RUIN THE PARTY, SHALL WE?
FATHER!
GODDAMMIT! WHAT NOW?!
FATHER!
DON'T YOU DARE PUSH THAT BUTTON!
CLICK
WHY WON'T YOU LET THIS GO?! MY CENTER IS NO THREAT TO YOU!
SEE, THAT'S YOUR PROBLEM.

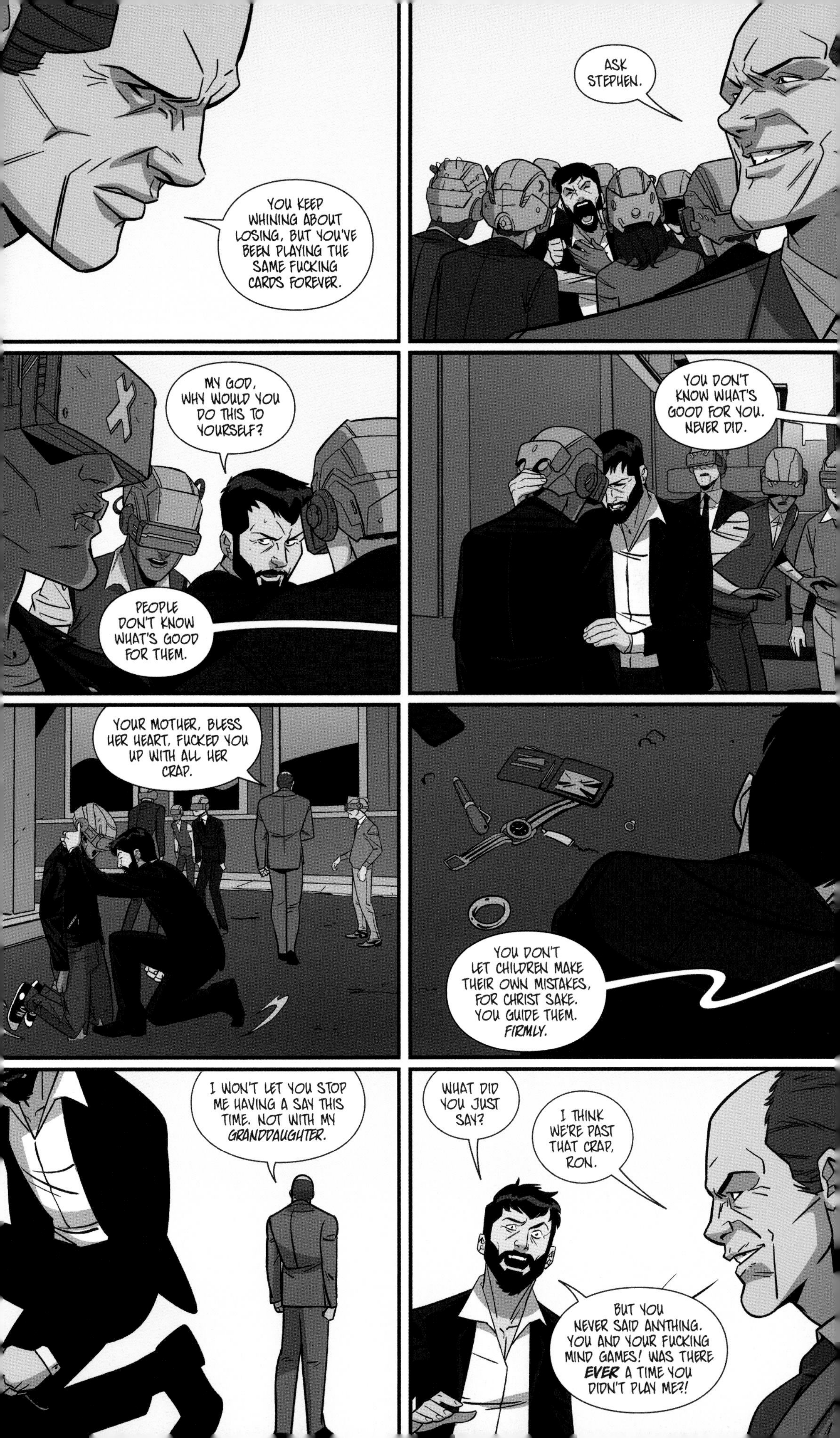
YOU KEEP WHINING ABOUT LOSING, BUT YOU'VE BEEN PLAYING THE SAME FUCKING CARDS FOREVER.
ASK STEPHEN.
MY GOD, WHY WOULD YOU DO THIS TO YOURSELF?
PEOPLE DON'T KNOW WHAT'S GOOD FOR THEM.
YOU DON'T KNOW WHAT'S GOOD FOR YOU. NEVER DID.
YOUR MOTHER, BLESS HER HEART, FUCKED YOU UP WITH ALL HER CRAP.
YOU DON'T LET CHILDREN MAKE THEIR OWN MISTAKES, FOR CHRIST SAKE. YOU GUIDE THEM. *FIRMLY*.
I WON'T LET YOU STOP ME HAVING A SAY THIS TIME. NOT WITH MY *GRANDDAUGHTER*.
WHAT DID YOU JUST SAY?
I THINK WE'RE PAST THAT CRAP, RON.
BUT YOU NEVER SAID ANYTHING. YOU AND YOUR FUCKING MIND GAMES! WAS THERE ***EVER*** A TIME YOU DIDN'T PLAY ME?!

OKAY, WHAT DO YOU WANT?

I BELIEVE THAT'S FAIRLY OBVIOUS.

ANSWER ME. WHAT DO YOU WANT?

YOU WANT A SPOT ON THE CHRISTMAS CARD? IS THAT IT? TO CUT THE FREAKING TURKEY AT THANKSGIVING?!

YOU DON'T HAVE TO BE CRUEL.

I WANT THE SAME AS YOU.

TO BE PART OF THIS.

TO SHAPE HER INTO A WOMAN THAT'D MAKE BOTH OF US PROUD.

ALL RIGHT, THEN.

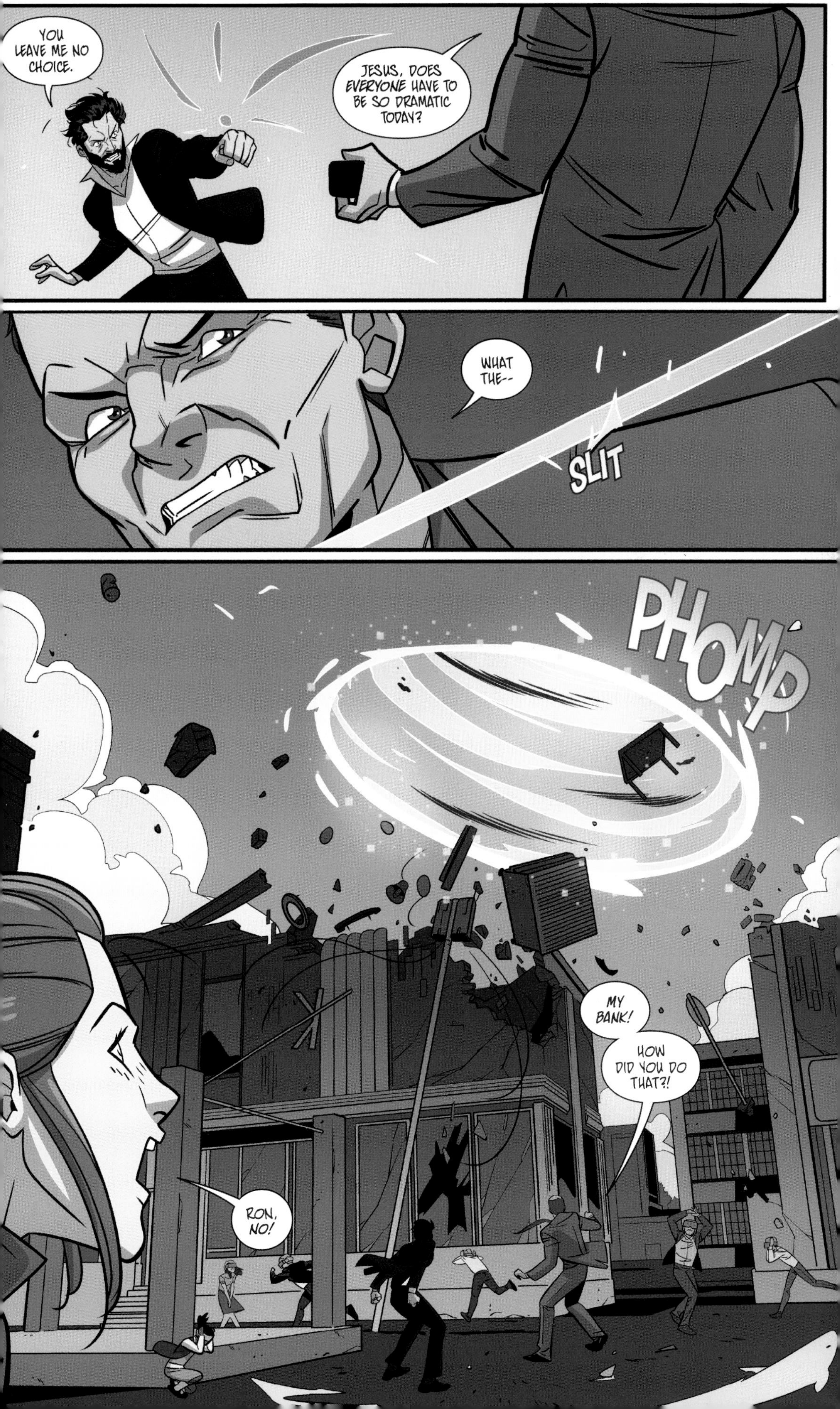
YOU LEAVE ME NO CHOICE.
JESUS, DOES EVERYONE HAVE TO BE SO DRAMATIC TODAY?
WHAT THE--
SLIT
PHOMP
MY BANK!
HOW DID YOU DO THAT?!
RON, NO!

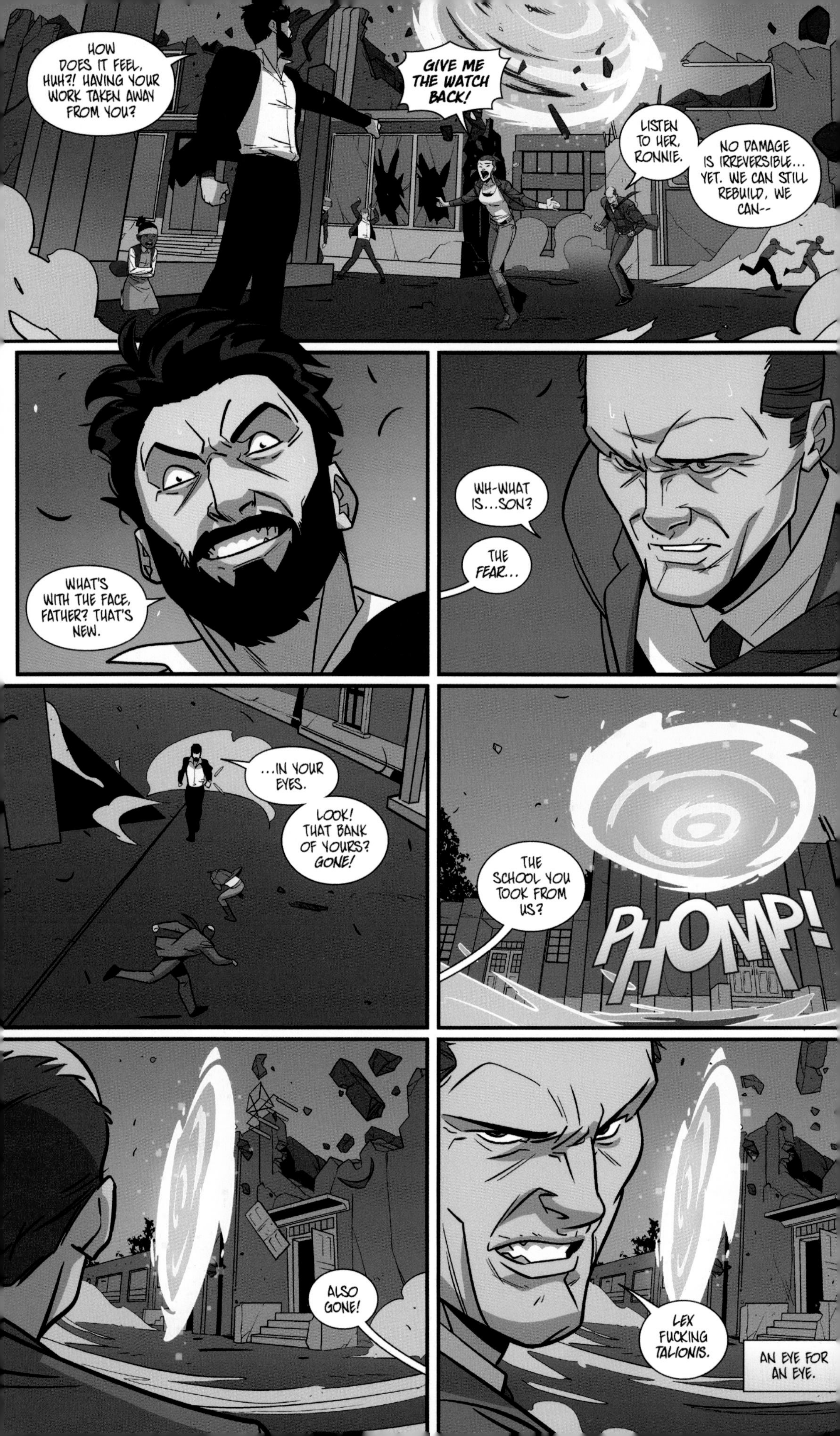
HOW DOES IT FEEL, HUH?! HAVING YOUR WORK TAKEN AWAY FROM YOU?
GIVE ME THE WATCH BACK!
LISTEN TO HER, RONNIE.
NO DAMAGE IS IRREVERSIBLE... YET. WE CAN STILL REBUILD, WE CAN--
WHAT'S WITH THE FACE, FATHER? THAT'S NEW.
WH-WHAT IS...SON?
THE FEAR...
...IN YOUR EYES.
LOOK! THAT BANK OF YOURS? GONE!
THE SCHOOL YOU TOOK FROM US?
PHOMP!
ALSO GONE!
LEX FUCKING TALIONIS.
AN EYE FOR AN EYE.

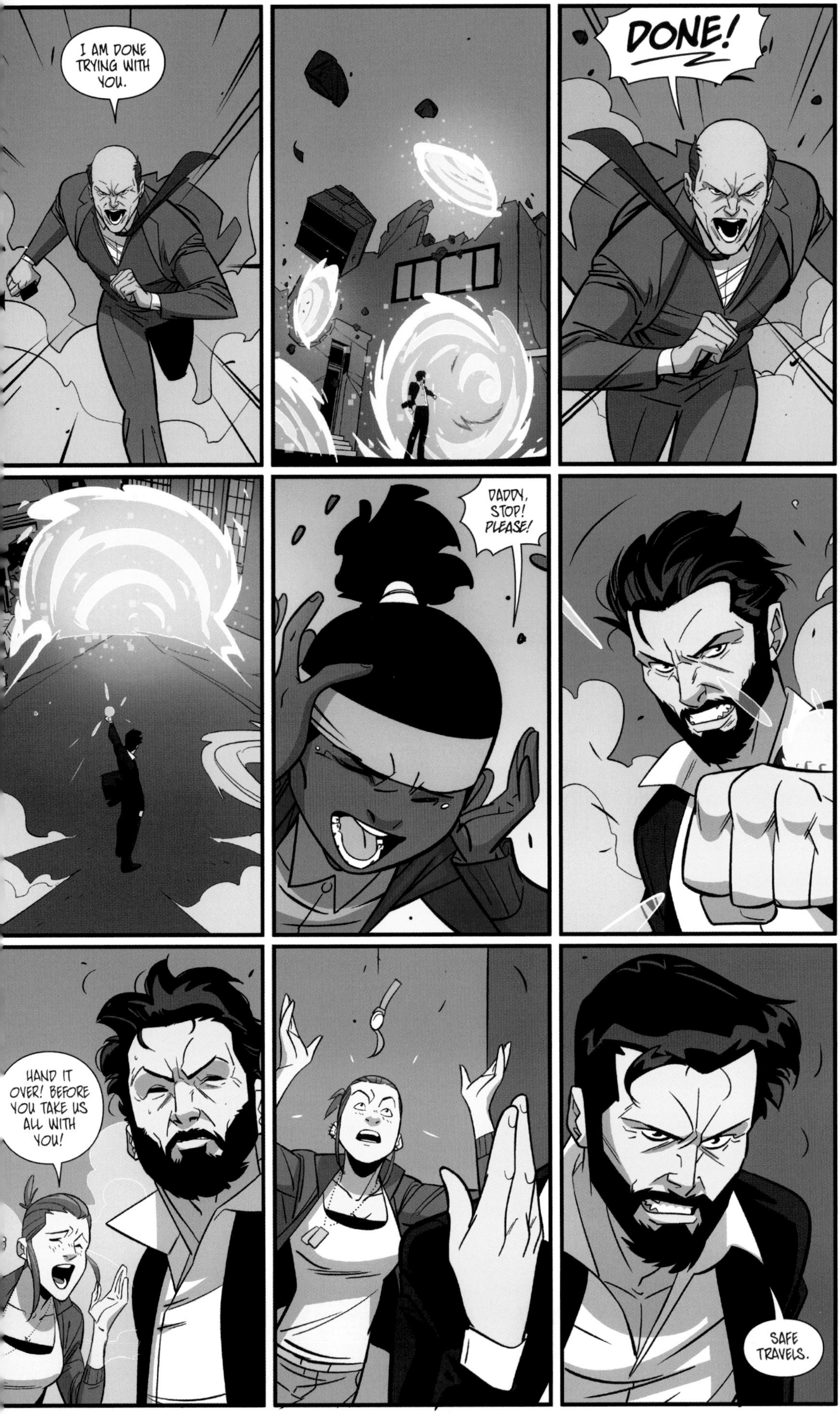
I AM DONE TRYING WITH YOU.
DONE!
DADDY, STOP! PLEASE!
HAND IT OVER! BEFORE YOU TAKE US ALL WITH YOU!
SAFE TRAVELS.

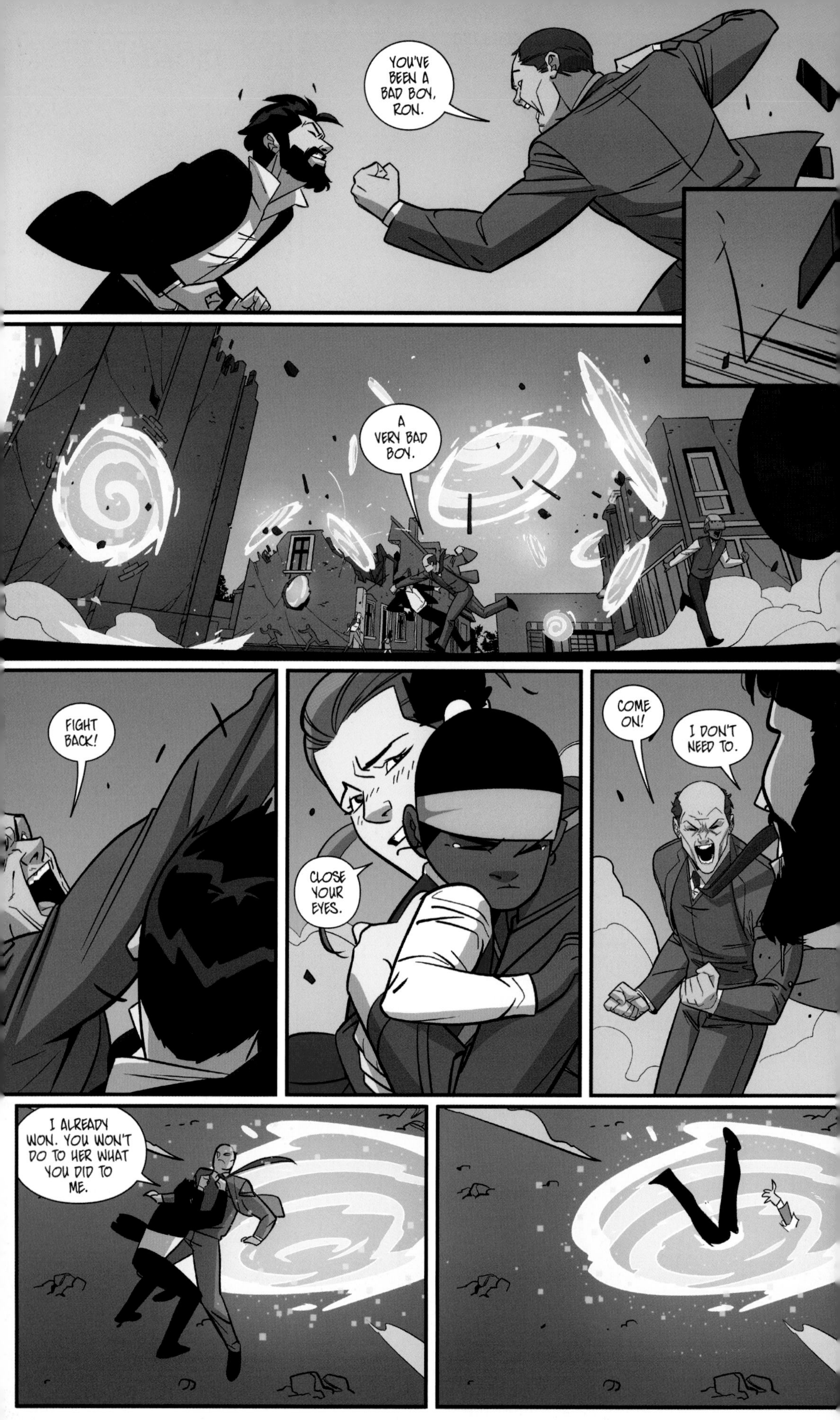
YOU'VE BEEN A BAD BOY, RON.
A VERY BAD BOY.
FIGHT BACK!
CLOSE YOUR EYES.
COME ON!
I DON'T NEED TO.
I ALREADY WON. YOU WON'T DO TO HER WHAT YOU DID TO ME.

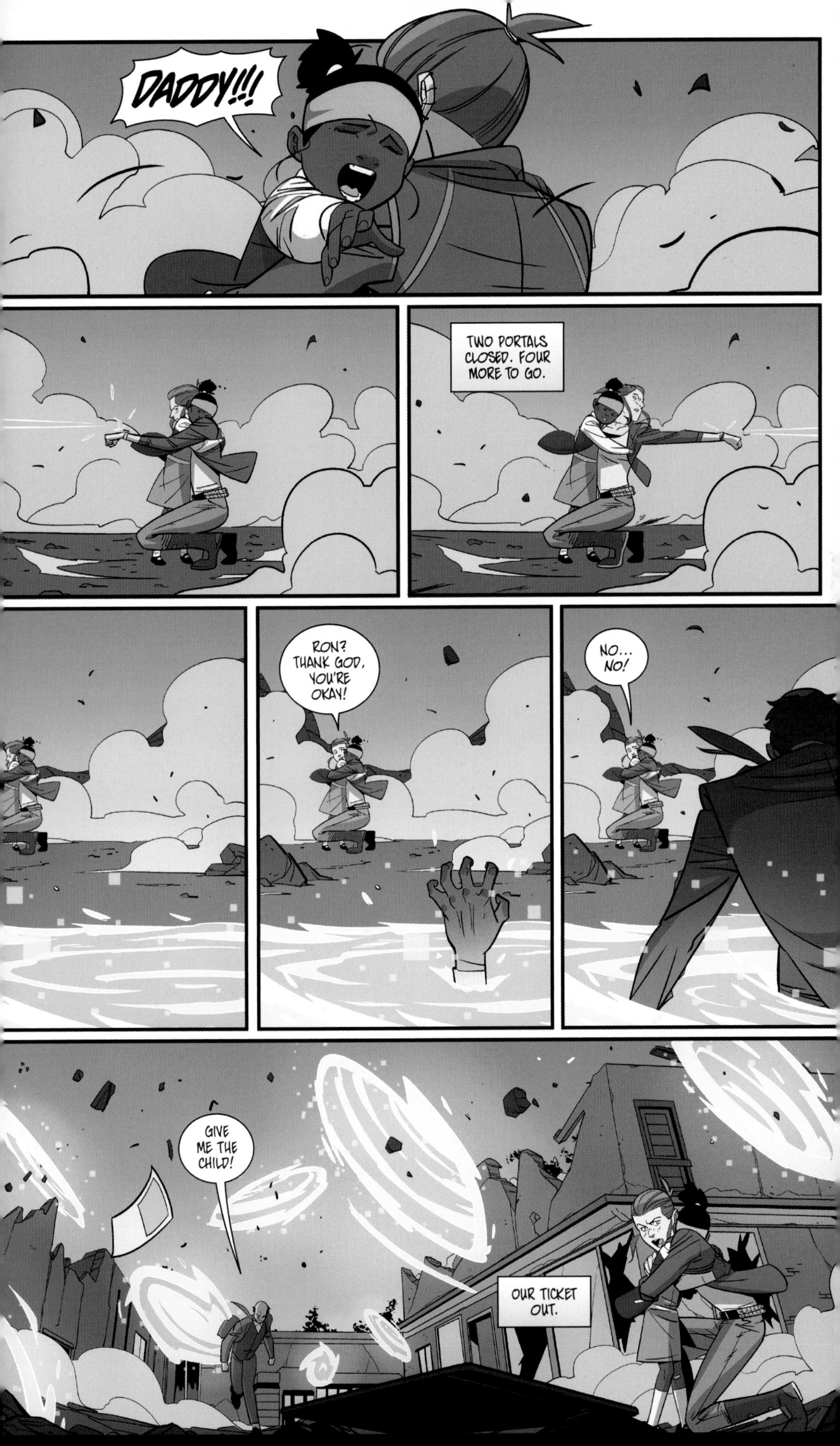
DADDY!!!
TWO PORTALS CLOSED. FOUR MORE TO GO.
RON? THANK GOD, YOU'RE OKAY!
NO... NO!
GIVE ME THE CHILD!
OUR TICKET OUT.

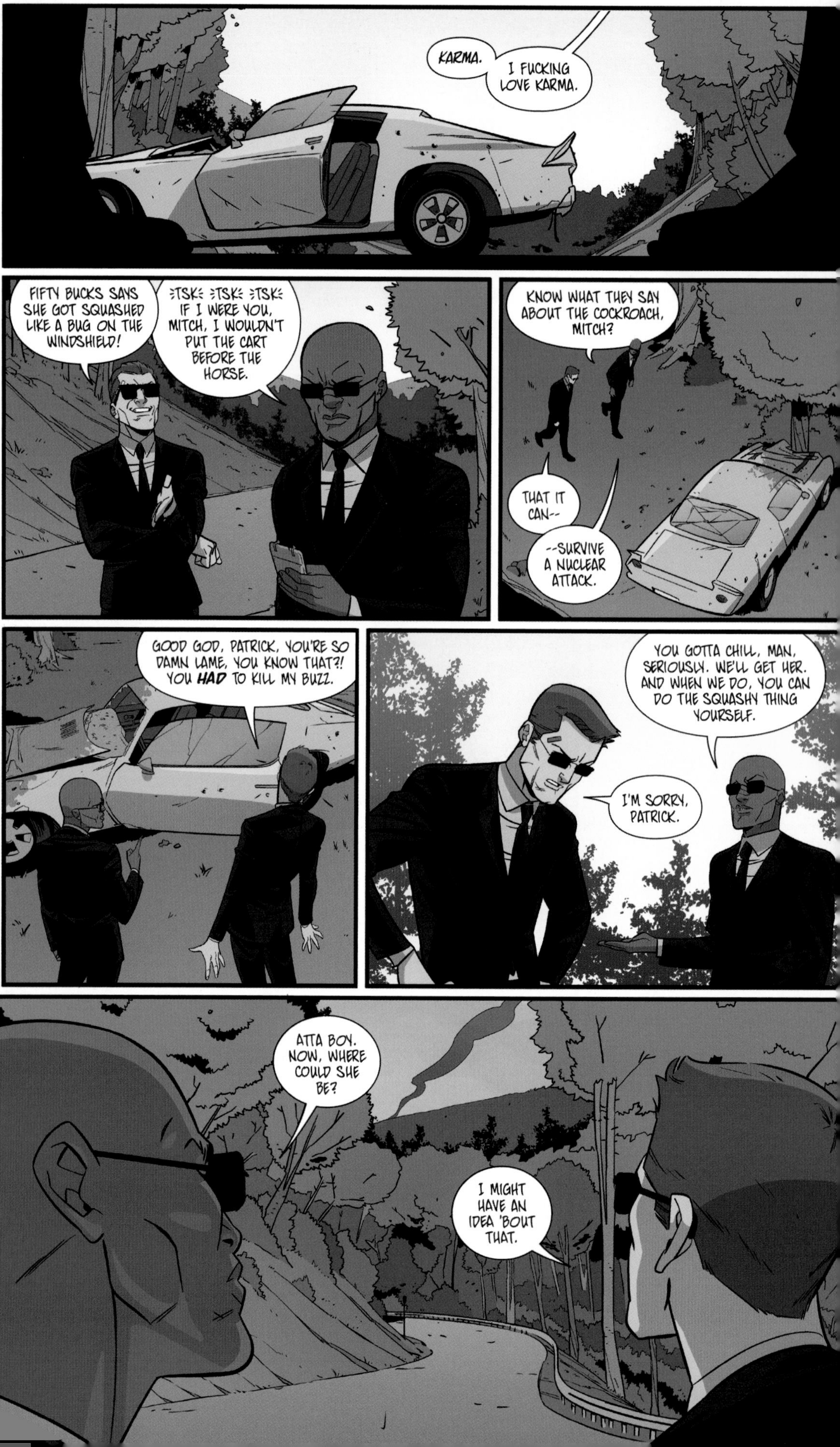
KARMA.
I FUCKING LOVE KARMA.
FIFTY BUCKS SAYS SHE GOT SQUASHED LIKE A BUG ON THE WINDSHIELD!
TSK TSK TSK IF I WERE YOU, MITCH, I WOULDN'T PUT THE CART BEFORE THE HORSE.
KNOW WHAT THEY SAY ABOUT THE COCKROACH, MITCH?
THAT IT CAN--
--SURVIVE A NUCLEAR ATTACK.
GOOD GOD, PATRICK, YOU'RE SO DAMN LAME, YOU KNOW THAT?! YOU **HAD** TO KILL MY BUZZ.
YOU GOTTA CHILL, MAN, SERIOUSLY. WE'LL GET HER. AND WHEN WE DO, YOU CAN DO THE SQUASHY THING YOURSELF.
I'M SORRY, PATRICK.
ATTA BOY. NOW, WHERE COULD SHE BE?
I MIGHT HAVE AN IDEA 'BOUT THAT.

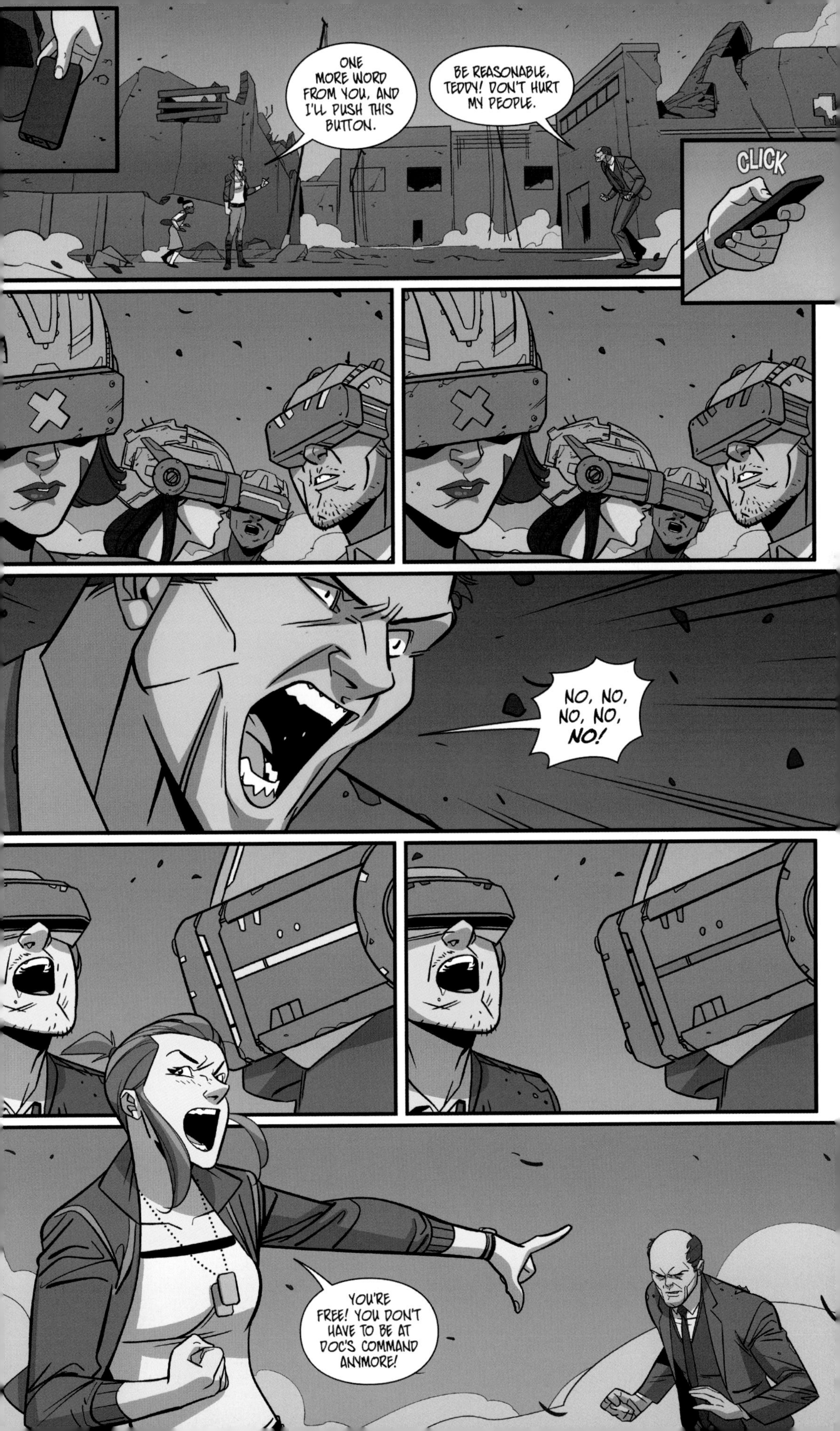
ONE MORE WORD FROM YOU, AND I'LL PUSH THIS BUTTON.
BE REASONABLE, TEDDY! DON'T HURT MY PEOPLE.
CLICK
NO, NO, NO, NO, NO!
YOU'RE FREE! YOU DON'T HAVE TO BE AT DOC'S COMMAND ANYMORE!

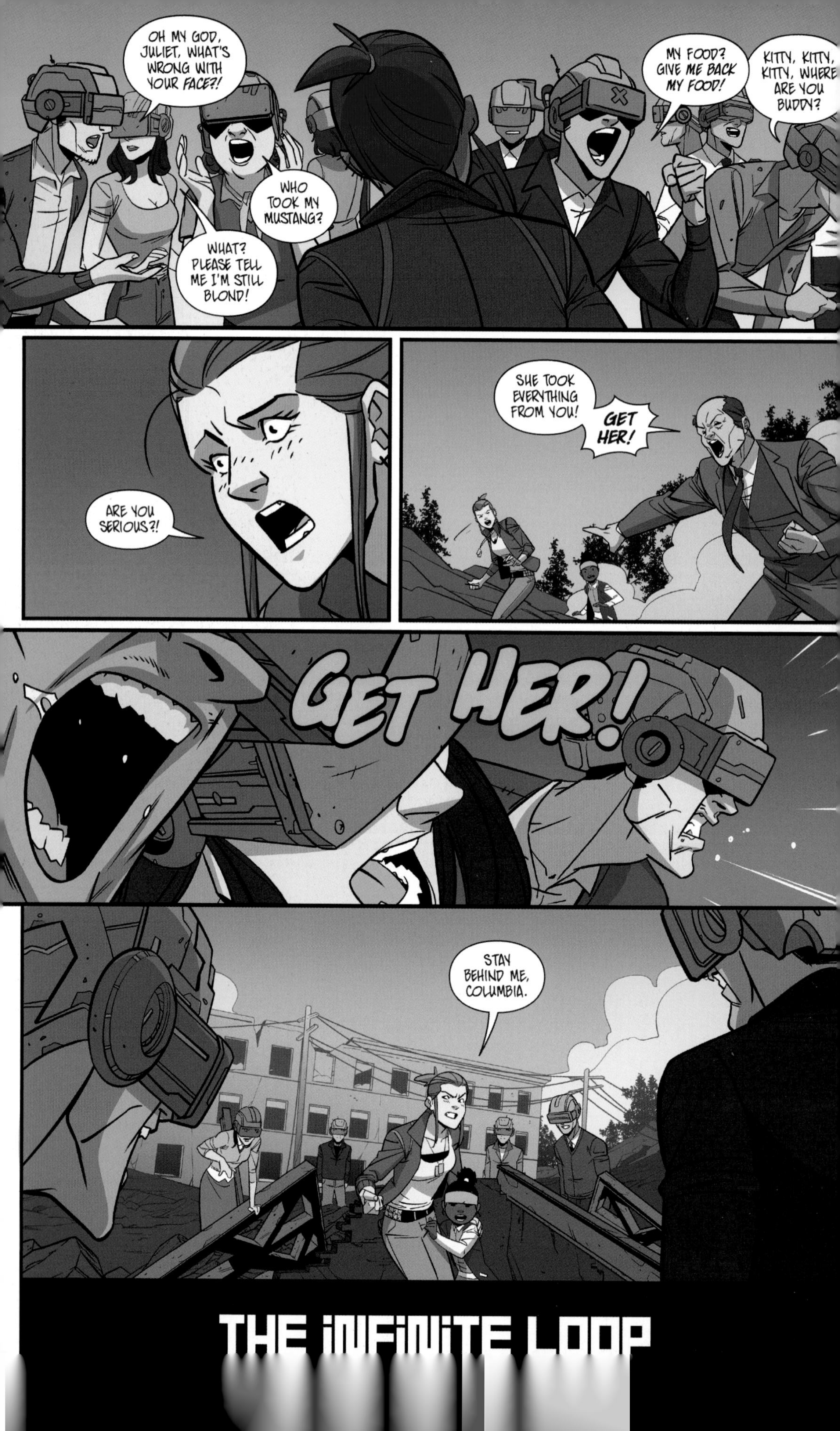

OH MY GOD, JULIET, WHAT'S WRONG WITH YOUR FACE?!
WHAT? PLEASE TELL ME I'M STILL BLOND!
WHO TOOK MY MUSTANG?
MY FOOD? GIVE ME BACK MY FOOD!
KITTY, KITTY, KITTY, WHERE ARE YOU BUDDY?
ARE YOU SERIOUS?!
SHE TOOK EVERYTHING FROM YOU!
GET HER!
GET HER!
STAY BEHIND ME, COLUMBIA.
THE INFINITE LOOP

Art by DAVE JOHNSON

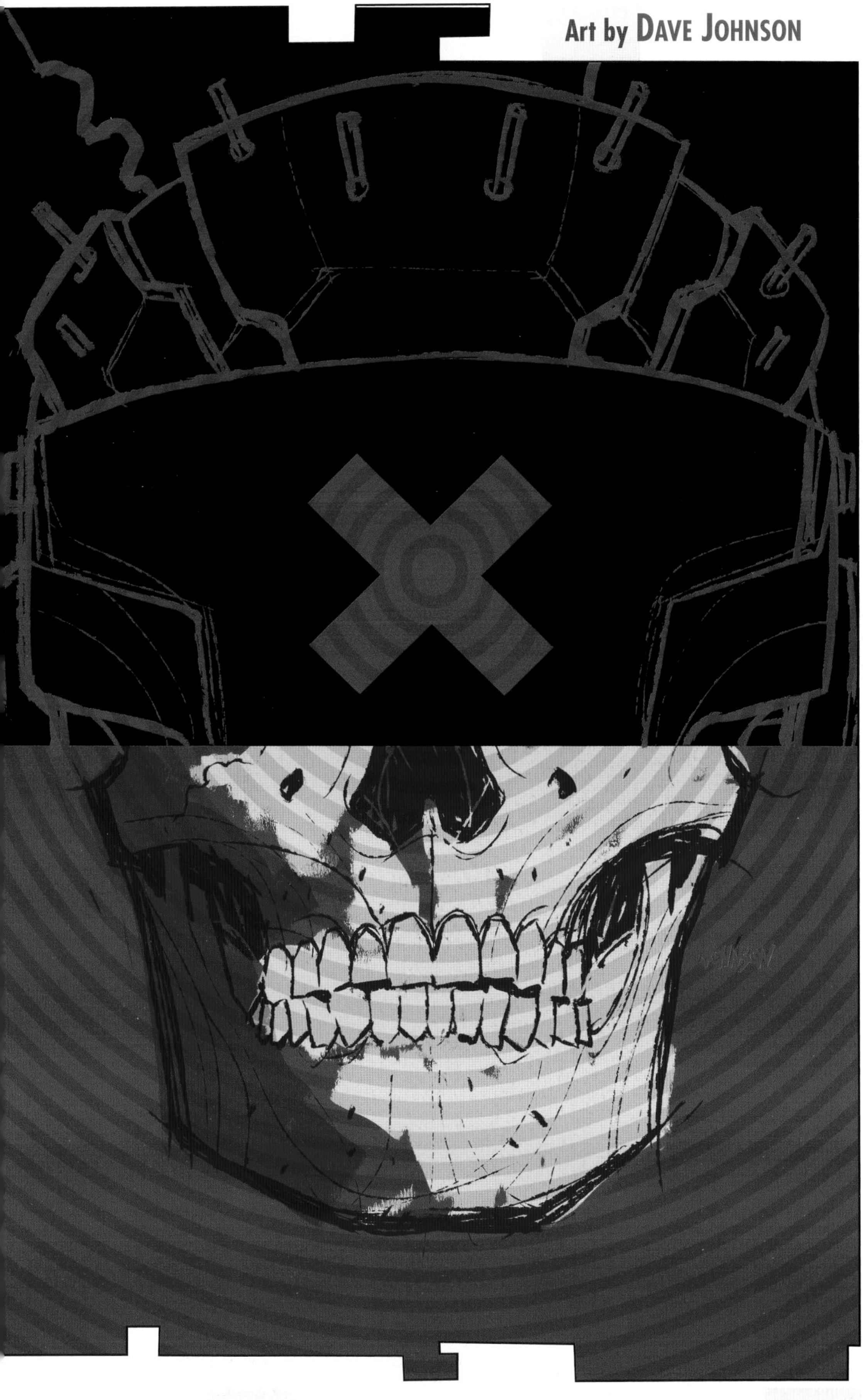

Art by
ELSA CHARRETIER

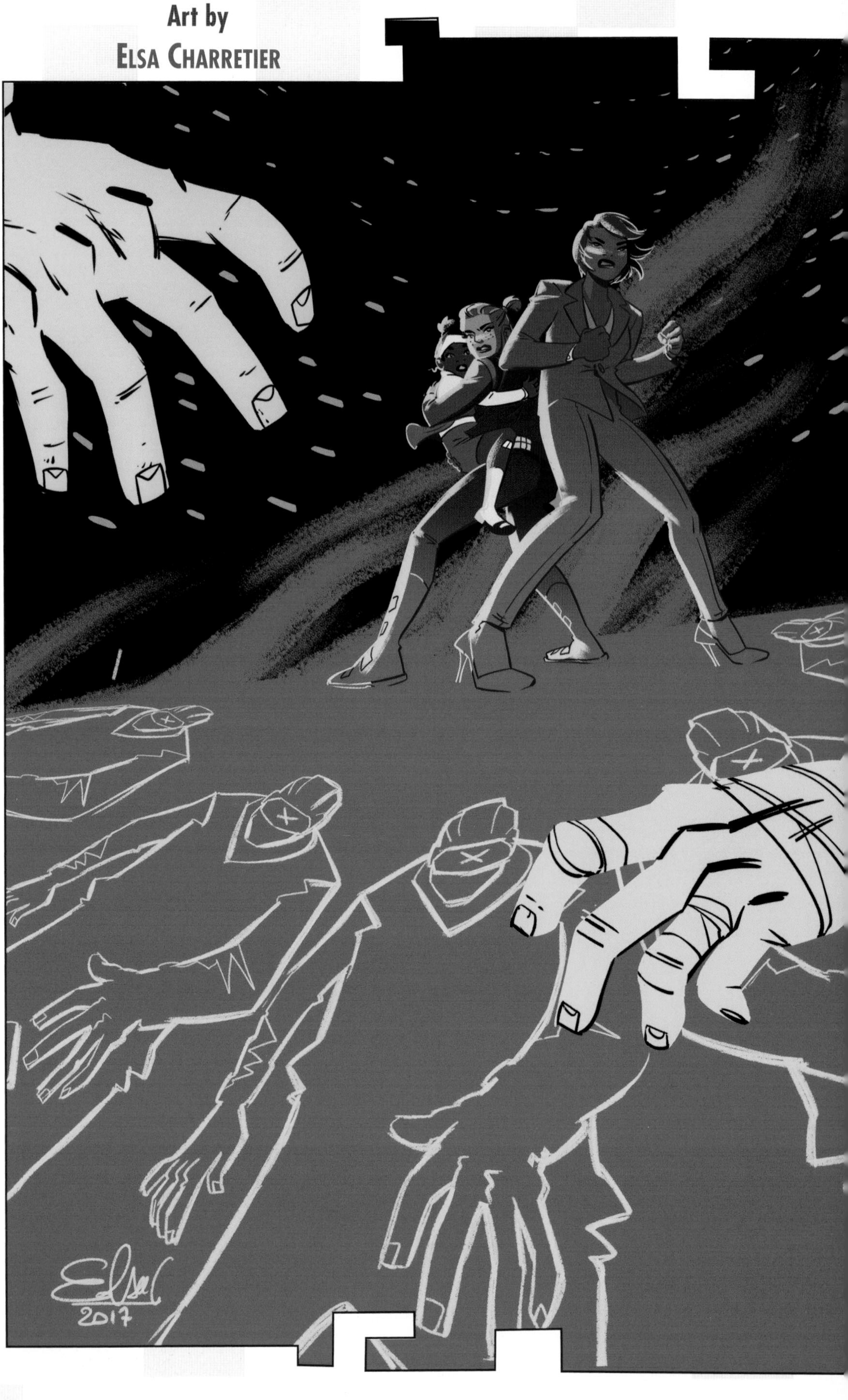

Elsa
2017

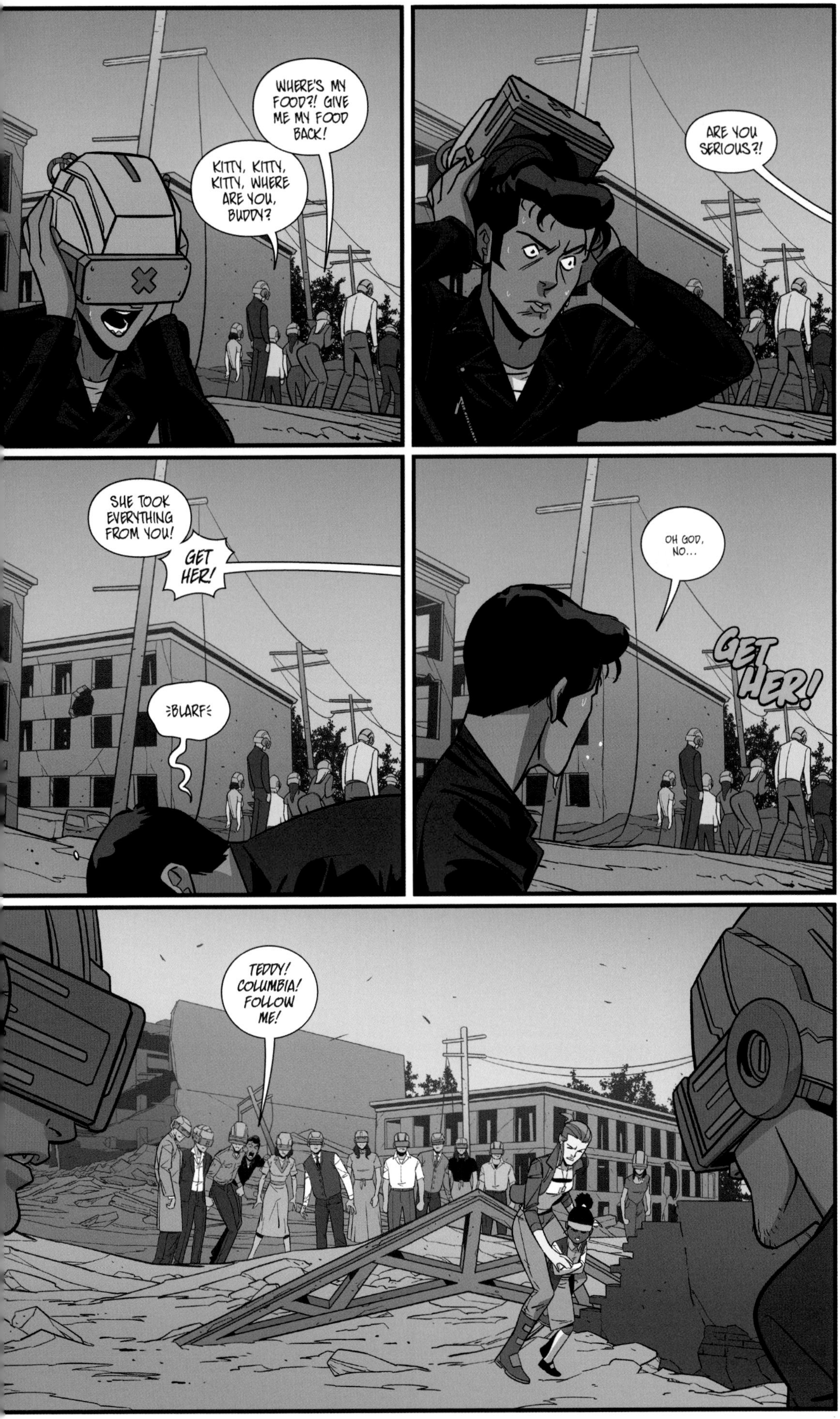
WHERE'S MY FOOD?! GIVE ME MY FOOD BACK!
KITTY, KITTY, KITTY, WHERE ARE YOU, BUDDY?
ARE YOU SERIOUS?!
SHE TOOK EVERYTHING FROM YOU!
GET HER!
BLARF
OH GOD, NO...
GET HER!
TEDDY! COLUMBIA! FOLLOW ME!

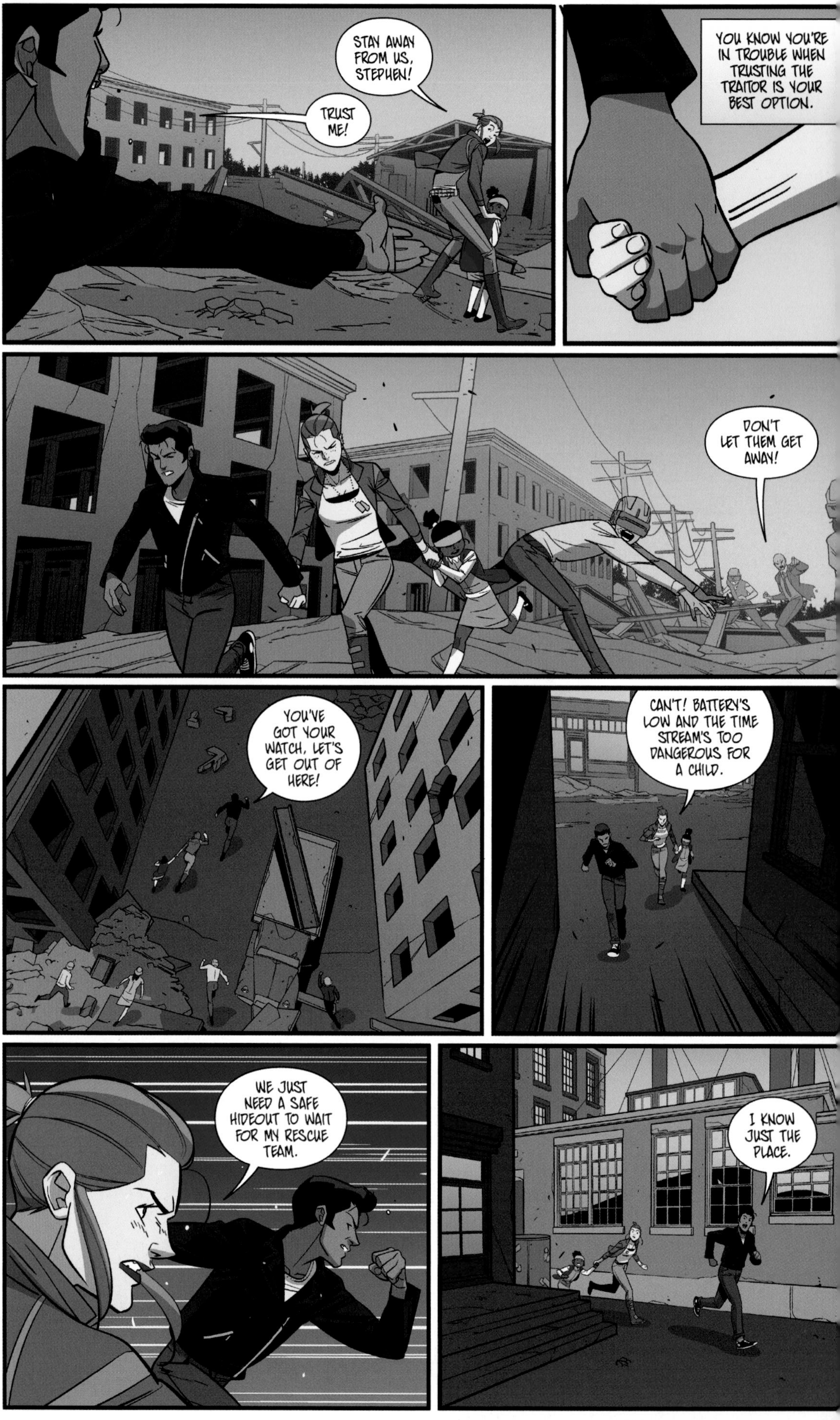
STAY AWAY FROM US, STEPHEN!
TRUST ME!
YOU KNOW YOU'RE IN TROUBLE WHEN TRUSTING THE TRAITOR IS YOUR BEST OPTION.
DON'T LET THEM GET AWAY!
YOU'VE GOT YOUR WATCH, LET'S GET OUT OF HERE!
CAN'T! BATTERY'S LOW AND THE TIME STREAM'S TOO DANGEROUS FOR A CHILD.
WE JUST NEED A SAFE HIDEOUT TO WAIT FOR MY RESCUE TEAM.
I KNOW JUST THE PLACE.

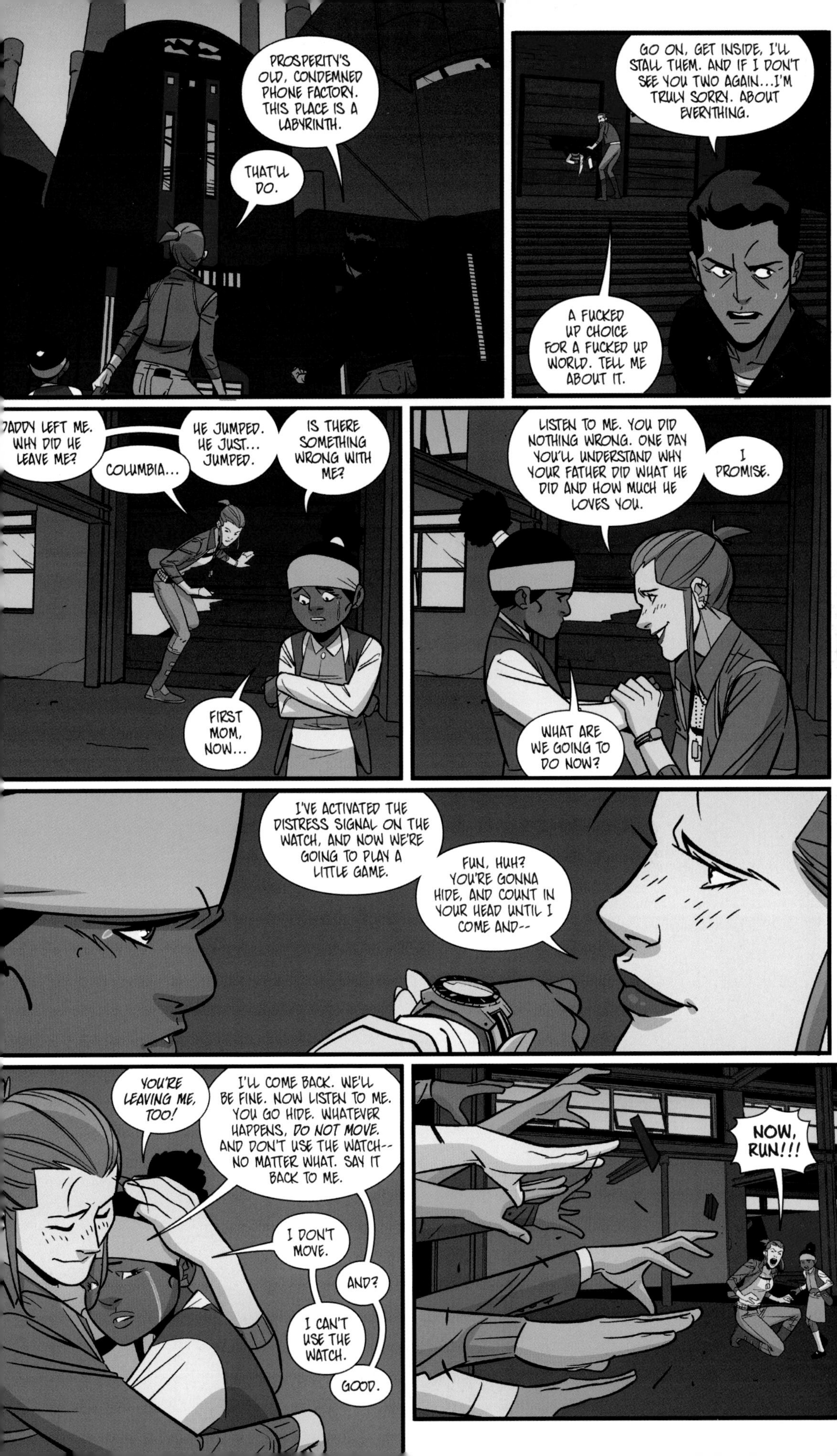
PROSPERITY'S OLD, CONDEMNED PHONE FACTORY. THIS PLACE IS A LABYRINTH.
THAT'LL DO.
GO ON, GET INSIDE, I'LL STALL THEM. AND IF I DON'T SEE YOU TWO AGAIN...I'M TRULY SORRY. ABOUT EVERYTHING.
A FUCKED UP CHOICE FOR A FUCKED UP WORLD. TELL ME ABOUT IT.
DADDY LEFT ME. WHY DID HE LEAVE ME?
COLUMBIA...
HE JUMPED. HE JUST... JUMPED.
IS THERE SOMETHING WRONG WITH ME?
FIRST MOM, NOW...
LISTEN TO ME. YOU DID NOTHING WRONG. ONE DAY YOU'LL UNDERSTAND WHY YOUR FATHER DID WHAT HE DID AND HOW MUCH HE LOVES YOU.
I PROMISE.
WHAT ARE WE GOING TO DO NOW?
I'VE ACTIVATED THE DISTRESS SIGNAL ON THE WATCH, AND NOW WE'RE GOING TO PLAY A LITTLE GAME.
FUN, HUH? YOU'RE GONNA HIDE, AND COUNT IN YOUR HEAD UNTIL I COME AND--
YOU'RE LEAVING ME, TOO!
I'LL COME BACK. WE'LL BE FINE. NOW LISTEN TO ME. YOU GO HIDE. WHATEVER HAPPENS, *DO NOT MOVE.* AND DON'T USE THE WATCH-- NO MATTER WHAT. SAY IT BACK TO ME.
I DON'T MOVE.
AND?
I CAN'T USE THE WATCH.
GOOD.
NOW, RUN!!!

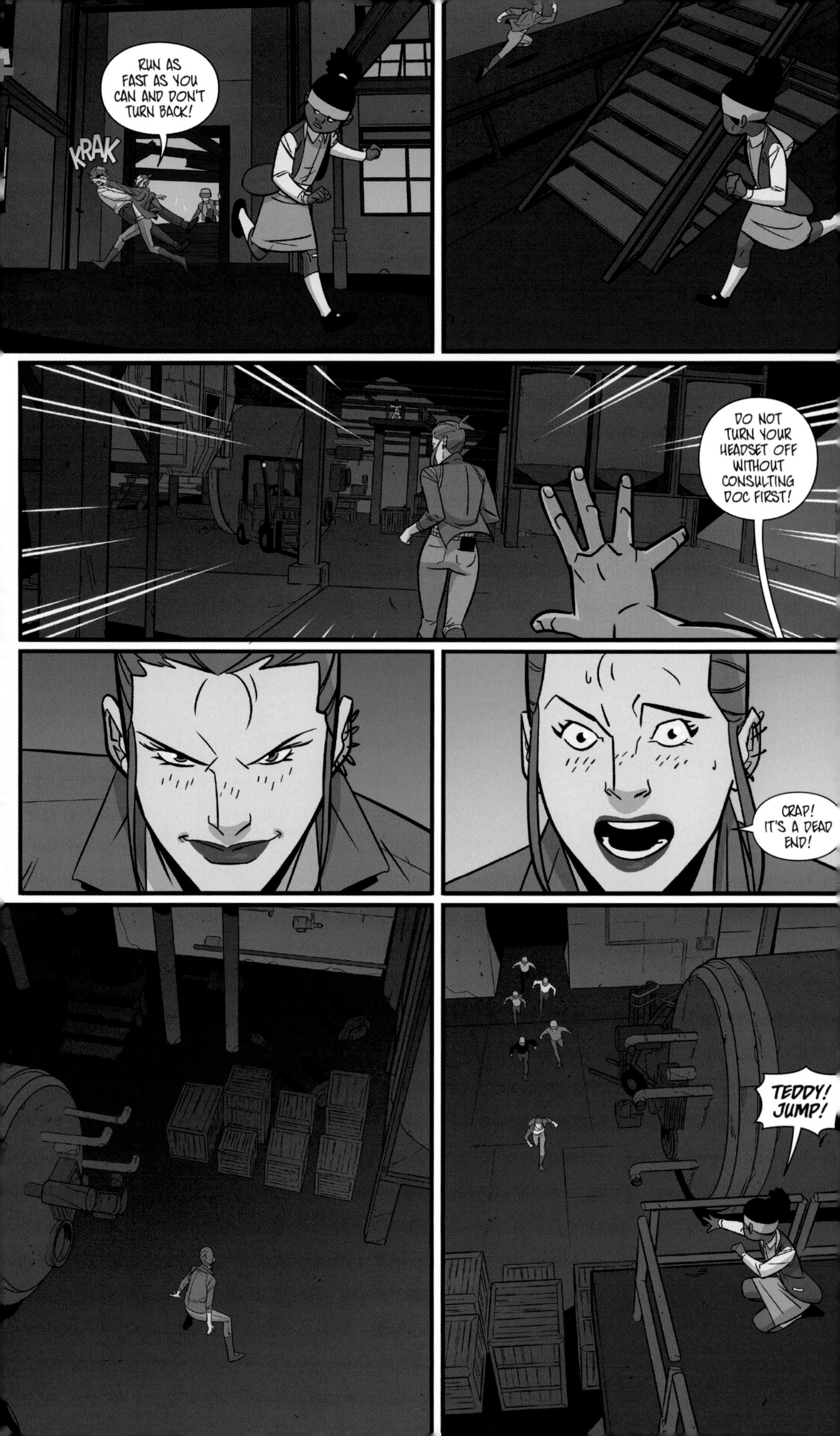
RUN AS FAST AS YOU CAN AND DON'T TURN BACK!
KRAK
DO NOT TURN YOUR HEADSET OFF WITHOUT CONSULTING DOC FIRST!
CRAP! IT'S A DEAD END!
TEDDY! JUMP!

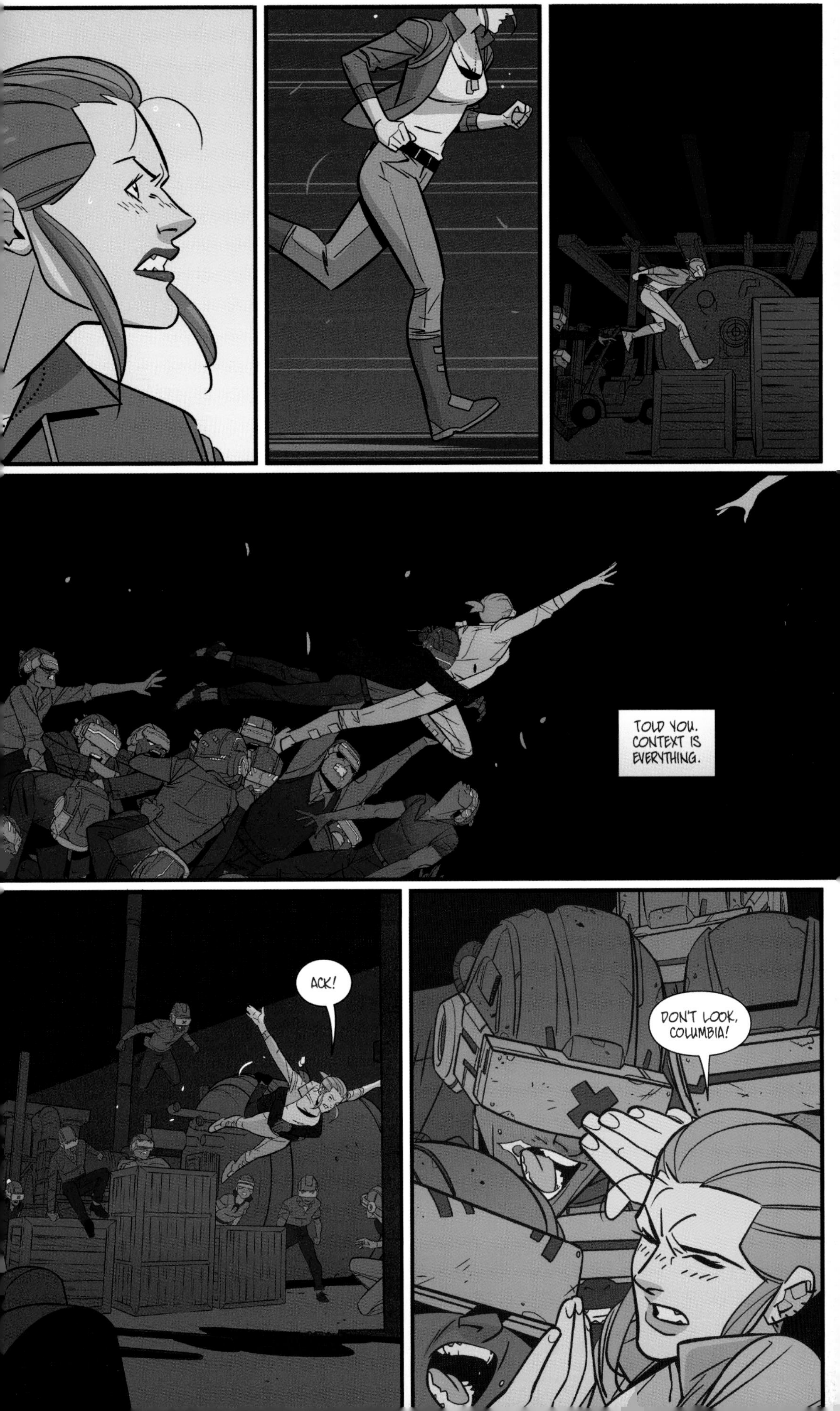
TOLD YOU. CONTEXT IS EVERYTHING.
ACK!
DON'T LOOK, COLUMBIA!

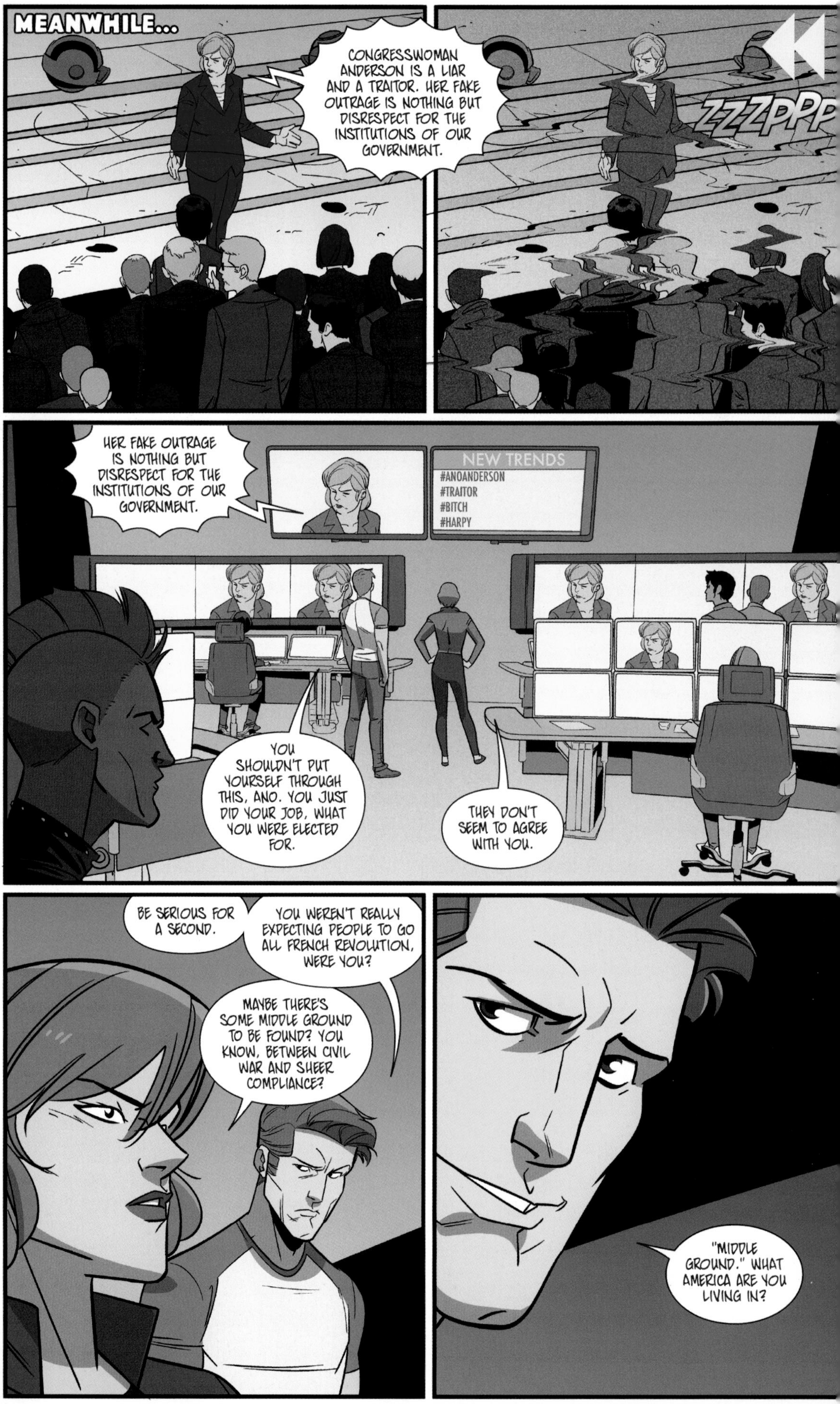

MEANWHILE...
CONGRESSWOMAN ANDERSON IS A LIAR AND A TRAITOR. HER FAKE OUTRAGE IS NOTHING BUT DISRESPECT FOR THE INSTITUTIONS OF OUR GOVERNMENT.
ZZZPPP
HER FAKE OUTRAGE IS NOTHING BUT DISRESPECT FOR THE INSTITUTIONS OF OUR GOVERNMENT.
NEW TRENDS
#ANOANDERSON
#TRAITOR
#BITCH
#HARPY
YOU SHOULDN'T PUT YOURSELF THROUGH THIS, ANO. YOU JUST DID YOUR JOB, WHAT YOU WERE ELECTED FOR.
THEY DON'T SEEM TO AGREE WITH YOU.
BE SERIOUS FOR A SECOND.
YOU WEREN'T REALLY EXPECTING PEOPLE TO GO ALL FRENCH REVOLUTION, WERE YOU?
MAYBE THERE'S SOME MIDDLE GROUND TO BE FOUND? YOU KNOW, BETWEEN CIVIL WAR AND SHEER COMPLIANCE?
"MIDDLE GROUND." WHAT AMERICA ARE YOU LIVING IN?

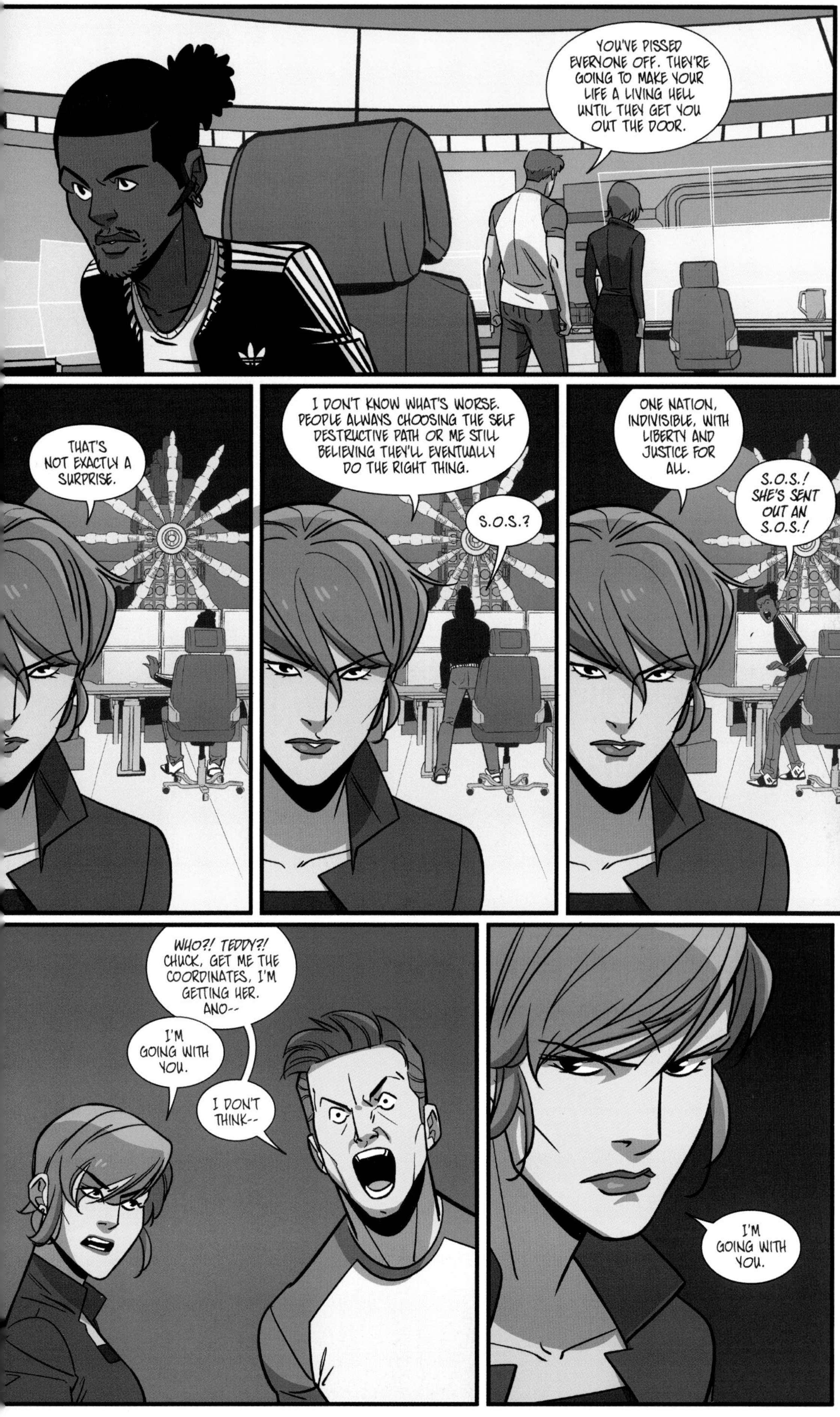
YOU'VE PISSED EVERYONE OFF. THEY'RE GOING TO MAKE YOUR LIFE A LIVING HELL UNTIL THEY GET YOU OUT THE DOOR.
THAT'S NOT EXACTLY A SURPRISE.
I DON'T KNOW WHAT'S WORSE. PEOPLE ALWAYS CHOOSING THE SELF DESTRUCTIVE PATH OR ME STILL BELIEVING THEY'LL EVENTUALLY DO THE RIGHT THING.
S.O.S.?
ONE NATION, INDIVISIBLE, WITH LIBERTY AND JUSTICE FOR ALL.
S.O.S.! SHE'S SENT OUT AN S.O.S.!
WHO?! TEDDY?! CHUCK, GET ME THE COORDINATES, I'M GETTING HER. AND--
I'M GOING WITH YOU.
I DON'T THINK--
I'M GOING WITH YOU.

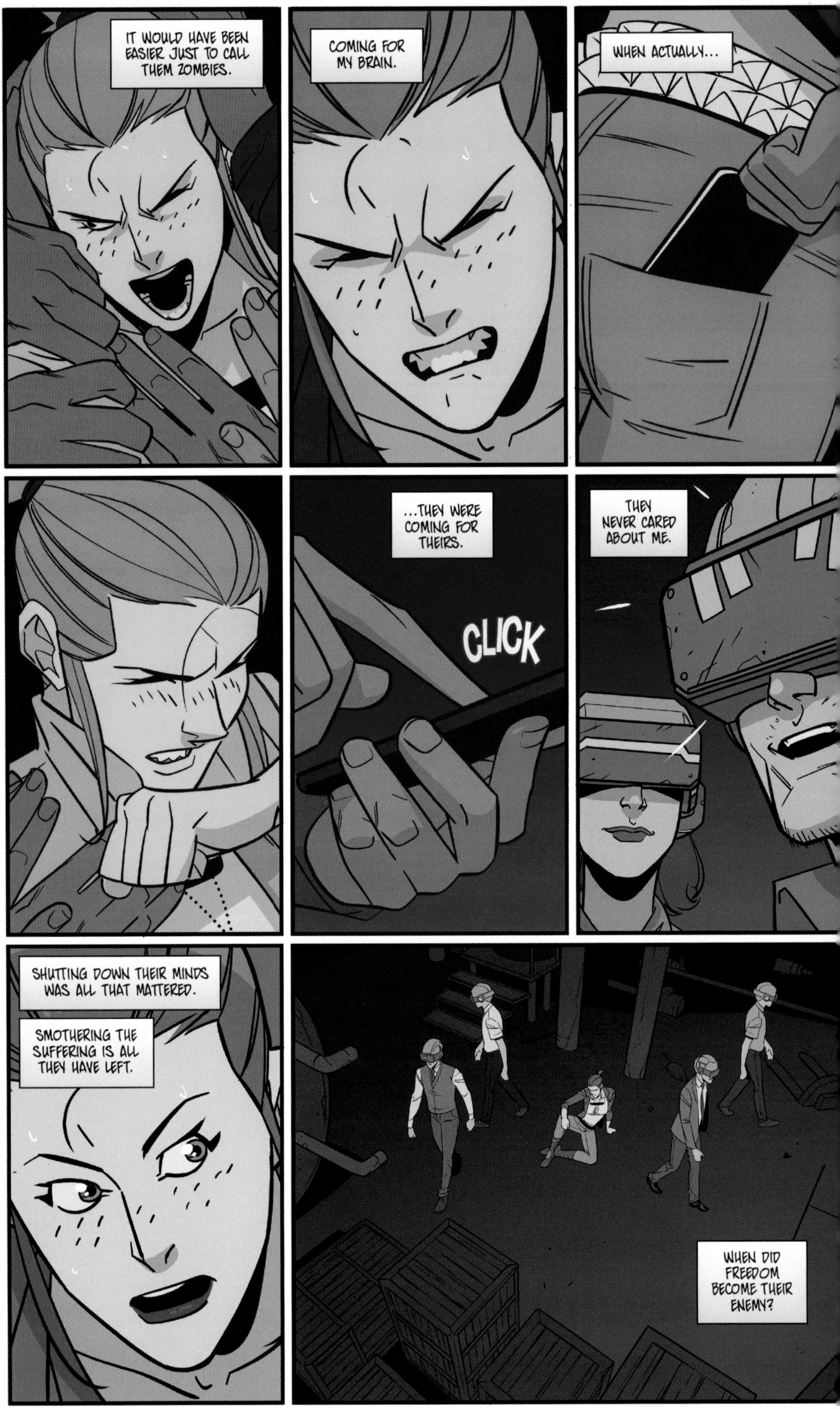
IT WOULD HAVE BEEN EASIER JUST TO CALL THEM ZOMBIES.
COMING FOR MY BRAIN.
WHEN ACTUALLY...
...THEY WERE COMING FOR THEIRS.
CLICK
THEY NEVER CARED ABOUT ME.
SHUTTING DOWN THEIR MINDS WAS ALL THAT MATTERED.
SMOTHERING THE SUFFERING IS ALL THEY HAVE LEFT.
WHEN DID FREEDOM BECOME THEIR ENEMY?

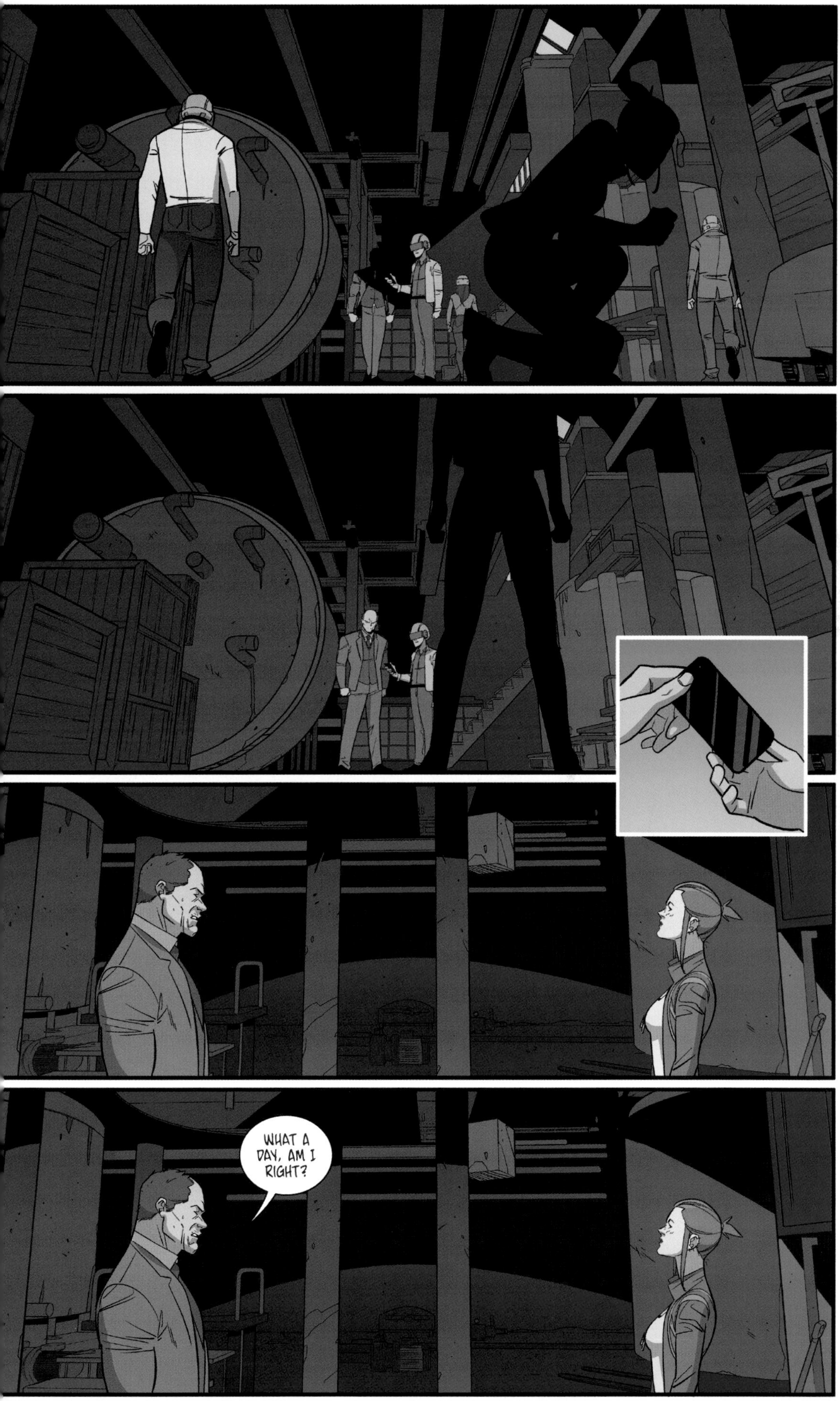
WHAT A DAY, AM I RIGHT?

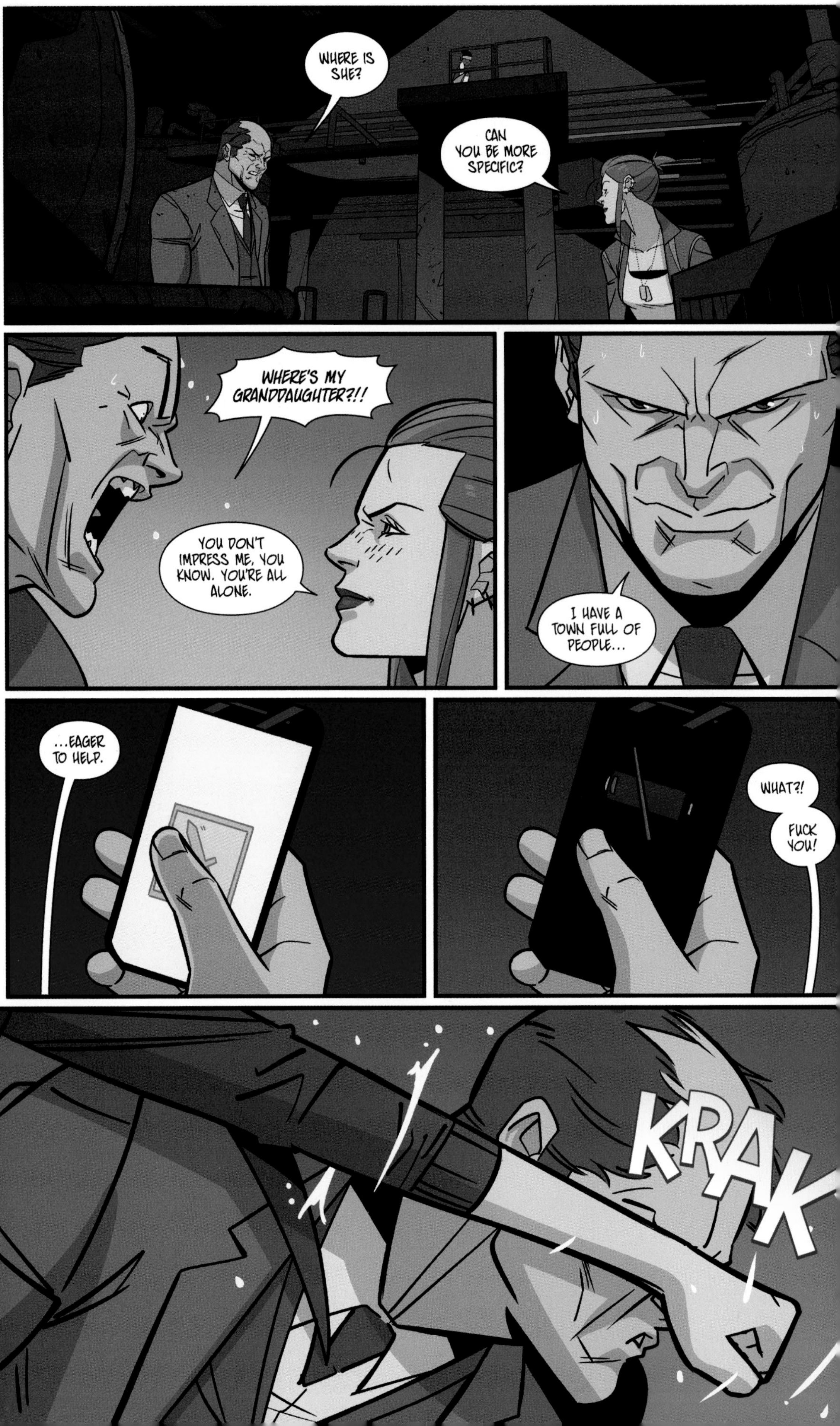
WHERE IS SHE?
CAN YOU BE MORE SPECIFIC?
WHERE'S MY GRANDDAUGHTER?!!
YOU DON'T IMPRESS ME, YOU KNOW. YOU'RE ALL ALONE.
I HAVE A TOWN FULL OF PEOPLE...
...EAGER TO HELP.
WHAT?!
FUCK YOU!
KRAK

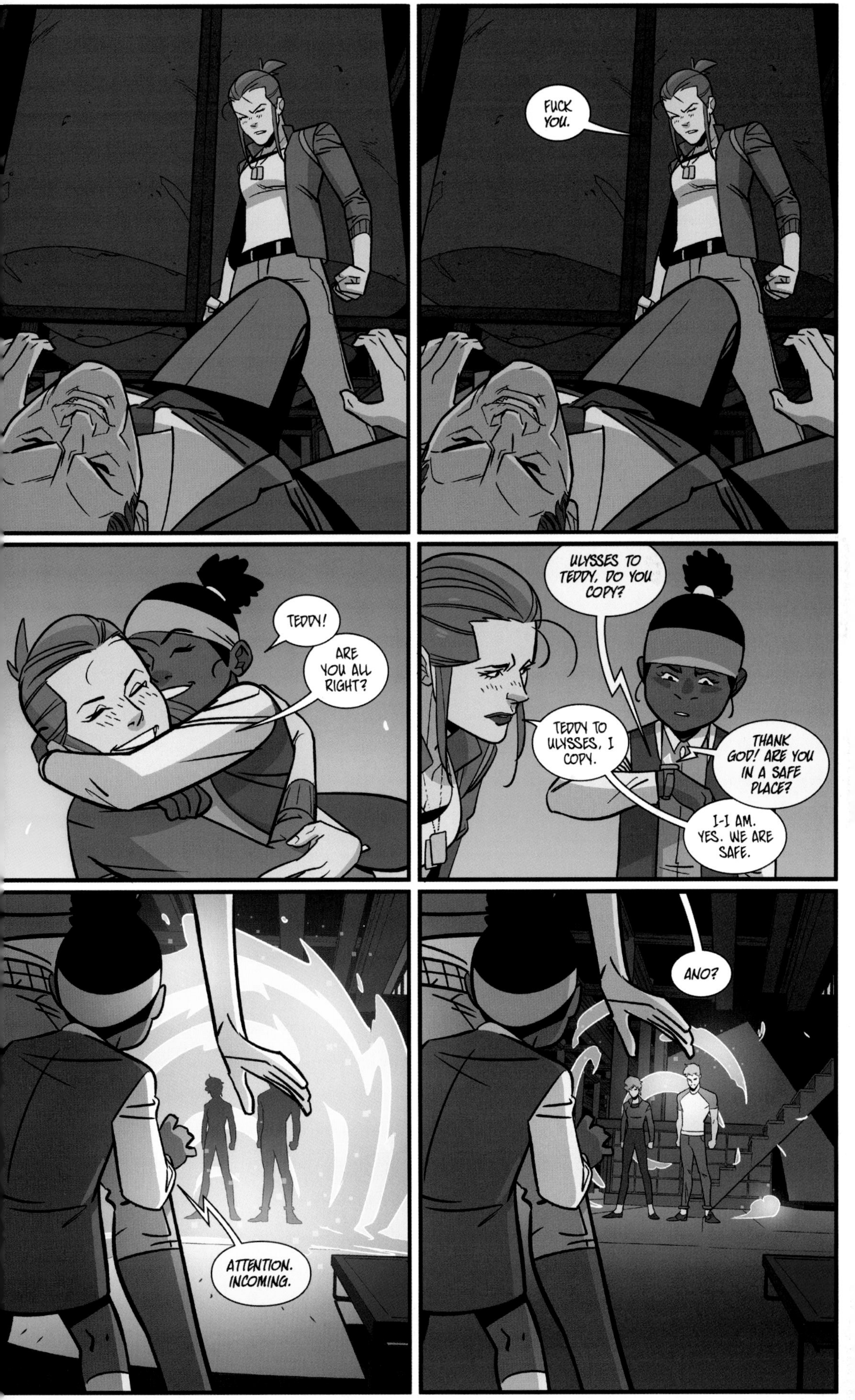
FUCK YOU.
TEDDY!
ARE YOU ALL RIGHT?
ULYSSES TO TEDDY, DO YOU COPY?
TEDDY TO ULYSSES, I COPY.
THANK GOD! ARE YOU IN A SAFE PLACE?
I-I AM. YES. WE ARE SAFE.
ATTENTION. INCOMING.
ANO?

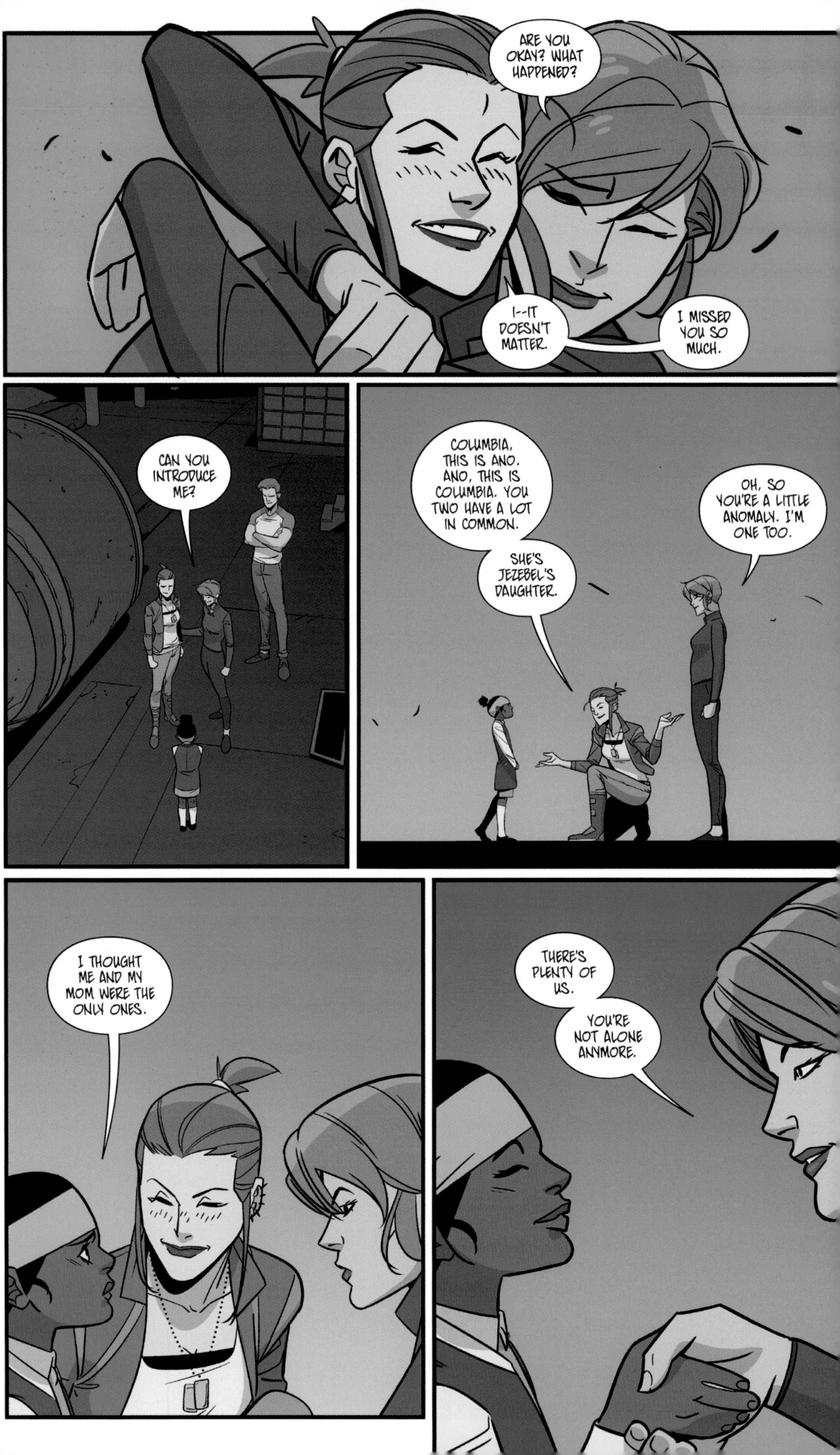
ARE YOU OKAY? WHAT HAPPENED?
I--IT DOESN'T MATTER.
I MISSED YOU SO MUCH.
CAN YOU INTRODUCE ME?
COLUMBIA, THIS IS ANO. ANO, THIS IS COLUMBIA. YOU TWO HAVE A LOT IN COMMON.
SHE'S JEZEBEL'S DAUGHTER.
OH, SO YOU'RE A LITTLE ANOMALY. I'M ONE TOO.
I THOUGHT ME AND MY MOM WERE THE ONLY ONES.
THERE'S PLENTY OF US.
YOU'RE NOT ALONE ANYMORE.

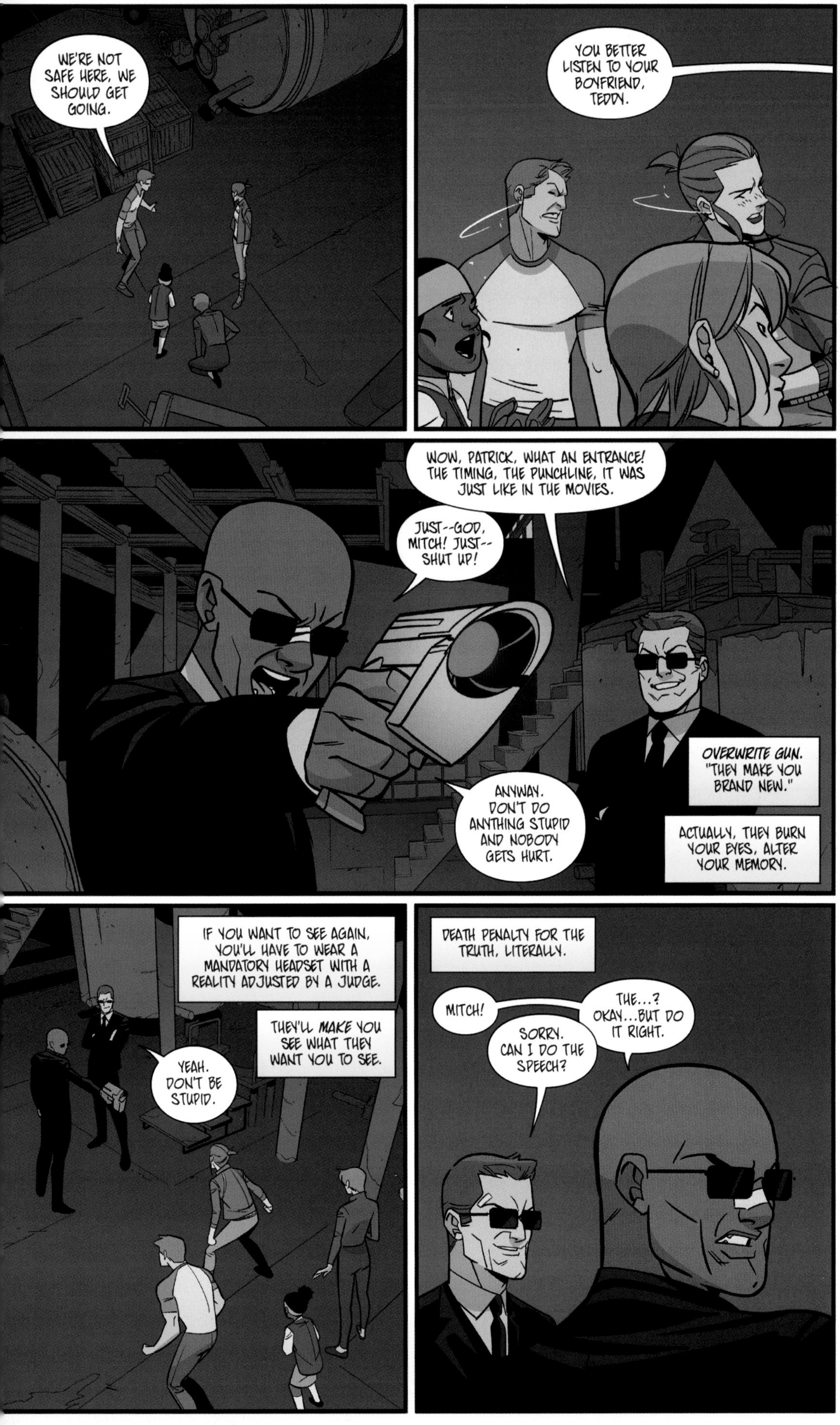
WE'RE NOT SAFE HERE, WE SHOULD GET GOING.
YOU BETTER LISTEN TO YOUR BOYFRIEND, TEDDY.
WOW, PATRICK, WHAT AN ENTRANCE! THE TIMING, THE PUNCHLINE, IT WAS JUST LIKE IN THE MOVIES.
JUST--GOD, MITCH! JUST--SHUT UP!
ANYWAY. DON'T DO ANYTHING STUPID AND NOBODY GETS HURT.
OVERWRITE GUN. "THEY MAKE YOU BRAND NEW."
ACTUALLY, THEY BURN YOUR EYES, ALTER YOUR MEMORY.
IF YOU WANT TO SEE AGAIN, YOU'LL HAVE TO WEAR A MANDATORY HEADSET WITH A REALITY ADJUSTED BY A JUDGE.
THEY'LL *MAKE* YOU SEE WHAT THEY WANT YOU TO SEE.
YEAH. DON'T BE STUPID.
DEATH PENALTY FOR THE TRUTH, LITERALLY.
MITCH!
SORRY. CAN I DO THE SPEECH?
THE...? OKAY...BUT DO IT RIGHT.

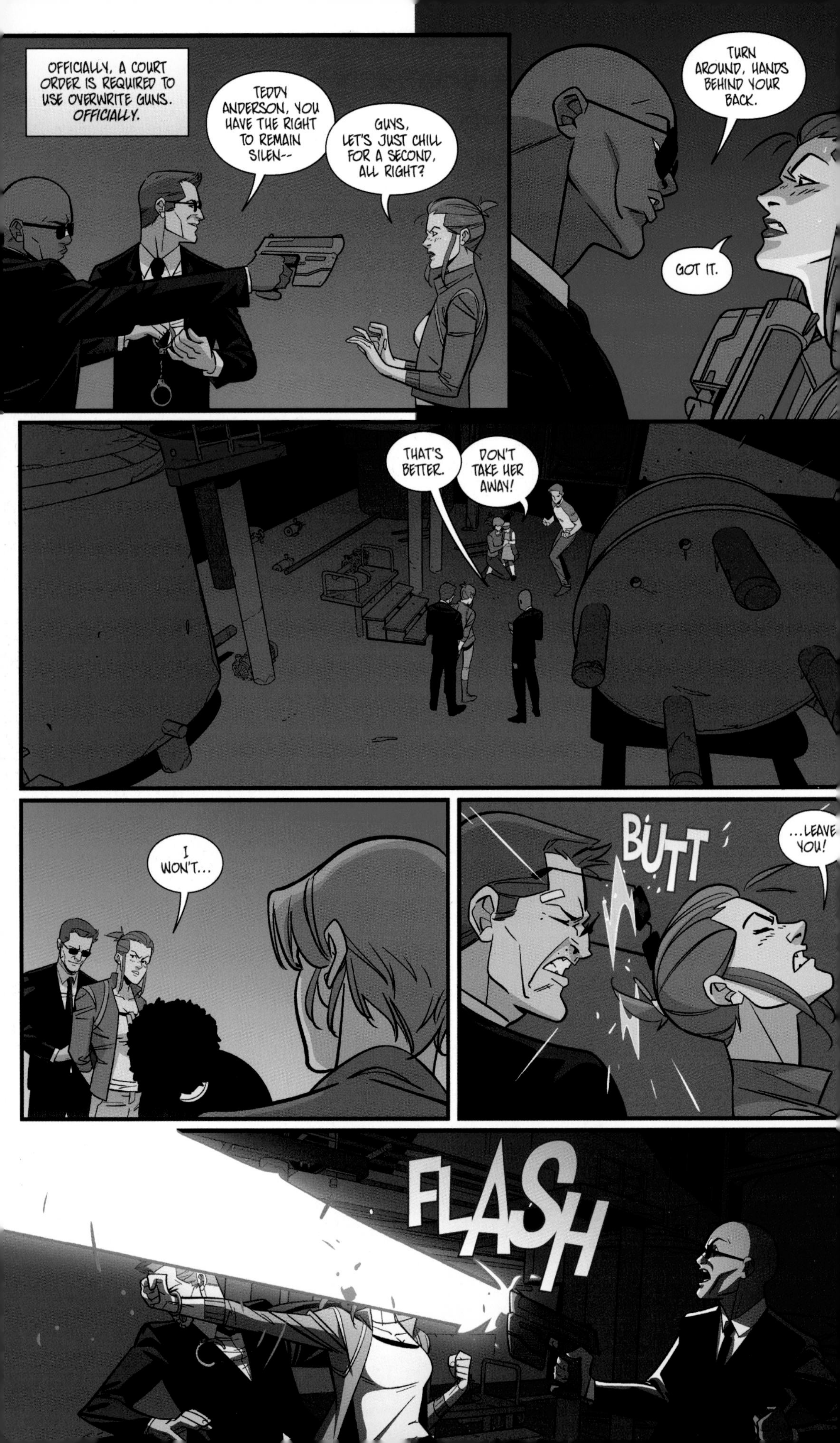
OFFICIALLY, A COURT ORDER IS REQUIRED TO USE OVERWRITE GUNS. OFFICIALLY.
TEDDY ANDERSON, YOU HAVE THE RIGHT TO REMAIN SILEN--
GUYS, LET'S JUST CHILL FOR A SECOND, ALL RIGHT?
TURN AROUND, HANDS BEHIND YOUR BACK.
GOT IT.
THAT'S BETTER.
DON'T TAKE HER AWAY!
I WON'T...
BUTT
...LEAVE YOU!
FLASH

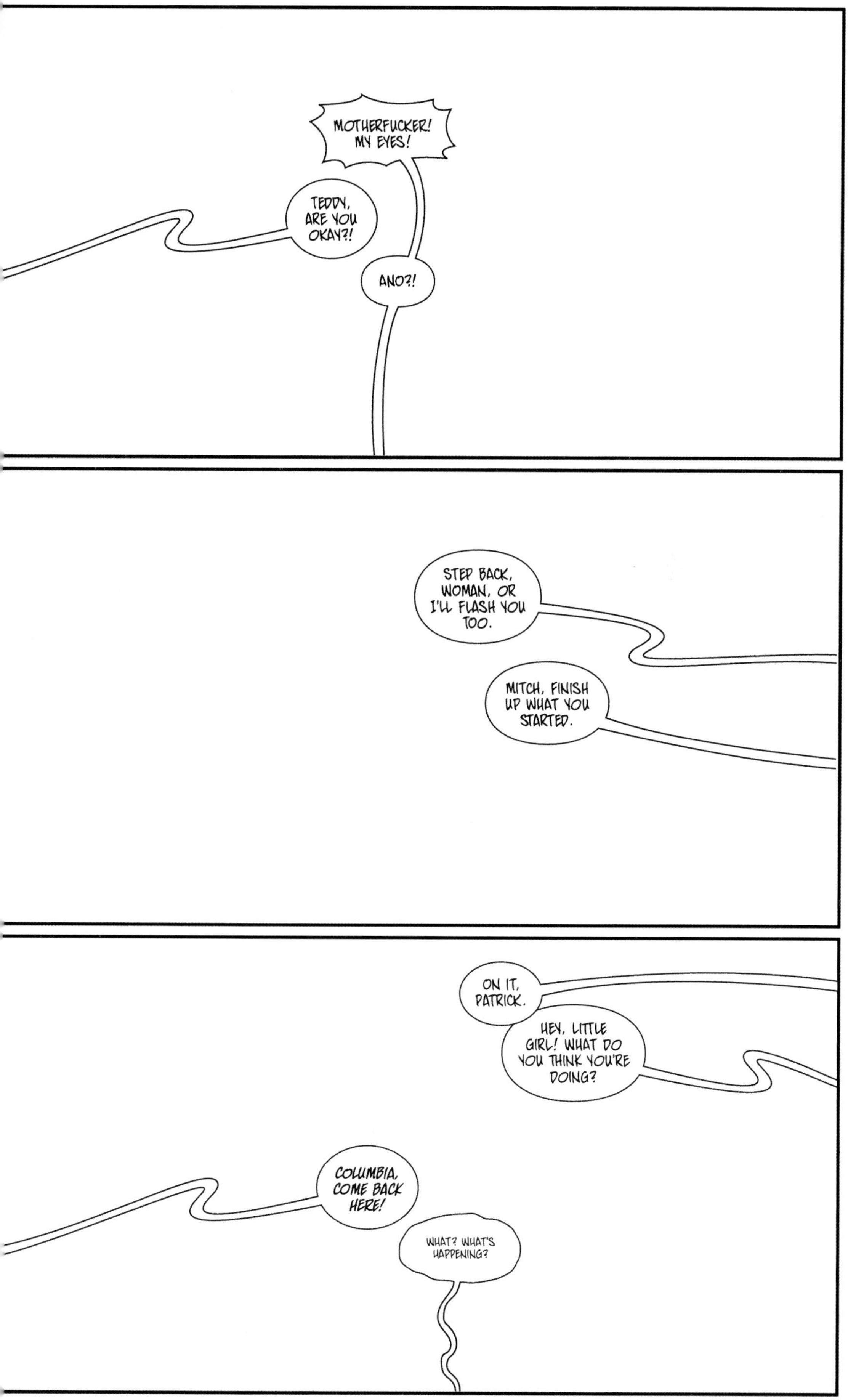
MOTHERFUCKER! MY EYES!
TEDDY, ARE YOU OKAY?!
ANO?!
STEP BACK, WOMAN, OR I'LL FLASH YOU TOO.
MITCH, FINISH UP WHAT YOU STARTED.
ON IT, PATRICK.
HEY, LITTLE GIRL! WHAT DO YOU THINK YOU'RE DOING?
COLUMBIA, COME BACK HERE!
WHAT? WHAT'S HAPPENING?

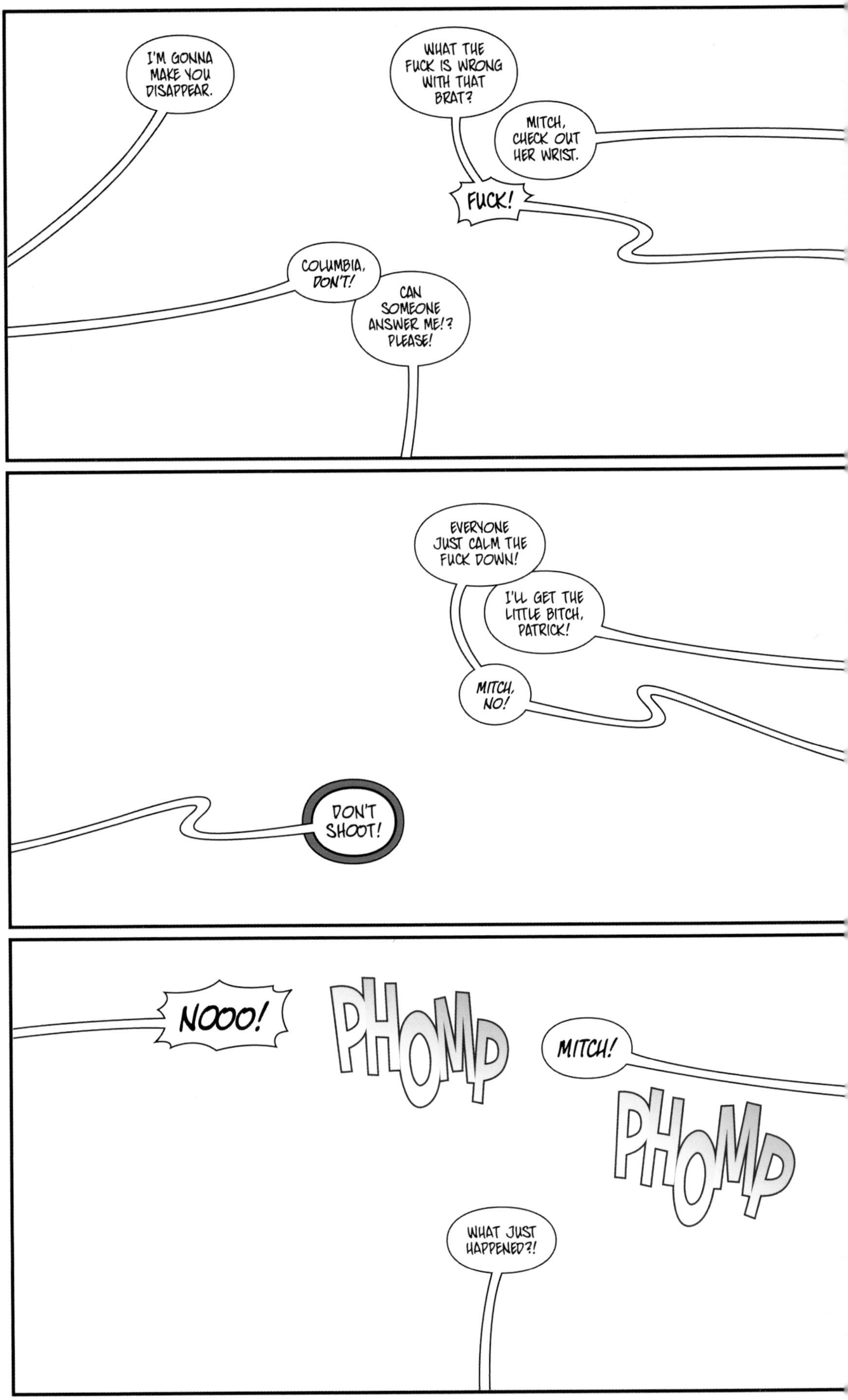
I'M GONNA MAKE YOU DISAPPEAR.
WHAT THE FUCK IS WRONG WITH THAT BRAT?
MITCH, CHECK OUT HER WRIST.
FUCK!
COLUMBIA, DON'T!
CAN SOMEONE ANSWER ME!? PLEASE!
EVERYONE JUST CALM THE FUCK DOWN!
I'LL GET THE LITTLE BITCH, PATRICK!
MITCH, NO!
DON'T SHOOT!
NOOO!
PHOMP
MITCH!
PHOMP
WHAT JUST HAPPENED?!

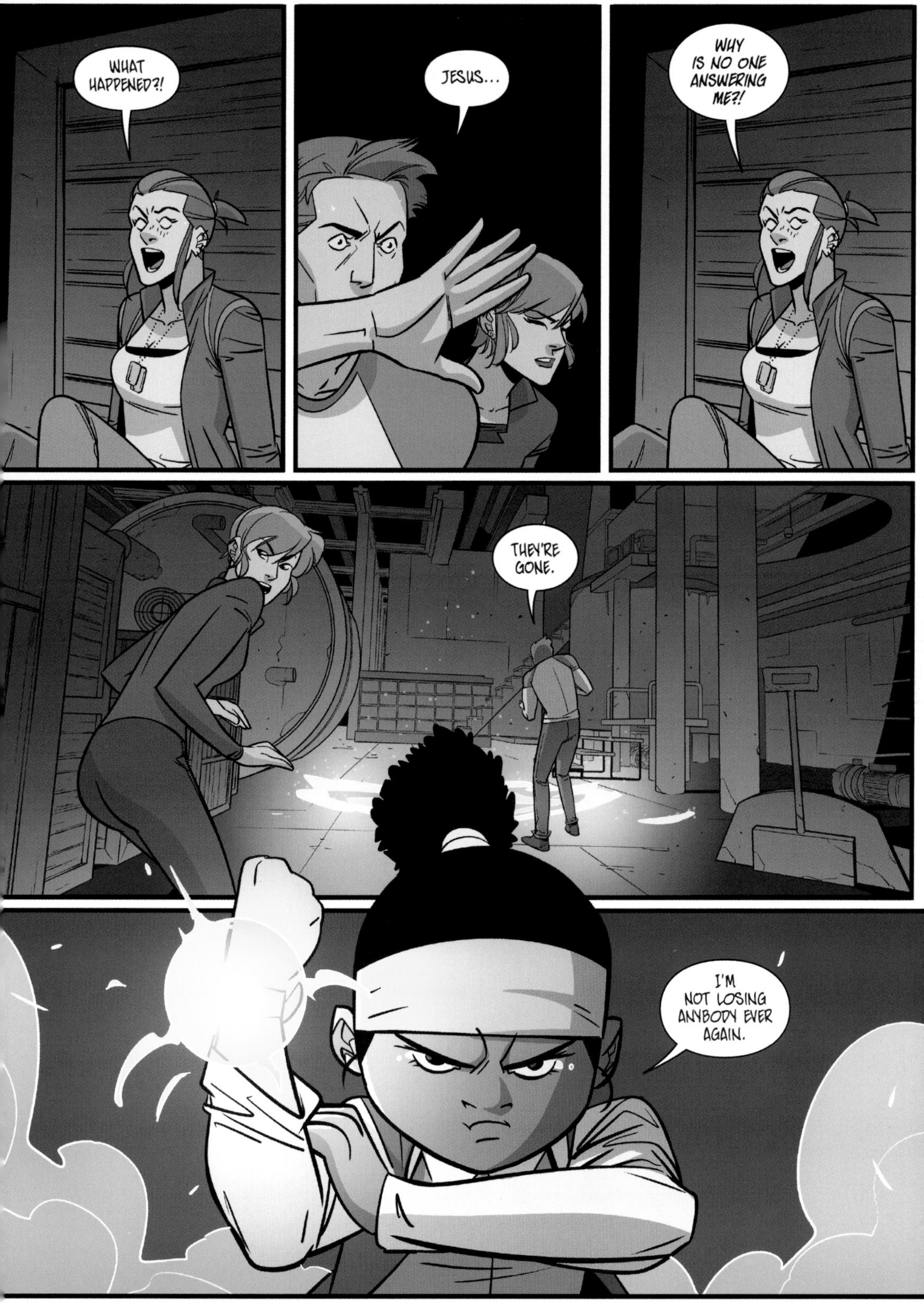
WHAT HAPPENED?!
JESUS...
WHY IS NO ONE ANSWERING ME?!
THEY'RE GONE.
I'M NOT LOSING ANYBODY EVER AGAIN.

THE INFINITE LOOP

4. LET'S GO HOME

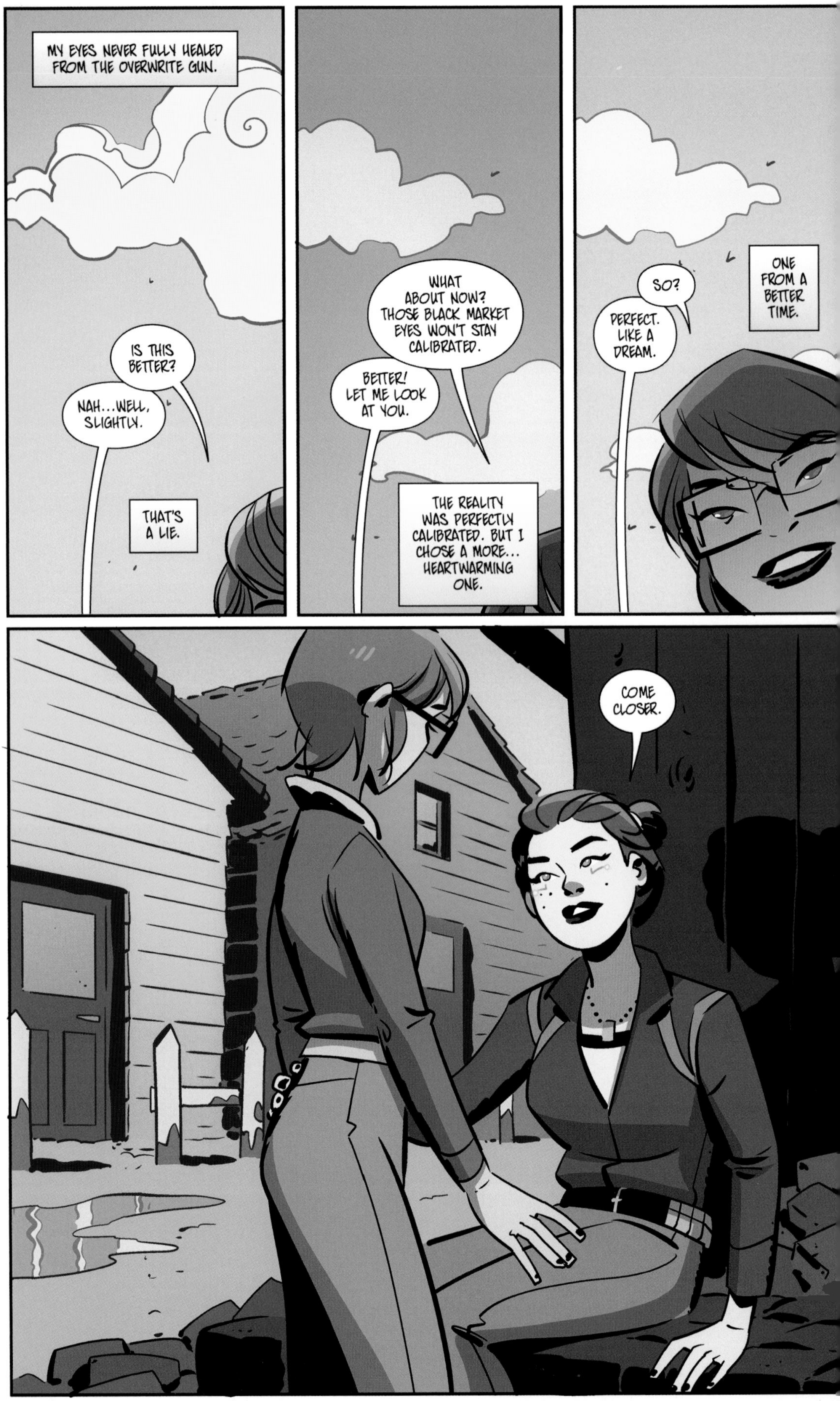
MY EYES NEVER FULLY HEALED FROM THE OVERWRITE GUN.
IS THIS BETTER?
NAH...WELL, SLIGHTLY.
THAT'S A LIE.
WHAT ABOUT NOW? THOSE BLACK MARKET EYES WON'T STAY CALIBRATED.
BETTER! LET ME LOOK AT YOU.
THE REALITY WAS PERFECTLY CALIBRATED. BUT I CHOSE A MORE... HEARTWARMING ONE.
SO?
PERFECT. LIKE A DREAM.
ONE FROM A BETTER TIME.
COME CLOSER.

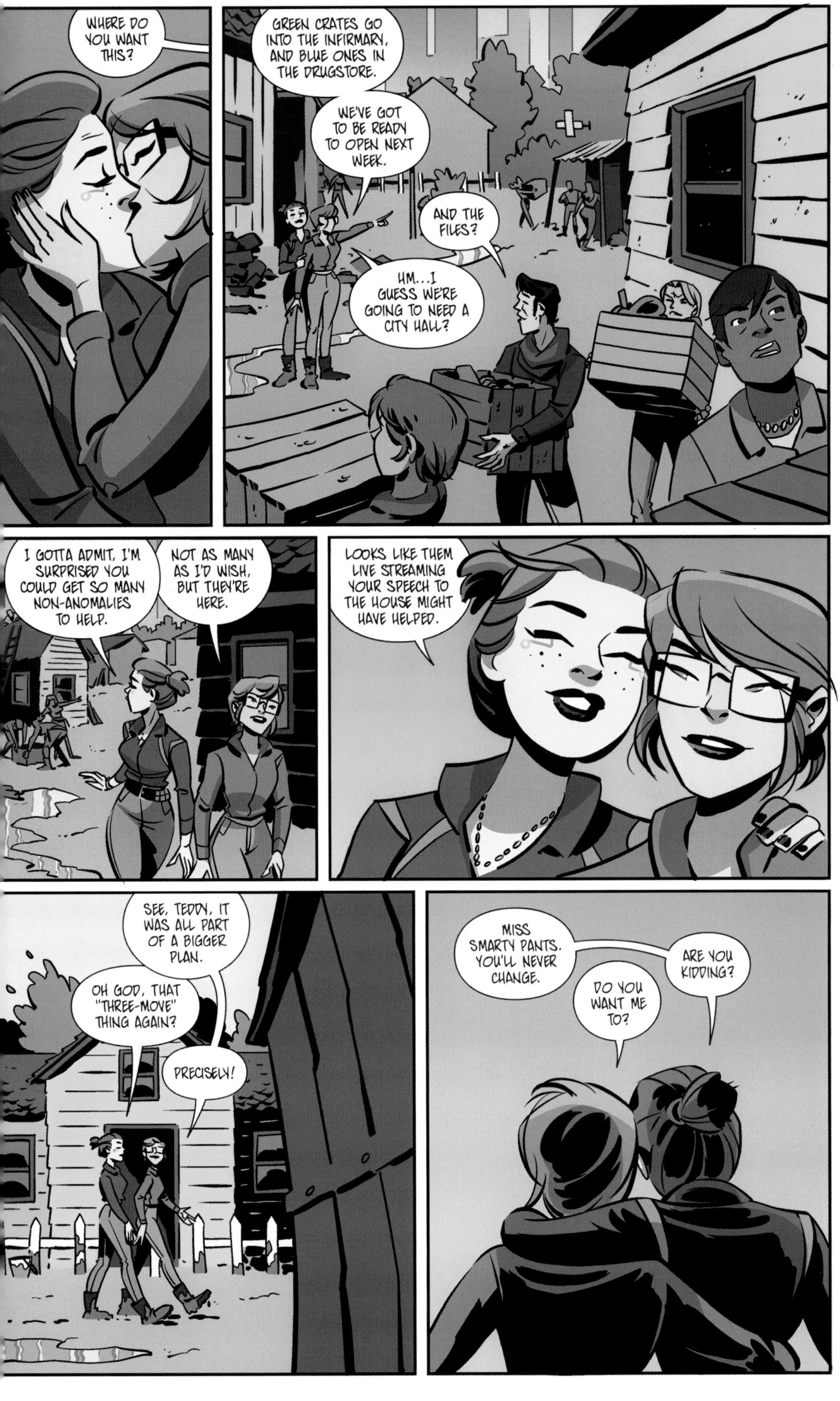
WHERE DO YOU WANT THIS?
GREEN CRATES GO INTO THE INFIRMARY, AND BLUE ONES IN THE DRUGSTORE.
WE'VE GOT TO BE READY TO OPEN NEXT WEEK.
AND THE FILES?
HM...I GUESS WE'RE GOING TO NEED A CITY HALL?
I GOTTA ADMIT, I'M SURPRISED YOU COULD GET SO MANY NON-ANOMALIES TO HELP.
NOT AS MANY AS I'D WISH, BUT THEY'RE HERE.
LOOKS LIKE THEM LIVE STREAMING YOUR SPEECH TO THE HOUSE MIGHT HAVE HELPED.
SEE, TEDDY, IT WAS ALL PART OF A BIGGER PLAN.
OH GOD, THAT "THREE-MOVE" THING AGAIN?
PRECISELY!
MISS SMARTY PANTS. YOU'LL NEVER CHANGE.
ARE YOU KIDDING?
DO YOU WANT ME TO?

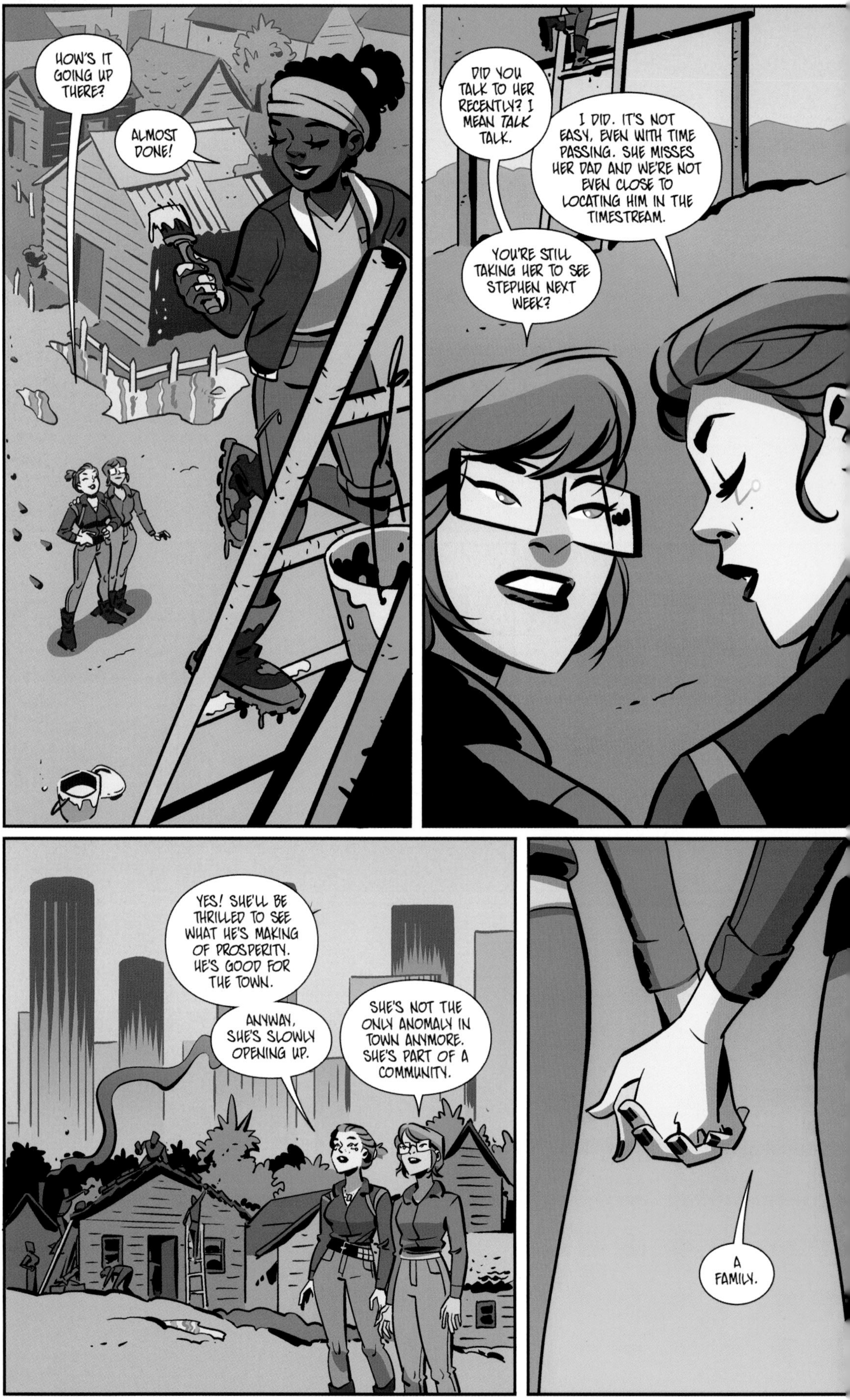
HOW'S IT GOING UP THERE?
ALMOST DONE!
DID YOU TALK TO HER RECENTLY? I MEAN *TALK* TALK.
I DID. IT'S NOT EASY, EVEN WITH TIME PASSING. SHE MISSES HER DAD AND WE'RE NOT EVEN CLOSE TO LOCATING HIM IN THE TIMESTREAM.
YOU'RE STILL TAKING HER TO SEE STEPHEN NEXT WEEK?
YES! SHE'LL BE THRILLED TO SEE WHAT HE'S MAKING OF PROSPERITY. HE'S GOOD FOR THE TOWN.
ANYWAY, SHE'S SLOWLY OPENING UP.
SHE'S NOT THE ONLY ANOMALY IN TOWN ANYMORE. SHE'S PART OF A COMMUNITY.
A FAMILY.

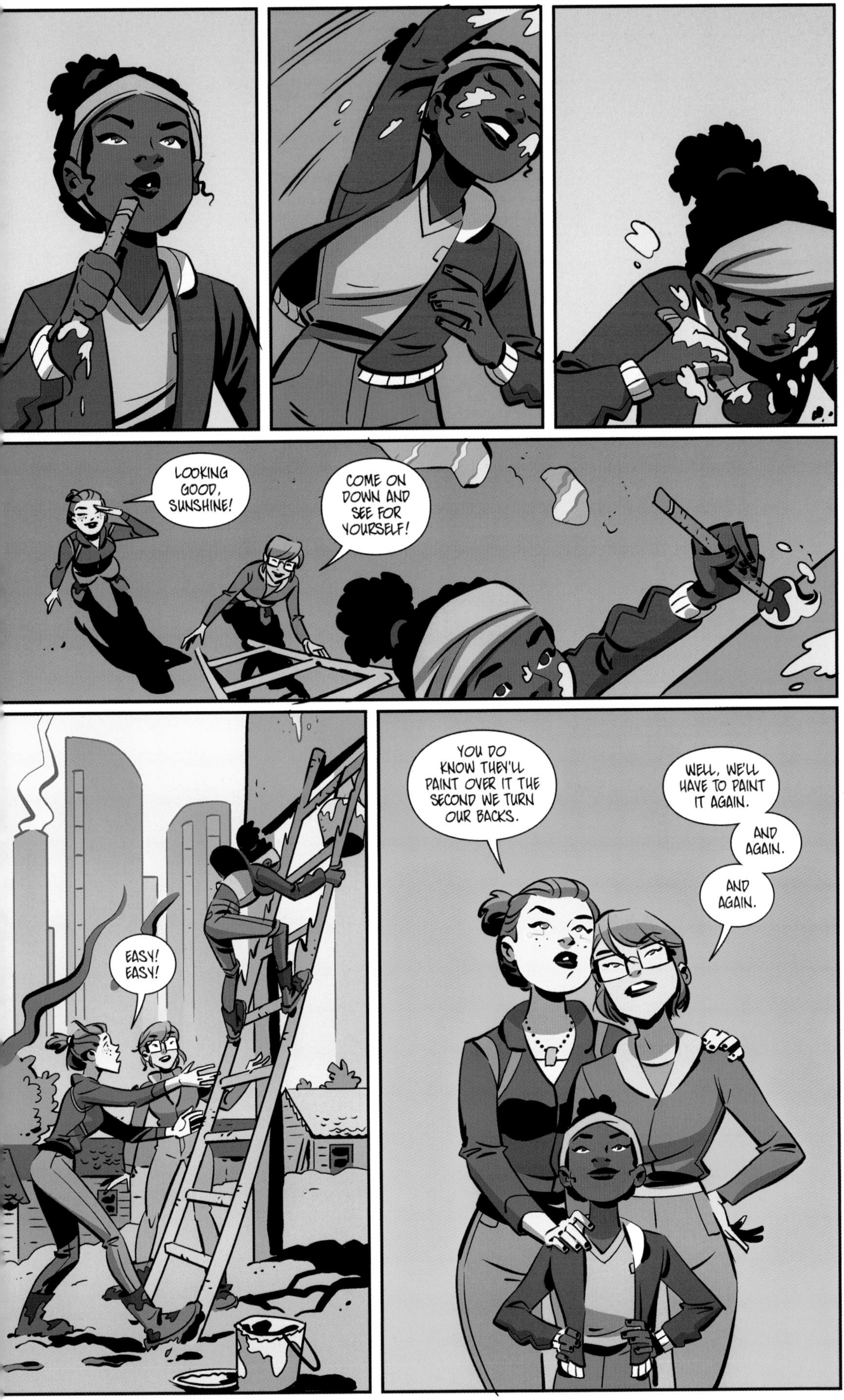
LOOKING GOOD, SUNSHINE!
COME ON DOWN AND SEE FOR YOURSELF!
EASY! EASY!
YOU DO KNOW THEY'LL PAINT OVER IT THE SECOND WE TURN OUR BACKS.
WELL, WE'LL HAVE TO PAINT IT AGAIN.
AND AGAIN.
AND AGAIN.

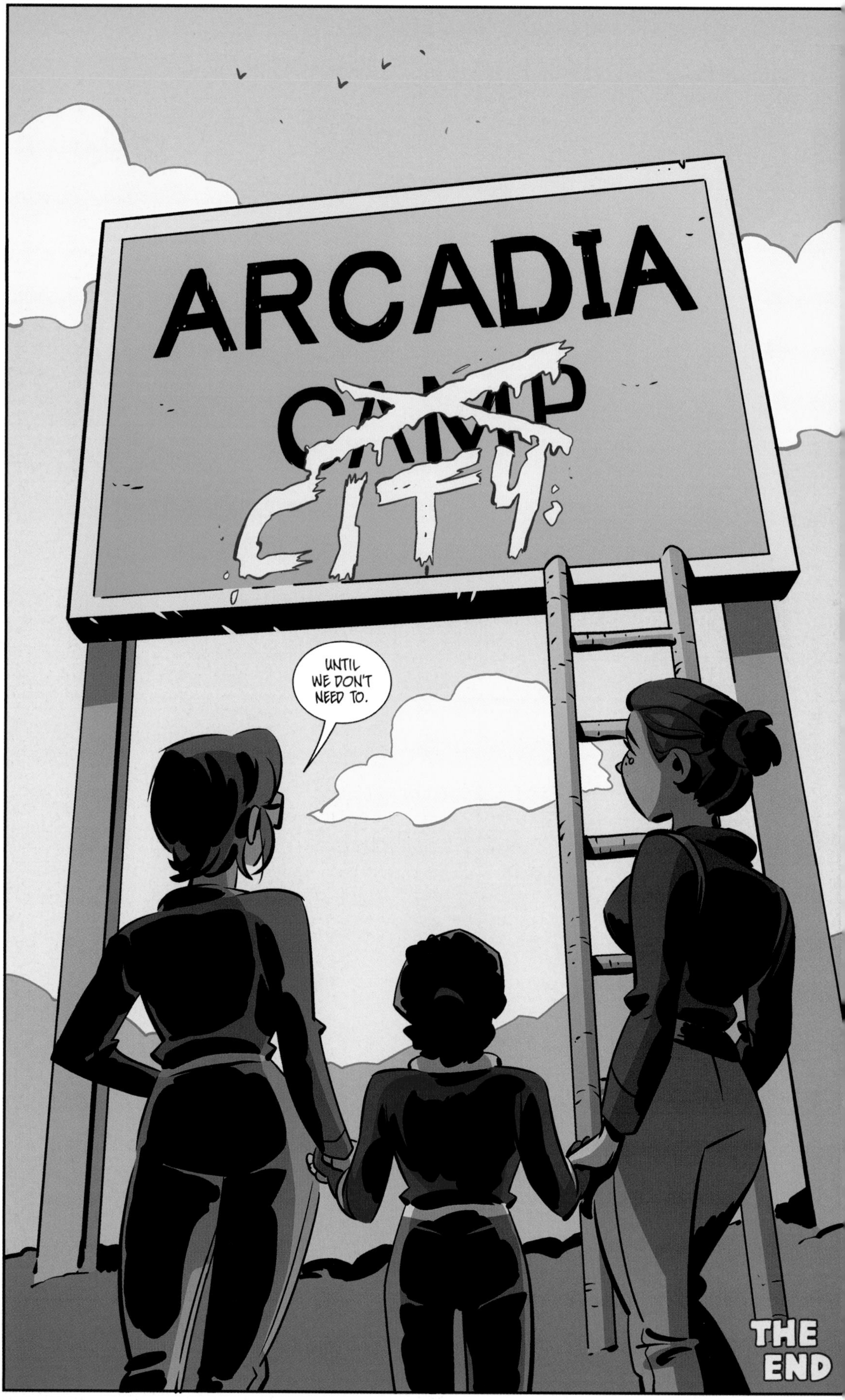
ARCADIA
CAMP
CITY
UNTIL WE DON'T NEED TO.
THE END

Art by MARGAUX SALTEL

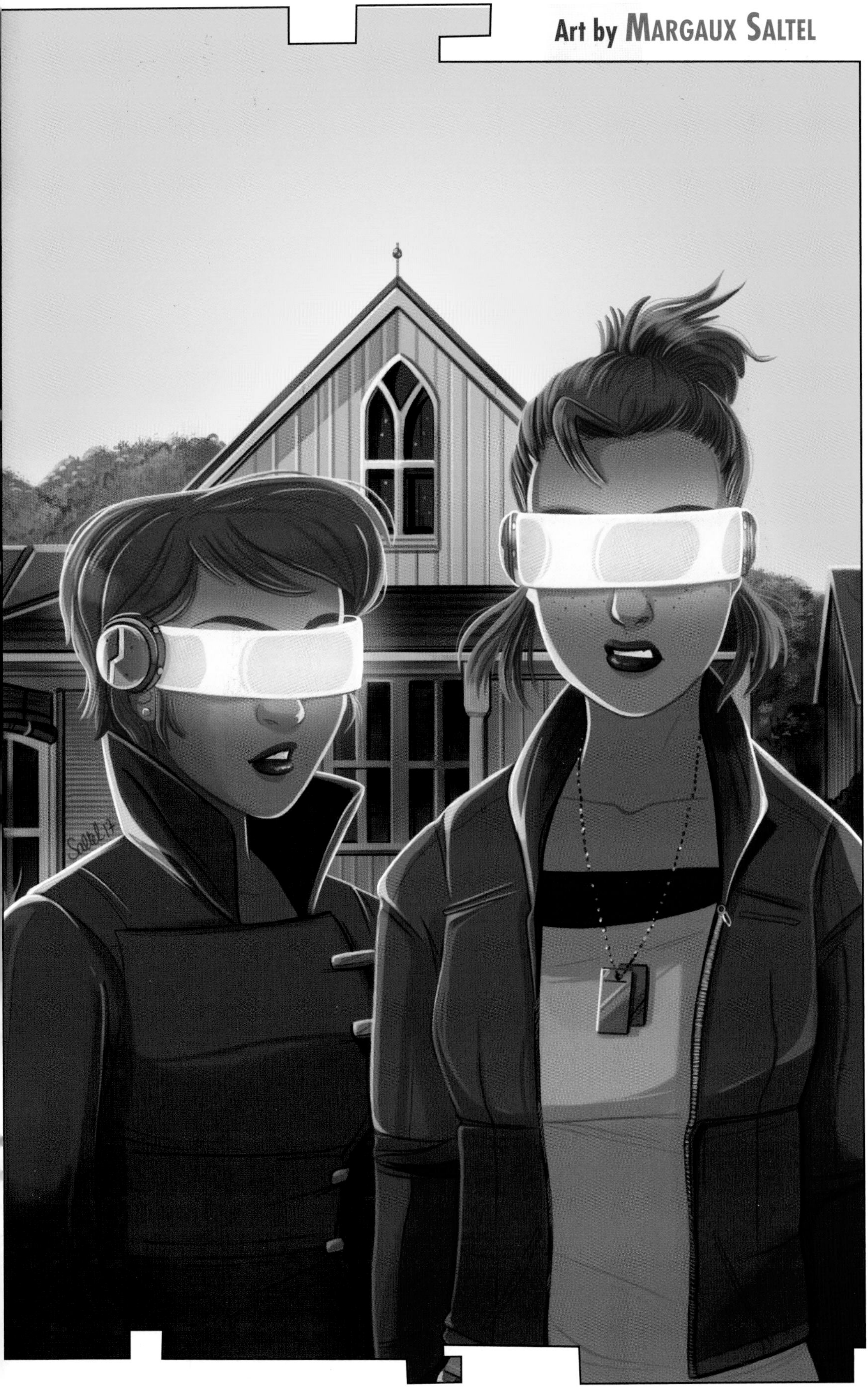
Saltel 17

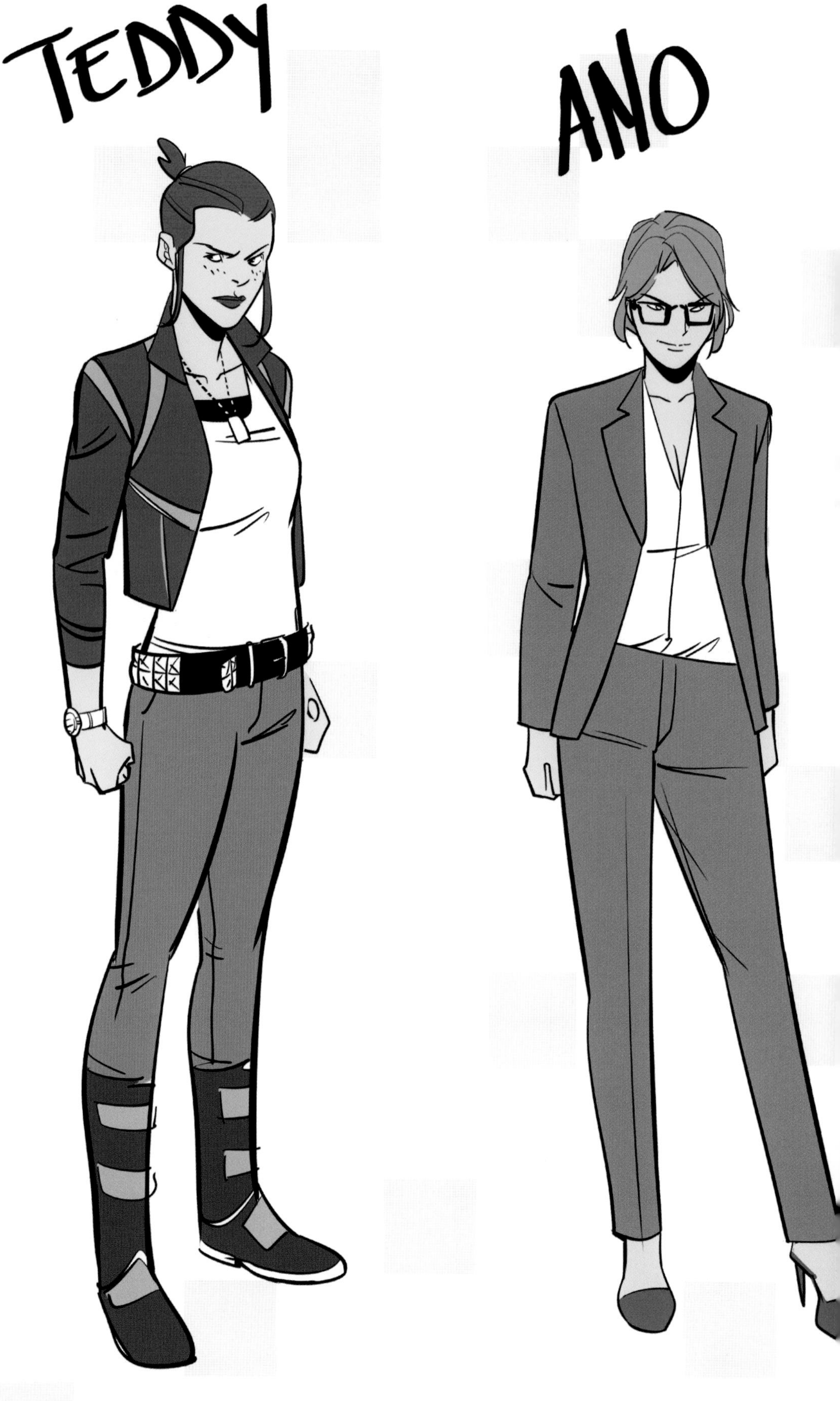
TEDDY
ANO

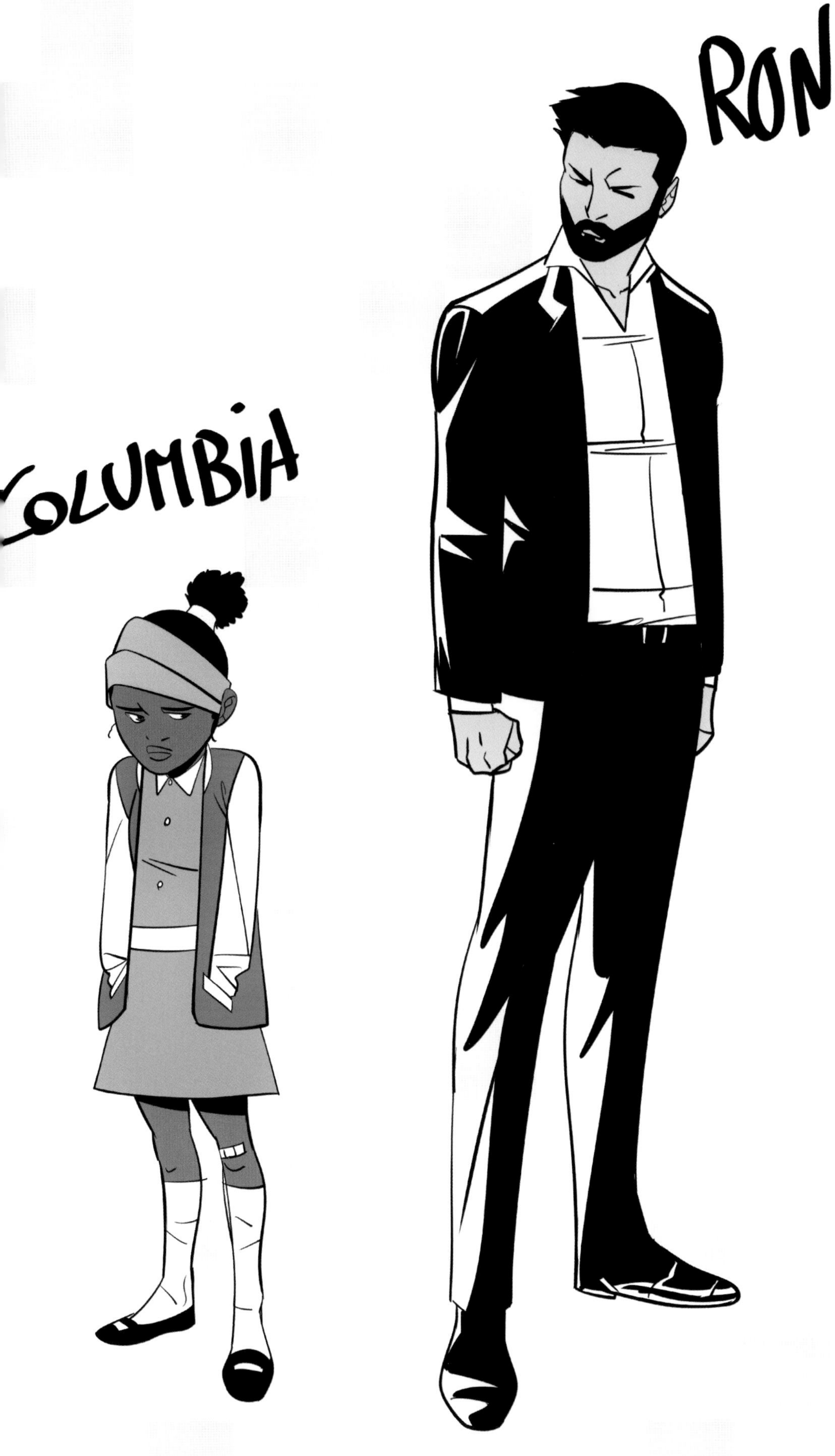
RON
COLUMBIA

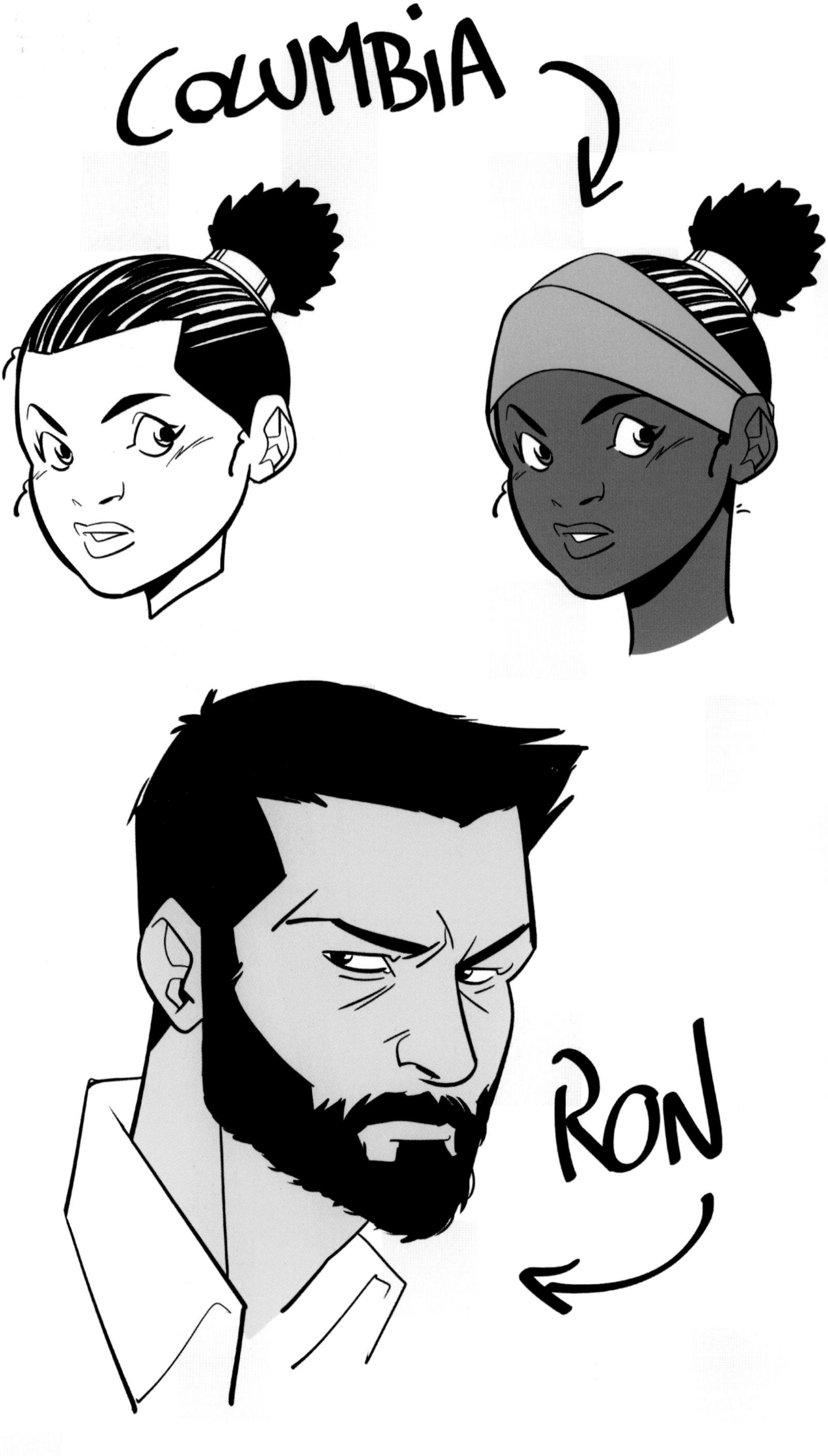
COLUMBIA
RON

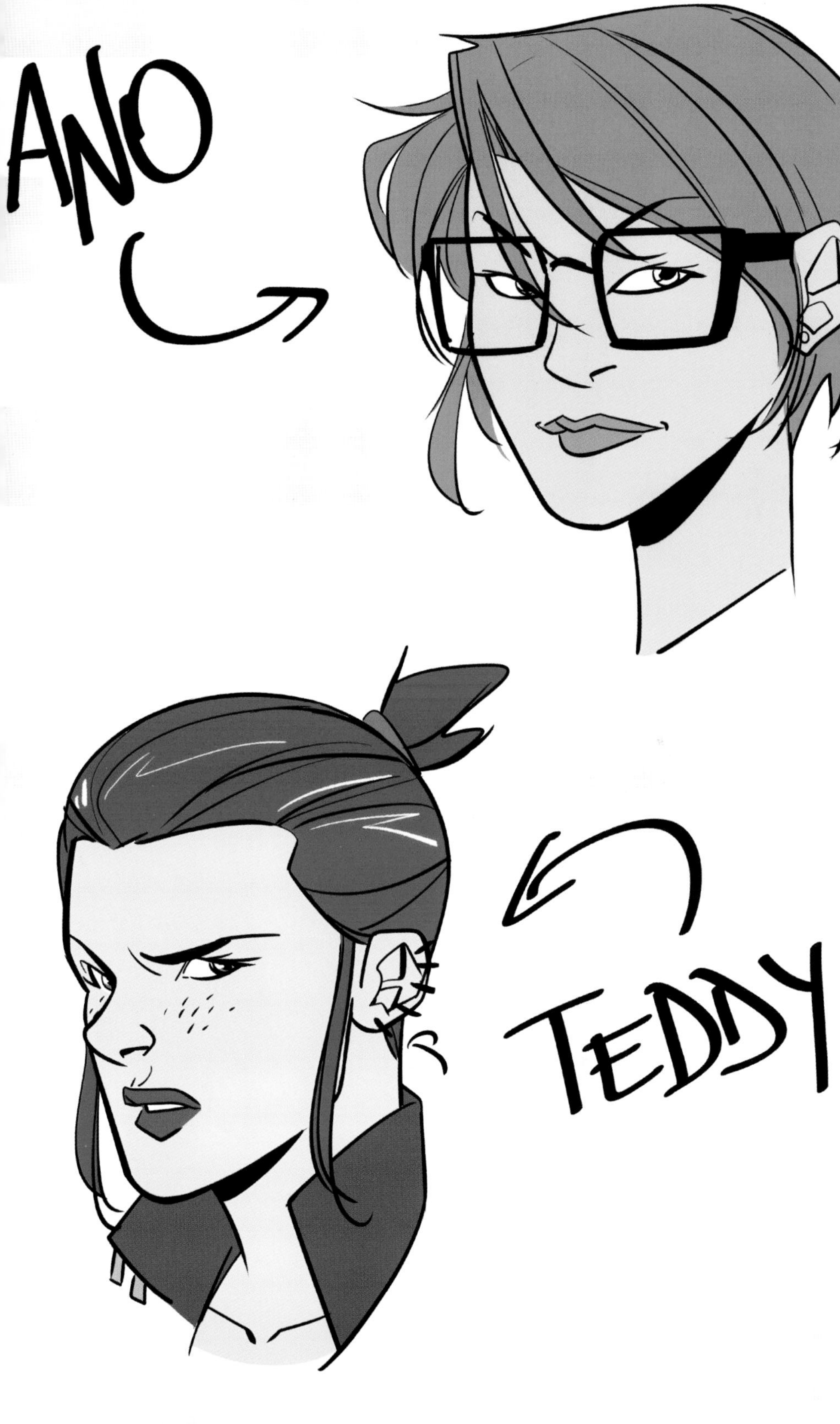
ANO
TEDDY

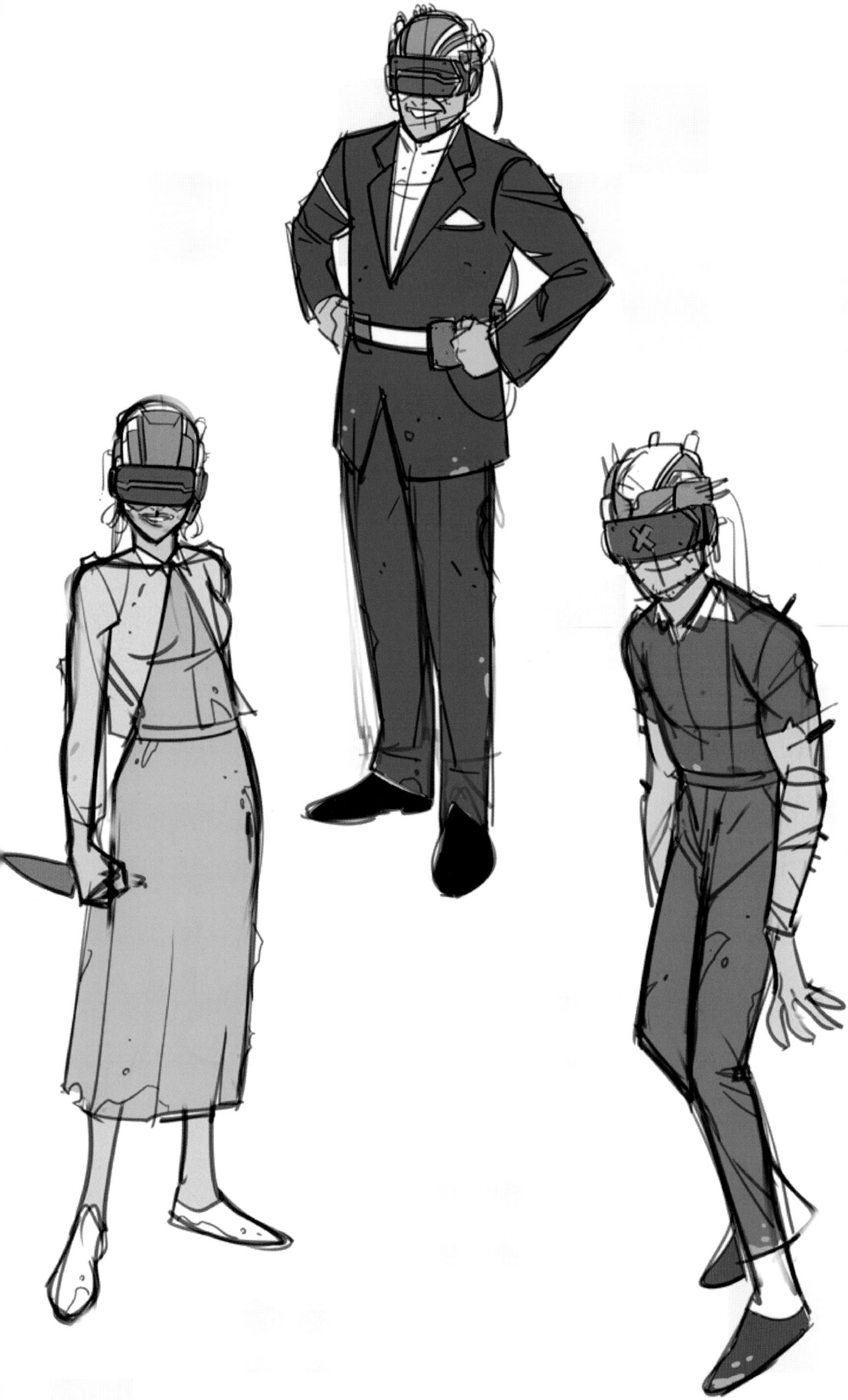

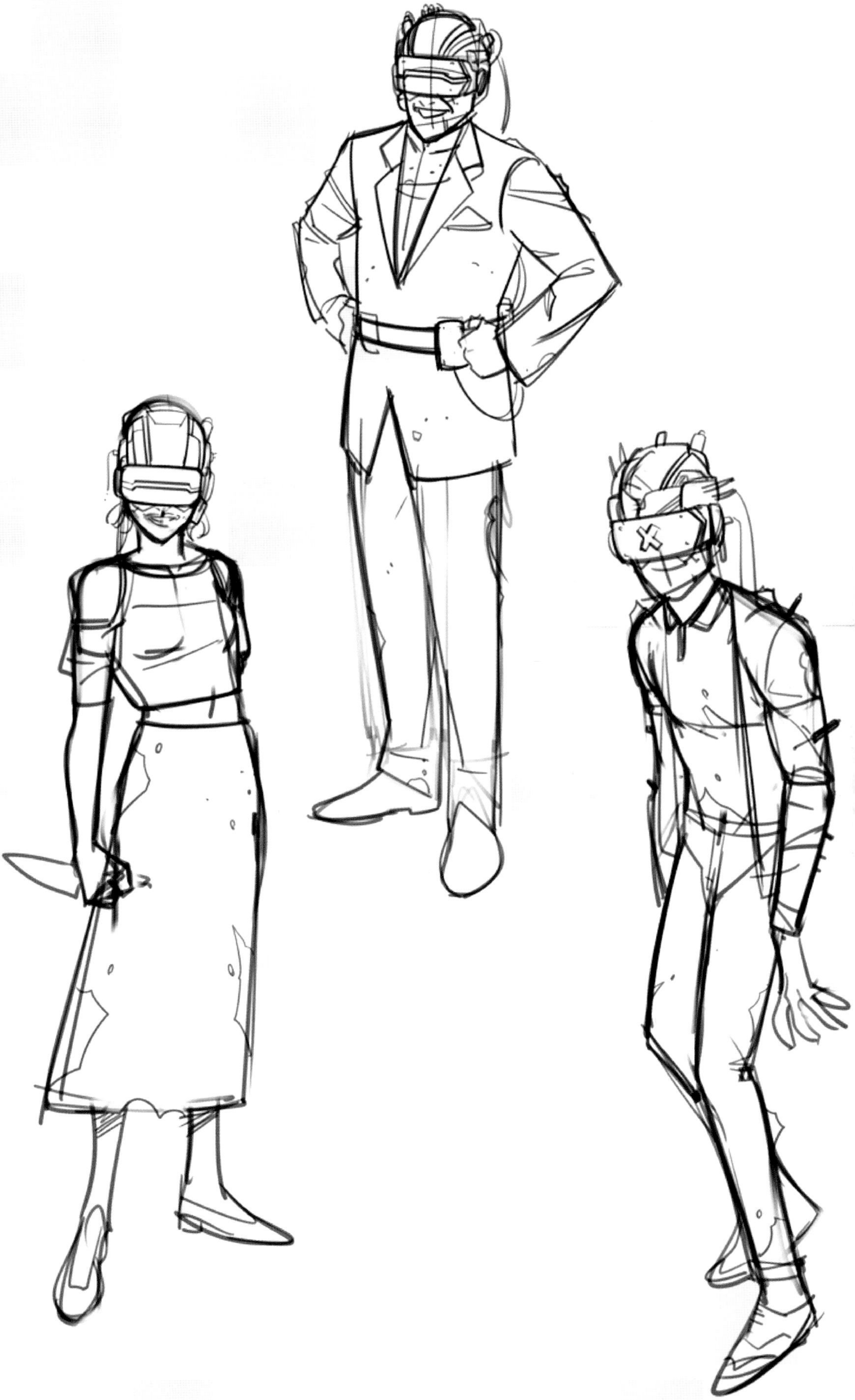

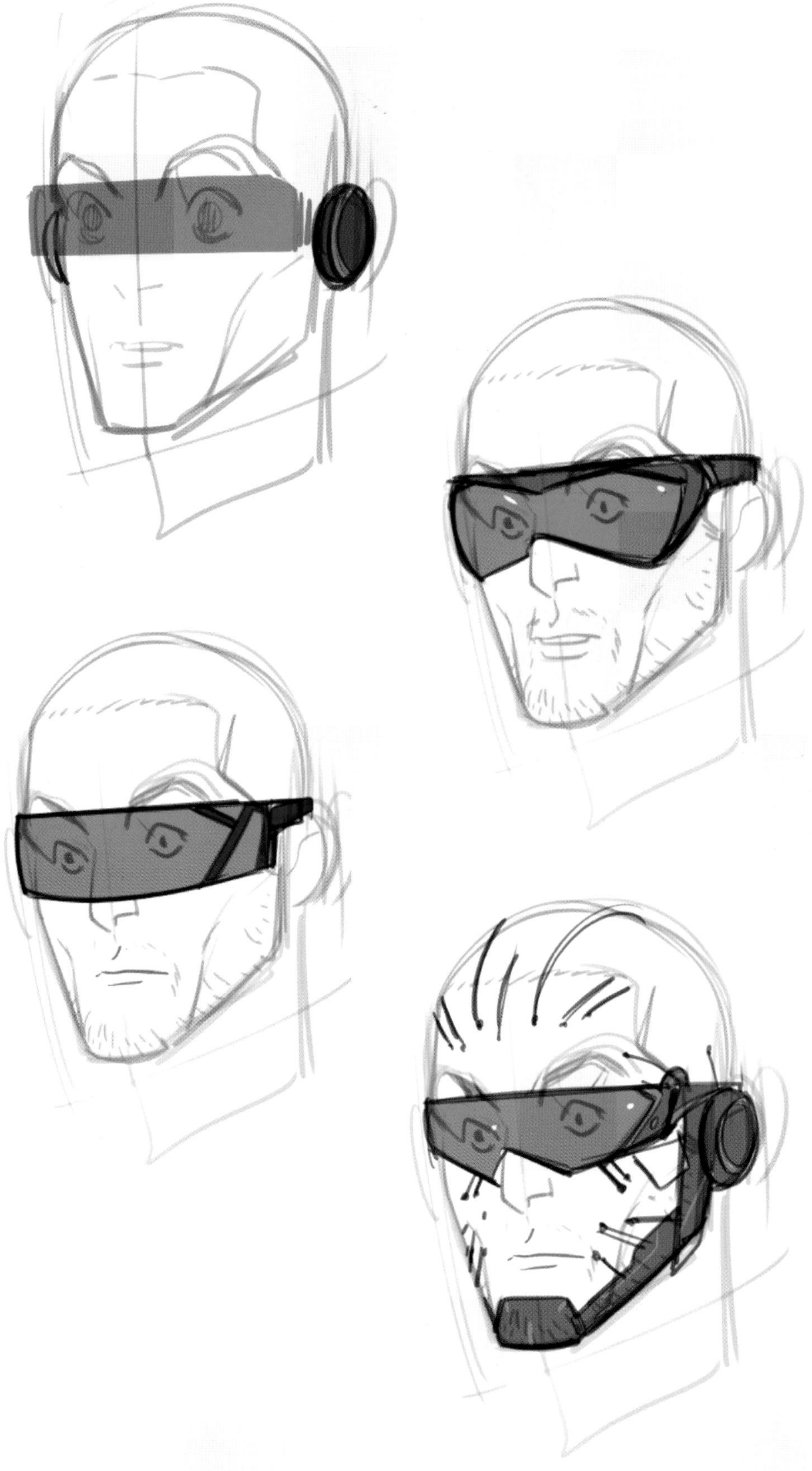

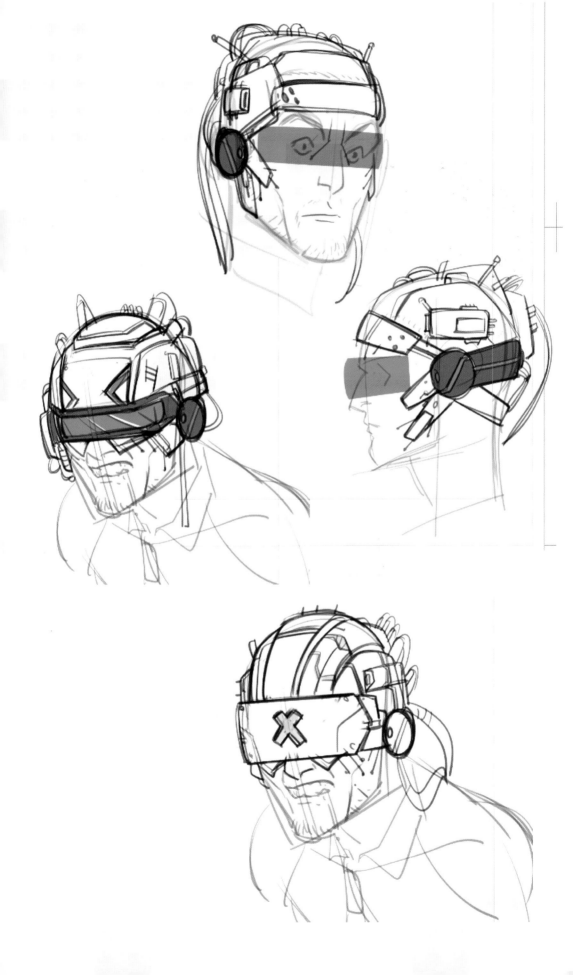

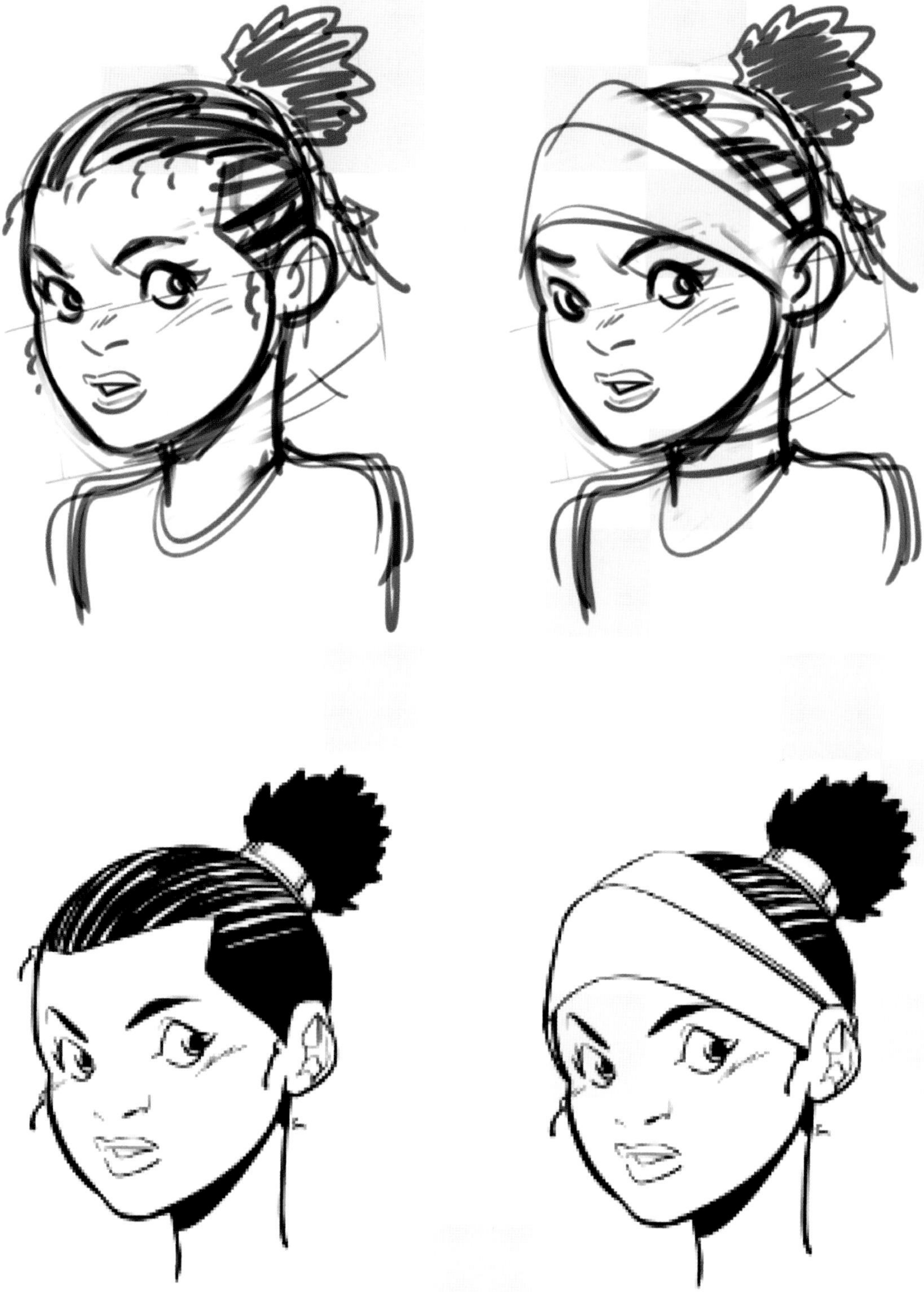

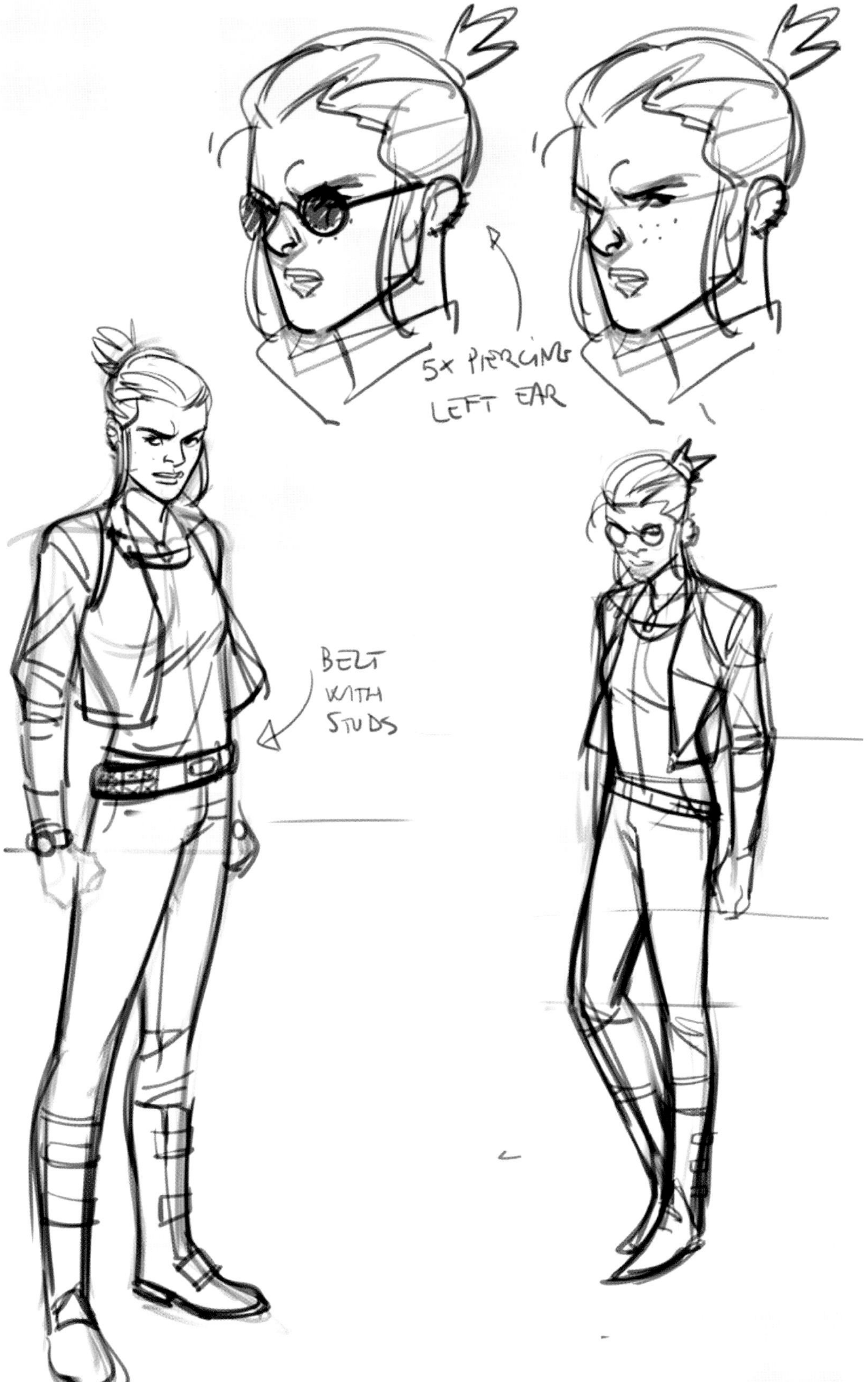

5x PIERCING LEFT EAR
BELT WITH STUDS

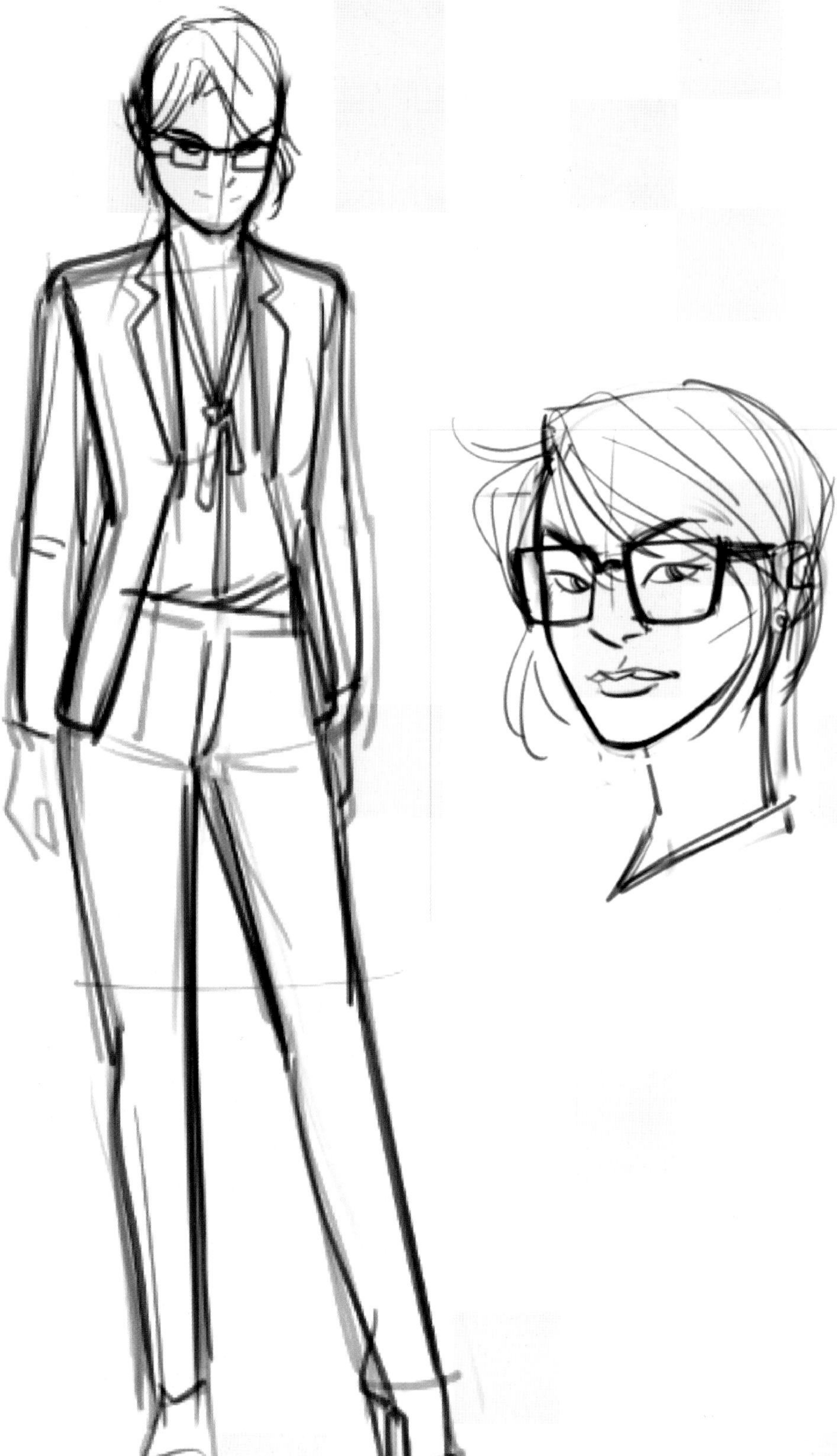

Art by **TIM SALE**

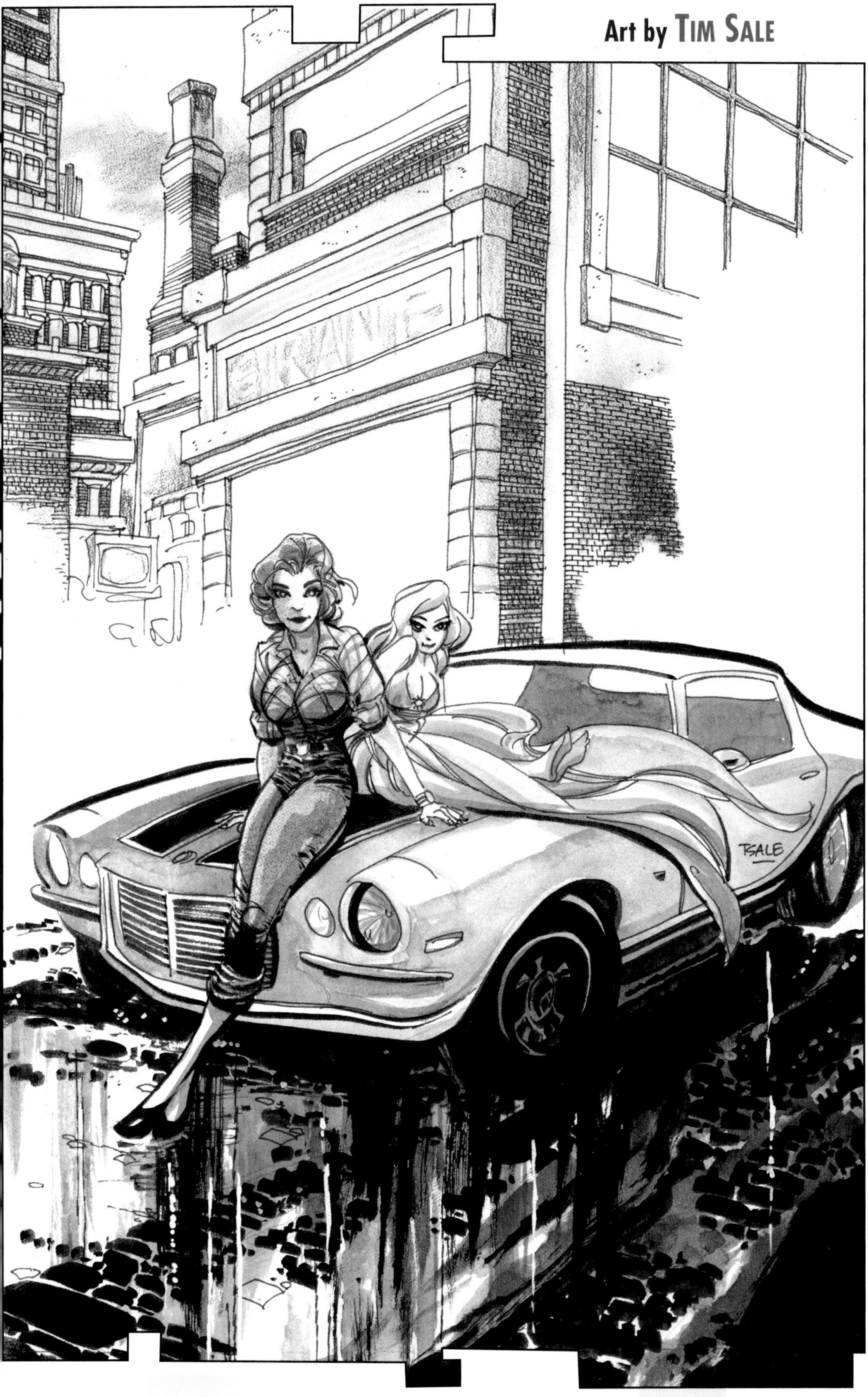
TSALE

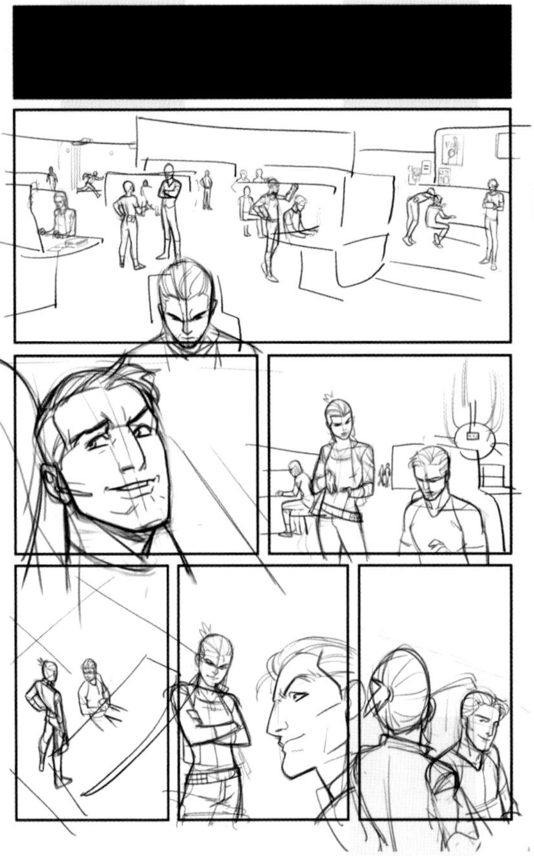

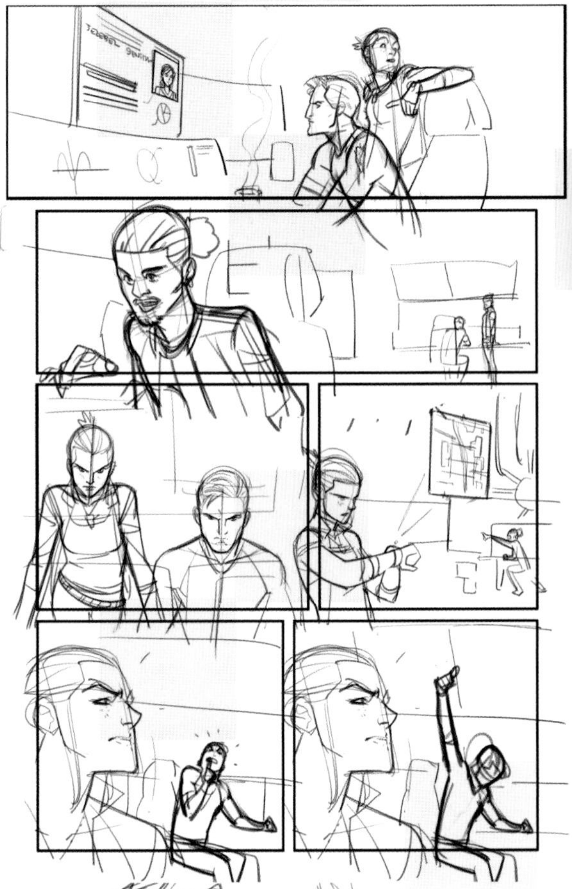

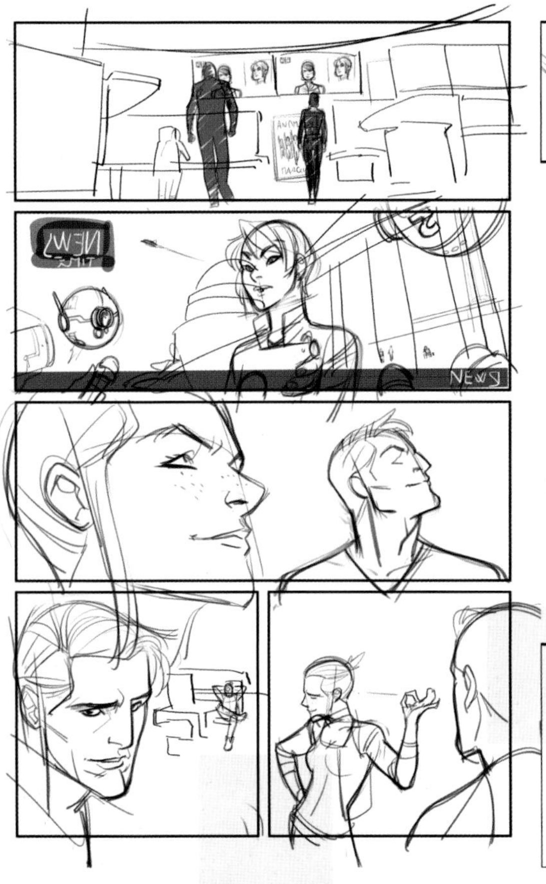
NEWS

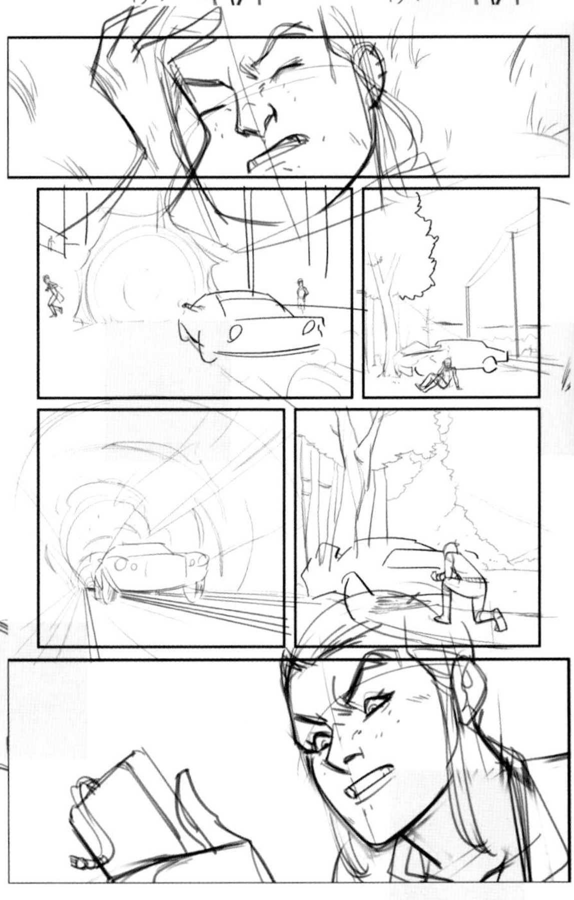

TEDDY
(V.O.)
"So help me God."

PANEL 2

Establishing shot of Teddy and Ulysse's company HQ. High-tech, futuristic although with a touch of start-up, in the sense that everyone could get their equipment -Holographic monitors, some other hi-tech devices (things like the Windows Surface table), everything looks professional and serious despite the start-up vibe. In terms of style, everything must looks coherent with the Head sets you designed. The office are designed in a circular pattern. Central station, Ulysses's, who's standing "inside" of it (his co-workers can be seated in fancy ergonomic chairs), and all the other work stations are set up in circle around him. There should be posters (not necessarily too obvious, because we want it all to feel organic) of Anomalies Marches, and all sort of Anomalies related events. Feel free to get creative for this environnement. One important we should clearly see is some sort of fancy futuristic Atomic clock, stating the time and year (28 September 2217).People are walking, going from one desk to another, collaborating on cases, some laughing, some more serious. Great dynamic, the office is full of life. There are personal stuff on their desks, pictures, mugs, anything that show they feel "at home".

Teddy is leaning against one of Ulysses's monitors while he is typing. His huge screen displays human anomalies files, maps, old pictures, recent ones... Teddy is holding a folder in her hands, reading it, puzzled. She's lifting the last page of the file, as if she was looking for some more information.

CAP
48 hours ago.

TEDDY
(V.O.)
Though it all started pretty well.

TEDDY
Uh... that's it?

PANEL 3

Ulysse is looking at her, amused.

ULYSSES
Are you really complaining?

PANEL 4

Teddy, Ulysse.

TEDDY
Where's the catch?

ULYSSES
No catch.

TEDDY
Ulysses, come on. It says right here I can take two backup agents with me. For a standard recon mission in West Virginia?

PANEL 5

Ulysses picks up he cup of tea that was on his desk. A fancy cup, Japanese style. Somewhere on his desk are lots of tea boxes, special pots and hi-tech kettle (Ulysse is a tea connoisseur ;))

ULYSSES
Let's say the area is... how do I put this... not exactly... welcoming.

TEDDY
Worse than the Cretaceous? Than Verdun? Than that horrifying timeline you sent me to...

PANEL 6

ULYSSES
The evilest One.

TEDDY
You need to come up with better names. Maybe in latin. Everything sounds smarter in latin.

ULYSSES
And douchy.

PANEL 7

TEDDY
Anyway, no need for backup. I'll go alone.

ULYSSES
Suit yourself, T.

PAGE 3

PANEL 1

Ulysses and Teddy are facing Ulysses's huge screen, showing a picture and a file (big enough so that we can read her name, Jezebel Bentman) Teddy looks back, talking to someone behind her.

TEDDY
When was our last contact with the anomaly, Chuck?

PANEL 2

Chuck is an African-American young man in his mid-twenties. He is at his desk, at the other end of the office (or at least, not too close). Lots of paperwork, boxes of files, he obviously has a lot of work. He checks Teddy's request on his computer.

CHUCK
Here. Her last Safety Check was eleven months ago. We think she could have disappeared between then and June's census, where she didn't show up.
(And then)
I'm forwarding her last known address to your watch.

PANEL 3

TEDDY
That's... quite a large window. Any chance the Feds found where we were hiding her?
(And then)
Ulysses, did we spot her in a refugee camp?

ULYSSES
No trace of her in Acardia Camp, Sunny Land or the smaller ones. But there's still a chance she might be held up in an Anomaly Detention center.

PANEL 4

Teddy is looking at her watch projecting a map of the city she's heading to.

TEDDY
Got the map, thanks Chuck.

In the background Chuck, excited, is pointing at a wall of screens displaying News channels.

CHUCK
Hey look at that, they're talking about your wife on TV!

PANEL 5

Teddy looks at the tv, jaded, almost irritated, but curious. Ulysses, behind her, is panicked, gesturing to Chuck to stop talking.

CHUCK
(OFF PANEL)
I mean ex-wife.

PANEL 6

Same shot, except now, Ulysses is giving a thumbs up.

CHUCK
(OFF PANEL)
I mean Congresswoman Ano Anderson.

PAGE 4

PANEL 1

Teddy and Ulysses are approaching the TV (holographic). This is a good panel to show one of two posters of Anomaly March. One of the channels is broadcasting a female news anchor. Close to her head is a frame showing Ano's picture.

TEDDY
Dude, just chillax. We're history.

TEDDY
(V.O)
Obviously, being married to an outlaw activist would have made a carrer government impossible.

TEDDY
Turn it up, would you?

ANCHOR WOMAN
It's a new setback for the Unity Bill, which was already facing major pushback from Republicans. Congresswoman Ano Anderson, first human anomaly ever elected to Congress, who introduced the bill, is now battling with her own Party. She briefly addressed the matter this morning.

PANEL 2

Closer to the TV. Ano is standing the Congress steps. She was on her way out, and has a coat on. Feel free to fit in some elements showing we're in the future, maybe some flying robot street cleaners, flying cars... Ano looks calm. It's important she doesn't look angry (despite what Teddy says in the next panel).

ANO
Rest assured that the Harmony Bill is on the right track. We've worked closely with all parties involved, and although it's a sensitive issue, I'm truly confident we will find common ground. The Bill will pass and soon it will be the end of these horrendous camps riddled with famine and disease.

THE INFINITE LOOP

NOTHING BUT THE TRUTH

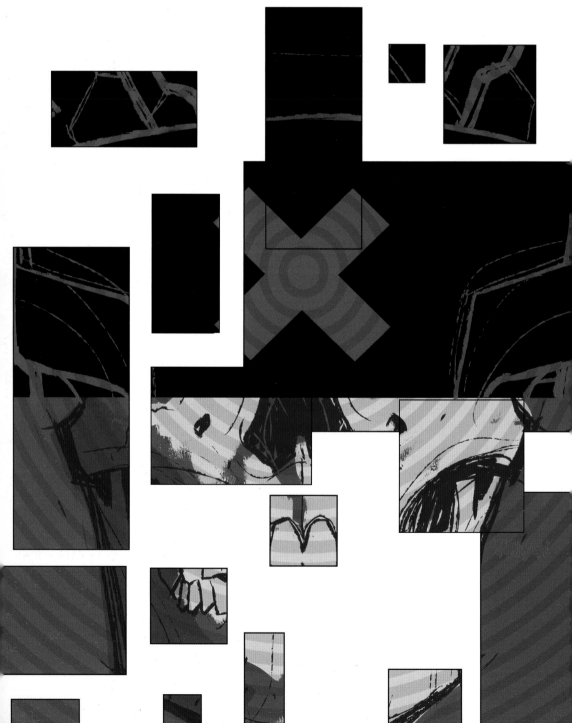

Teach Yourself to Sew Better

A STEP-BY-STEP GUIDE TO YOUR VIKING

Jan Saunders

Chilton Book Company
Radnor, Pennsylvania

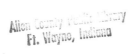
Published in Radnor, Pennsylvania 19089, by Chilton Book Company

Designed by Kevin Culver and Teddi Jensen

Produced by Cynthia Berglund

Manufactured in the United States of America

Illustrations by Pamela Poole

Photography by Lee Phillips

Library of Congress/Cataloging-in-Publication Data

Saunders, Janice S.
A Step-by-Step guide to your Viking / Jan Saunders.
p. cm. —(Teach yourself to sew better)
Includes bibliographical references and index.
ISBN 0-8019-8014-3 (pbk.)
1. Machine sewing. 2. Sewing machines. I. Title. II. Series.
TT713.S26 1990
646.2'044—dc20   89-45965
1 2 3 4 5 6 7 8 9 0   9 8 7 6 5 4 3 2 1 0   CIP